SHATTERING THE GLASS

SHATTERING

The Remarkable History of Women's Basketball

THE GLASS

PAMELA GRUNDY AND

SUSAN SHACKELFORD

THE NEW PRESS

NEW YORK
LONDON

Requests for permission to reproduce selections from this book
should be mailed to: Permissions Department, The New Press,
38 Greene Street, New York, NY 10013

Published in the United States by The New Press, New York, 2005
Distributed by W. W. Norton & Company, Inc., New York

LIBRARY OF CONGRESS CATALOGING-IN-PUBLICATION DATA

Grundy, Pamela.
Shattering the glass : the remarkable history of women's basketball / Pamela
Grundy and Susan Shackelford.
p. cm.
Includes bibliographical references (p.) and index.
ISBN 1-56584-822-5 (hc.)
1. Basketball for women—United States—History.   2. Women basketball
players—United States—History.   3. College sports—United States—History.
I. Shackelford, Susan.   II. Title.
GV886.G78   2005
796.323'082—dc22   2005041670

The New Press was established in 1990 as a not-for-profit alternative to the large,
commercial publishing houses currently dominating the book publishing industry.
The New Press operates in the public interest rather than for private gain, and is
committed to publishing, in innovative ways, works of educational, cultural, and
community value that are often deemed insufficiently profitable.

www.thenewpress.com

Book design by Kelly Too
Composition by dix!

Printed in the United States of America

2   4   6   8   10   9   7   5   3   1

To Pat and George Shackelford,
devoted parents who nurtured both a love of
basketball and a passion for the written word

and to Susan Cahn, who led the way

CONTENTS

NOTE ON CITATION

Any quotations not footnoted in the text come from the oral history interviews listed in the bibliography.

In the text, married women who appear primarily as players are generally referred to by their maiden names, while those who appear primarily as coaches are referred to by their married names. There are three main exceptions—Margie Hunt McDonald, Marianne Crawford Stanley and Theresa Shank Grentz—who appear as coaches and players in roughly equal measure. They are referred to by their maiden names as players and married names as coaches.

Because so many maiden names are used in the text, the oral history interviews have been alphabetized by first name for ease of reference.

SHATTERING THE GLASS

Introduction

Sometime in the mid-1940s, Mary Alyce Alexander's father put a bas-ketball hoop in the family backyard. It was a homemade affair—a plywood backboard with an improvised rim, more or less ten feet high. Almost instantly, her Charlotte, North Carolina yard became a commu-nity center, packed with eager neighbors who played through the day and then, after Mrs. Alexander turned on the porch light, well into the night. "Nobody ever waited on the sidelines," Mary Alyce recalled. "You just played till you dropped. Sometimes it might be two on three. It might be three on four, or four on four. But everybody always played. Everybody always played. And we played and played and played and played, until we couldn't anymore. And then when they left, I would start shooting."

Mary Alyce Alexander's love for basketball echoes across a century of American women's history. Women first took up the game in 1892, al-most as soon as it was invented. Throughout the twentieth century, and into the twenty-first, more American women have played basketball than any other sport. Players have been tall and short, fast and slow, gay and straight, from every income level and ethnic background. They have played in cow pastures and on city playgrounds; in immigrant communities and on Native American reservations; in YWCAs and on urban black streets; in schoolyards and gymnasiums without number. They have reveled in the magic of watching the ball drop cleanly through the basket, and in the heady camraderie of no-look passes and perfect plays.

But their story is also one of struggle. For most of basketball's history, competitive athletics has been considered a man's realm. The components of athletic success—discipline, determination, strength, stamina, assertiveness—have been cast as male, not female, birthrights. As a result, female athletes have found their efforts hemmed in by cautions and restrictions designed to "protect" them from the strains of heated competition. Many have also faced questions about whether excelling at a "masculine" activity somehow jeopardized their womanhood, whether through threatening their ability to have children, rendering them unattractive to men or nudging them toward lesbianism.[1]

In 1949, when Mary Alyce Alexander graduated from West Charlotte High School, she ran straight into those assumptions. The boys who had flocked to her backyard and joined her on clandestine forays to the local college gym could take their shot at college varsities. But few schools fielded female teams. Although she excelled in class, her basketball career was over.

Reality hit hard. "I guess it would be tantamount to saying you're forced to give up a childhood dream, or you're forced to grow up suddenly," she concluded. "Because I thought I would play basketball until I couldn't move anymore. But it didn't work out like that. Didn't work out that way at all."

Such restrictions have meant that even as female players have tested themselves, have dug deep for the courage and the will to rise to athletic challenges, they have also confronted the society around them. Battles for women's sports have gone hand in hand with those for women's rights. Both athletes and activists have worked to highlight women's physical and mental abilities, to win women greater roles in public life and to push views of womanhood beyond fixed definitions of distinctly "feminine" appearance and behavior. These efforts have taken place at local levels, where advocates of women's sports have battled for the resources required to build teams and institutions. They have also entered the arenas of national politics and mass culture, realms that have wielded growing influence over the shape of local institutions and the way that Americans view themselves.

This history is full of extraordinary individuals. While this work is far from comprehensive—there is just too much to tell—the net we cast is wide. We tell the stories of several generations of basketball pioneers—Ora Washington, Hazel Walker, Harley Redin, Nera White—whose achievements deserve to be far better known. We also delve into the lives and actions of more familiar figures—Sue Gunter, Vivian Stringer, Nancy Lieberman, Leon Barmore, Dawn Staley—charting the roles they have played not only on the court, but in building up the sport they love. Their passion for the game, the joy of sport, rings through the narrative.

But this is no simple tale of steady forward progress. In many ways, our story resembles a game itself, a collection of shifting strategies and challenges, hot shooting streaks and scoreless slumps. A game plan that once was effective falters, forcing players to regroup. Substitutions are required: an emphasis on speed gives way to a need for height and strength, a zone defense to a full-court press. An opponent who tired early on returns refreshed. It is a heated contest, requiring participants to summon all their forces and dig deep within themselves for the resolve to carry on.

Still, there are differences. The players are on their own, forced to size up the opposition on the spot, set their own goals and devise their own plans. The rules change from time to time, requiring entirely new strategies. Most important, their opponents are not individuals but a range of presumptions that limit women's ambitions and opportunities: chief among them the idea that men and women are fundamentally different, in character as well as physically, and that each sex is "naturally" inclined toward particular activities and destined for specific social roles. Competitors meet these preconceptions in concrete form: the athletic director who views women's sports as a waste of time and money; the mother who fumes because her daughter cares more about her jump shot than her hair; the high school classmates who whisper words like "dyke" and "butch." But the real opposition springs from the

ideas that drive such actions, the pervasive assumptions that, often un-
noticed, shape our society and our lives.

Our story starts in the late nineteenth century, with a group of college
teachers trained in the fledgling field of physical education. Section I
details the forceful challenge they mounted to the widespread notion
that women were frail by nature, and thus hopelessly dependent on men
for protection and support. Physical educators prized the Victorian traits
of female decorum and restraint and, when they took up basketball,
fashioned distinctive women's rules that restricted movement and
downplayed competition. But they also used the game to help their students prepare for new social and political roles, encouraging the development of "masculine" qualities such as teamwork, determination and
physical confidence.

The scene then shifts to the 1920s, and to the rise and fall of a far
more energetic game. The chapters in Section II recount the ways that
rural, working-class and African American communities developed
highly competitive women's teams during the 1920s, 1930s and 1940s.
In contrast to physical educators' focus on middle-class gentility, these
communities drew on a deeply grounded understanding of female fortitude. Their efforts were also buoyed by a new energy coursing through
national popular culture, a trend that downplayed dignity and propriety
in favor of high-spirited female energy and flirtatious sexual appeal. In
many parts of the country, beloved teams grew up at high schools, business colleges, factories and African American colleges. The Amateur
Athletic Union sponsored a flourishing set of leagues and an acclaimed
national championship.

Still, the balance that these players struck between high-level play
and conventional femininity remained precarious. In the 1950s, a period of social realignment and conservative cultural retrenchment undercut local institutions and flooded popular culture with visions of
womanhood that focused almost exclusively on the roles of wife and
mother. Many teams did not survive.

Even as teams faltered, however, momentum picked back up in the
college realm. In 1972, spurred by a blossoming women's liberation
movement, Congress passed a landmark piece of legislation known as

Title IX, which requires colleges and high schools to offer men and women equal opportunity in all programs—including sports. The chapters in Section III detail the work that led up to Title IX and the long, hard fight to turn that promise into reality—efforts that stretched beyond the development of teams and players to encompass a broad range of legal, political, financial and promotional campaigns.

Today, a century of effort has produced a marvelous game, a fast, tough, artistic sport that nurtures individual talents and promotes a sense of womanhood grounded in strength, confidence and accomplishment. Section IV surveys these burgeoning improvements and examines current efforts to move women's basketball, along with the vision of womanhood that it embodies, into the popular culture mainstream.

THIS LONG HISTORY OFFERS AN INVIGORATING STORY OF ACHIEVEment to which countless individuals—women and men—have contributed. It also details the many challenges that remain. In the summer of 2004, longtime national star Dawn Staley spoke to these issues. Four decades after Mary Alyce Alexander first picked up a basketball, Staley spent every moment she could spare running and shooting with the boys in her North Philadelphia neighborhood. Although no one in her family had ever been to college, when she graduated from high school in 1988 she had a full athletic scholarship. In the subsequent two decades, she played on three gold medal–winning Olympic teams and in two U.S. professional leagues. Today she is both a professional player and a women's college coach. "I'm proof," she wrote, "that odds can be beaten and that dreams really do come true."[2]

But she also noted the work left to do. Sports are still masculine terrain. Although female stars play as hard, practice as long and care as much as their male counterparts, the broader acclaim—and far higher salary—a top man receives make it clear that as a society "we place more value on what he does." Too many young women still grow up with limited views of their own physical abilities. Too often, talented players feel called upon to "prove" that they are women as well as athletes. In this, women's sports resembles many other realms of U.S. life, where women have made great strides but still face daunting obstacles. The glass ceiling that blocks women's upward rise is cracked in spots, but far from wholly shattered. Pursuing this dream will require—as in the past—a panoply of efforts on many fronts and an unrelenting determination. In such a struggle, the stories of past warriors, of challenges confronted and of goals achieved, can prove both guide and inspiration.

"We've come a long way," Staley wrote, "but we still have miles to go." We hope this book will help.

SECTION I

ORIGINS

1892–1920

· 1 ·

College Ladies on the Court

Senda Berenson stood at the center of the Smith College gymnasium, a petite woman clad in a black gym suit, basketball in hand. Around her, players in the school's first-ever basketball game listened eagerly to her last-minute instructions, dispensed in a voice that still bore the lilt of her Lithuanian childhood. Students from the all-female college crammed the balcony above the floor, many of them dangling their feet through the rails. It was the fall of 1892, and the twenty-four-year-old Berenson was just a few months into her job as director of "physical culture" at the Northampton, Massachusetts, school. But already she perched on the edge of history. In a few short years, basketball would be the most popular sport at women's schools across the nation, and Berenson would be its leading advocate.

That first game, which pitted the school's freshmen against the sophomores, got off to a rocky start. "As I threw the ball for the beginning of the game," Berenson later recalled, "it struck the uplifted hand of the center player, the captain of the freshman team, in a peculiar way so that it threw her shoulder joint out of place." But the incident did not deter either coach or players: "We took the girl into the office and pulled the joint into place, another center took her place, and the game went on."[1]

Senda Berenson at Smith College, Northhampton, Massachusetts. COURTESY OF
THE SMITH COLLEGE ARCHIVES, SMITH COLLEGE.

A few years and many contests later, Berenson described her students' love for basketball in elegant Victorian prose. "Many of our young women are well enough in a way, yet never know the joy of mere living, are lazy, listless and lack vitality," she wrote. "Let such a person try this game, she will forget herself at the first throw of the ball, will take deep draughts of air with the unaccustomed exercise and 'tingle and throb with the joy of the game.' "[2]

Such sporting enthusiasm swept the country in the late nineteenth century. The pace of American life had quickened after the Civil War as growing numbers of citizens moved from farms to factories and from small towns to bustling cities. The keys to athletic success—physical endurance, strategic thinking, teamwork, competitive drive—seemed to mesh neatly with the demands of an increasingly competitive industrial society, and the connections sparked athletic zeal across the country. The recently invented game of football had grown into an obsession among the nation's male college students. Professional baseball teams were expanding their audiences and solidifying their leagues. The sporting goods industry thrived, selling equipment for golf, tennis, croquet, bicycling, hockey, lacrosse and a host of other sports. Americans had played games for centuries, but they had never been so serious before.

For Berenson's students, and for countless other women of the era, athletic competition became an integral part of a newly energetic version of American womanhood. By the end of the nineteenth century, women from the nation's educated middle classes were beginning to step beyond traditional roles of wife and mother, moving into professions such as teaching and social work and agitating for the right to vote. As they surveyed the challenges that lay before them, it became clear that reaching their new goals would require women to develop new strengths—physical as well as mental. Educators such as Berenson plunged into that task. The version of basketball that emerged from their endeavors still bore a Victorian stamp, stressing refinement and gentility as well as confidence and strength. But it represented a profound shift in standard views of womanhood, trading fragility for determined resolve.

An essay by Atlanta University student L.I. Mack, published in 1900 in the school's student magazine, announced the change in ringing terms. "Educated women who seek employment must keep in mind the fact that only by the sweat of the brow is man's bread won," Mack told her colleagues at the all-black school. "They must also remember that if they descend into the arena, they cannot hope for success unless they accept the conditions under which an athlete must strive. They must be prepared for hard work, for persevering work, because the race will be the same for them as for the men. The men will go beside them, struggling for the same prize; and, since men have, in the start, the advantage of the women, they must brace up every energy, and bring into play every faculty, to avoid defeat and ensure victory. Whatsoever they undertake, they must, and will, and do go through with it to the end."[3]

Perhaps not surprisingly, Mack's essay was published barely a month after a brief athletic notice appeared in the university's alumni bulletin. "Through the liberality of some friends," the school announced, "supplemented by the work of our own shop, a basket ball outfit has been procured for the girls."[4]

THE GAME OF BASKETBALL HAD BEEN BORN AT THE HEART OF THE country's new sporting enthusiasm. In the fall of 1891, in Springfield, Massachusetts, a young Canadian named James Naismith was ordered to create an indoor game to tame a rowdy gym class at the International Training School of the Young Men's Christian Association (YMCA). Naismith wrestled with the job for several weeks, seeking to shape a game that would be fun to play and that would encourage discipline and teamwork rather than brute force. Finally, he came up with thirteen rules that would form basketball's foundation. The game consisted of two fifteen-minute halves. The players scored by shooting a ball into a peach basket nailed above the gymnasium floor. They moved the ball by passing—running with the ball was prohibited and the dribble would not be invented until several years later. Hitting, tripping and other forms of rough conduct were penalized by fouls. In early December,

Players at Hampton Institute,
Hampton, Virginia, 1907.
COURTESY OF THE HAMPTON
UNIVERSITY ARCHIVES.

Naismith tacked the typewritten list on the school's gymnasium wall and chose teams for the first game.[5]

The initial contest, Naismith later recalled, left something to be desired. "There was no team work, but each man did his best," he explained. "The forwards tried to make goals and the backs tried to keep the opponents from making them. The team was large, and the floor was small. Any man on the field was close enough to the basket to throw for goal, and most of them were anxious to score."[6] Still, it seemed a promising start. A month later, Naismith agreed to write up a description of the game for the YMCA's monthly newsletter. A few months after that, Senda Berenson picked up a copy.

Berenson was immediately intrigued. Most of the era's popular team sports were considered too rough for college women. Basketball, however, looked more promising. Players shot the ball upwards at a basket, rather than forcing it across a line, as in football. They could not hold the ball close to their body, nor hit it with their fists. The rules specifically forbade "shouldering, holding, pushing, tripping or striking in any way the person of an opponent." Although the game had been designed for men, she saw no reason that women could not try it too. Soon after reading the article, she began teaching Smith students how to play.[7]

The new game would hold special significance for women. Men found the game an enjoyable addition to sports such as football and baseball, as well as a welcome alternative to winter gymnastics. For women, most of whom had never played team sports, basketball was a revelation. The sport became especially popular among college women, who were already pressing eagerly at the boundaries of conventional womanhood.

SENDA BERENSON, WHO HAD SURMOUNTED MANY OBSTACLES OF her own, was a fitting model for these young, ambitious students. She was born in a small Jewish community in Lithuania during a time of economic depression and rising, often violent anti-Semitism. When she was six, her father, Albert Valvrojenski, took a hard look at the family's future and decided to seek his fortune in the United States. In 1874, Albert joined two cousins in Boston. Like many of his fellow immigrants, he changed his name in the process, adopting the more American-sounding Berenson. He acquired a pushcart and began to work as a street peddler, buying and selling old clothes. In 1875, he sent for his family. That summer, seven-year-old Senda Valvrojenski stepped onto Boston soil, and became Senda Berenson.[8]

Like many of their peers, the Berensons found America no paradise. Albert Berenson was known for his independent mind and his short temper. His children inherited both, which made for a stormy household. Although Albert was well educated and well read, Boston was packed with ambitious, hardworking newcomers such as himself. Despite years of work, he was never able to abandon his peddler's cart. The financial strains of his business struggles and the Berensons' cramped quarters in Boston's crowded, noisy West End only added to family tensions. Senda and her four siblings spent much of their time reading books, dreaming of far-off places and longing for a better life.

Senda's older brother Bernard found his escape in study. He was a brilliant young man, and as a teenager he caught the eye of Boston's intellectual elite. Their patronage helped him leave home for good, first earning a degree at Harvard and then launching a long and distinguished career as an interpreter of Italian Renaissance art.

Senda had a harder time. Nineteenth-century women had few ways to make an independent living, and Senda was not only small but frail. Like her beloved brother, she loved books, art and music. But throughout much of her youth, she was unable to sit up long enough to stay in school.

Specifically what ailed her is not clear. But her frailty fit neatly into the dominant worldview of nineteenth-century Americans, many of whom took women's physical weakness for granted. By the mid-nineteenth century, American intellectual and cultural institutions were dominated by the nation's white urban middle class, whose members held to a strict set of Victorian beliefs that stressed self-discipline, social refinement and carefully defined distinctions between men and women. From this vantage point, biology had fitted each sex for a specific social role. Men were best suited for the competitive stresses of the modern economic and political worlds. Women, the "weaker" sex, needed male protection and the shelter of a home. In this protected space, they could create refined, nurturing environments that shielded their frail bodies and delicate nerves from worldly pressures.[9]

These perceptions were bolstered by the science of the times. Although nineteenth-century Americans were fascinated by the scientific method, many of the era's most influential theories reflected assumptions about the way the world should operate, rather than careful observation of how it actually worked. In the case of women, these assumptions usually meant that "scientists" discussed female biology almost exclusively in terms of childbearing. "Women have small brains!" announced one typical study, in which a German doctor compared male and female brains and conveniently concluded that "the difference in the sexes is due to the fact that the principal duty of women is motherhood, and nature cannot afford to waste on her either physical or mental powers which are not essential to that function."[10]

Assumptions of female frailty and dependence were woven throughout almost every facet of nineteenth-century American society. They were reinforced by the legal system—women were barred from voting and for much of the century were not allowed to own property. They also limited the way that women dressed and moved. As well as being frail, Victorian theories ran, women also possessed delicate sensibilities, especially regarding sexuality, and thus needed physical protection. Accordingly, nineteenth-century fashion freighted women with yards of heavy material, bound them into corsets that restricted breathing and hobbled them with cumbersome skirts that turned a simple stroll across a room into a challenge.

IN A WORLD THAT DEFINED WOMEN AS FRAGILE AND DEPENDENT, A young woman wishing to escape a domineering father was expected to seek refuge with a husband. But Senda Berenson did not choose that route. By the time she turned twenty she was still at home, chafing at her father's outbursts and writing long letters to Bernard, who had embarked on a lengthy European sojourn. Her brother sympathized with her plight and at one point gallantly exclaimed: "Oh, if only I were home already to take you at once out of the hell in which you are. I know father well enough."[11] But despite such noble sentiments, he showed no signs of coming back. If Senda were to escape her "hell," she would have to find the path herself.

In the fall of 1890, she did. On the advice of friends, she enrolled in the recently organized Boston Normal School of Gymnastics, which was dedicated to an emerging profession known as "physical education." The decision would transform her life.

The Boston Normal School, which opened in 1889, was dedicated to building female strength—a goal that had broad ramifications. Opponents of expanding female rights often rested their case on assumptions of female frailty. As Berenson herself would later write: "One of the strong arguments in the economic world against giving women as high salaries as men for similar work is that women are more prone to illness than men. They need, therefore, all the more to develop health and endurance if they desire to become candidates for equal wages."[12] Women's leaders also recognized the psychological havoc that weak muscles, tight corsets and constraining skirts could wreak on individuals. When thousands of American women took up bicycling during the 1890s, suffrage leader Susan B. Anthony remarked that the sport did "more to emancipate women than anything else in the world," because it produced a "feeling of freedom and self-reliance."[13]

Boston Normal was designed specifically to build such confidence. Its founder, the aristocratic Amy Morris Homans, embodied the ideals of both female vigor and female refinement. The "personification of self-sufficiency and self-mastery," she had little tolerance for weakness and little interest in pampering her students. Berenson spent much of her first three months at the school lying flat across three stools, an exercise designed to strengthen her back muscles. She had never cared for exercise of any kind and found such authority little more tolerable than her father's. "How I hated it at first!" she once recalled. But the program worked. At the time, "physical education" consisted of detailed gymnastic routines, as well as systematic work with weights, ropes, vaulting horses and other apparatuses. As her health improved, she began to tackle these challenges with zeal. Soon she had mastered all the school's requirements, transforming her understanding of exercise and of herself.[14]

"It is impossible to tell how my life had altered," she later explained. "I had changed an aching body to a free and strong mechanism, ready and eager for whatever might come. My indifference had changed to deep conviction and I wanted to work only in physical education so that I might help others as I had been helped."[15] Her enthusiasm was evident to everyone. The next year, when a job came open at prestigious Smith College, Homans recommended Berenson.

THE GAMES THAT BERENSON ORGANIZED AT SMITH WERE ONLY A beginning. As soon as basketball was deemed a suitable sport for women, the women's game spread rapidly across the country, sparking excitement almost everywhere it landed. "There is not an instant of ennui in basket ball," wrote an early California enthusiast. "All is motion, change, excitement. The ball is caught and instantly thrown. No one is allowed to fall on it and stay there. Five feet is the furthest you can run with it, and five seconds the longest you can hold it, and all in all, it's the jolliest kind of a romp."[16]

New Orleans became one center for the game. In 1891, when

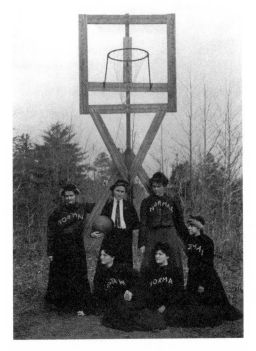

Team from State Normal College, Greensboro, North Carolina, 1901. COURTESY OF THE UNIVERSITY ARCHIVES, JACKSON LIBRARY, UNIVERSITY OF NORTH CAROLINA AT GREENSBORO.

Louisiana native Clara Baer began a physical education program at the city's exclusive Sophie Newcomb College, she faced considerable opposition. Parents protested that exercise would render their daughters unladylike. Many students only abandoned their corsets when Baer's insistence on vigorous gymnastics, aided by the city's humid climate, managed to "sweat" them off. But by 1895, when two Sophie Newcomb basketball teams met in a game at New Orleans' Southern Athletic Club, attitudes had changed. One of the school's students proudly displayed her muscles to a reporter from the city's *Daily Picayune,* proclaiming that "there is nothing like physical culture for a woman who wants to be strong and healthy." [17]

The whole event, in the reporter's words, demonstrated "how thoroughly the [turn-of-the-century] woman is capable of enjoying herself without the time-honored masculine attendant." The game was played with verve. "No bones had been injured, no limbs broken, no blood shed, and congratulations were in order," the report ran. "But the floor was strewn with hairpins, and as for handkerchiefs, there was a deluge of them and no one could tell hers from the other." One enthusiastic participant dubbed the match "the beginning of a new era in this quiet old southern metropolis." [18]

As at most schools, Sophie Newcomb students organized their games by class—freshmen, sophomores, juniors and seniors. Class loyalties ran strong, heightening students' enthusiasm. "The annual championship basket ball series opened . . . with the Senior-Sophomore game," read a typical report. "The usual feeling of sisterly love between these two classes had in some miraculous way been 'wafted aloft,' and when the score showed an overwhelming defeat of the Seniors with a score of 52–19, the hilarity of the Sophomores was not to be withstood." A few days later, however, the seniors "redeemed themselves and were restored to their respected position by defeating the Juniors by a score of 36–27." The report concluded with a promise of more action to come. "There is much speculation as to the final outcome of these games and no one dares prophesy who the winners will be." [19]

The sense of expansive well-being the sport gave its participants was often reflected in the names players chose for their teams. In San Francisco, players at Girls' High School named themselves the Atlantas, after the fleet-footed Greek goddess. At Elizabeth College in Charlotte, North Carolina, students dubbed their intramural teams the Amazons and the Olympians. In Richmond, Virginia, two teams of African American schoolteachers competed as the Suffragists and the Feminists.[20]

BY THE MID-1890S, SOME YOUNG WOMEN HAD BEGUN TO TURN THIS growing confidence to a wider field of play. Restless with the limits of intramural games, teams from Stanford University and the University of California at Berkeley staged the nation's first women's intercollegiate contest on April 4, 1896.

The game, held at a San Francisco armory, created an enormous sensation. More than seven hundred spectators jammed the gallery and "roared until the glass doors in the gun cases shivered at the noise." Although the final score was remarkably low—Stanford triumphed 2–1—there had apparently been no shortage of action. Both of San Francisco's major newspapers gave the game extensive coverage. The *Examiner*'s account occupied a full page, presenting drawings of the action, a lengthy account of the events and analyses by the captains of both teams, as well as an independent "expert." The *Chronicle* assigned its story to Mabel Craft, an aspiring young writer who would later become one of the state's leading reporters, as well as an outspoken advocate for the rights of women and African Americans.[21]

Craft's ardor showed clearly in her account. The game was "snappy" from the start, with "many calls for time and some disputes," she wrote. "Enthusiastic captains claimed fouls, and some were allowed. . . . Sometimes with a slump and a slide three girls would dive for the ball, and end in an inextricable heap of red, white and blue. In less time than it takes to read it they were all planted firmly on their two feet, flushed, perspiring, intensely in earnest and oblivious of everything except that ball. . . ."[22]

The players' conduct, she asserted, offered a convincing demonstration of women's physical strength and energetic spirit. Basketball "wasn't invented for girls, and there isn't anything effeminate about it," she wrote. "It was made for men to play indoors and it is a game that would send the physician who thinks the feminine organization 'so delicate,' into the hysterics he tries so hard to perpetuate."

As onlookers marveled at the young women's play, students on the two campuses eagerly awaited word of the game. In Palo Alto, a telegraph announcing Stanford's victory produced "a wild outburst of enthusiasm" in the men's dormitory. "The boys came pouring out of the rooms," ran one report, "and the halls of the building were soon filled with a mass of yelling students." The team was scheduled to take an evening train back to Palo Alto. Their classmates "began assembling at the railroad station an hour before the train was due, and whiled the time away with songs and college yells. . . . An omnibus profusely decorated with flags and cardinal was waiting to receive the players at the station. From the station to the University the team met with an ovation. The houses in 'Faculty Row' were illumined in their honor." Each member of the team was subsequently presented with a coveted varsity letter—the only Stanford women to have received the honor.[23]

THE STANFORD–BERKELEY CONTEST MARKED A MILESTONE IN women's basketball history. But for one of the victorious revelers, it was only a beginning. Clelia Mosher, the young Stanford coach, stood at the threshold of a distinguished scientific career that would transform understanding of women's physical abilities. Mosher resembled Senda Berenson in many ways. She had been born in New York State in 1863, into a family deeply rooted in the independent thinking of the Quaker and Huguenot faiths. She had also been forced to overcome physical challenges. Mosher's father, a doctor, nurtured her scientific interests from an early age, and she spent much of her youth in the greenhouse he built for her, experimenting with plants and animals. When it came time for college, however, he was less supportive. Like Berenson, Mosher had always been frail, and an older sister had died of tuberculosis. Worried that college would prove too great a strain, her father refused to pay her tuition.[24]

Mosher had greater confidence in her abilities. She took a teaching job and turned her greenhouse into a plant and florist business. Two years later, she had saved enough to enroll at nearby Wellesley College.

Stanford University team, victors in the nation's first women's intercollegiate basketball game, Palo Alto, California, 1896. COURTESY OF THE DEPARTMENT OF SPECIAL COLLECTIONS, STANFORD UNIVERSITY.

Although she struggled with her health, she persevered. Subsequently, she traveled to far-off Stanford, the first four-year college in the country to institute a physical education curriculum. She graduated in 1893 and was hired the next year to direct the school's gymnasium. In 1910, after obtaining an MD from Johns Hopkins Medical School, she became the head of Stanford's newly formed department of women's physical education.

Mosher made it her life's work to disprove common assumptions about female frailty. She used rigorous scientific studies to argue that most observations of female weakness resulted not from distinctly female anatomy but from the circumstances of women's lives. Like many activists, she took corsets as a prime example. With their confining arrays of whalebones, laces, straps and buckles, corsets offered an especially striking demonstration of the way that social assumptions could become physical realities. Many middle-class Victorians believed that women could not stand properly without a corset's support. But the constricting garments did far more harm than good, restricting breathing, displacing ovaries and sometimes fracturing ribs. In one of Mosher's early studies, she demonstrated that the weak, shallow breaths that so many doctors used as evidence of innate female weakness were a direct result of tightly cinched corsets. She forcefully challenged the widespread assumption that women should stay in bed while menstruating. She also carried out a pioneering study into female sexuality that indicated Victorian portraits of middle-class women as afraid of or uninterested in sex were well off the mark.[25]

In her physical education endeavors, Mosher worked not only to improve her students' health but also to combat the psychological effects of widespread presumptions about female weakness. Menstruation was a case in point. "From the minute a girl hears of it, she is taught . . . to regard it as a periodic illness," Mosher wrote. "The terms 'sick time,' [and] 'being unwell' have long been grafted into our ordinary speech. The result upon the mind of constantly anticipated misery can scarcely be measured." During her years at Stanford, she devised a wide-ranging curriculum that encouraged young women to take pride in their abilities and in the female body. Along with teaching gymnastics and sports, she assigned readings on the accomplishments of distinguished modern women and encouraged her students to study the graceful female nudes chiseled by ancient Greek sculptors.[26]

The relatively open society of the American West, which was less thoroughly tradition bound than its eastern counterpart, proved a boon not only for Mosher's scientific endeavors but for women's intercollegiate basketball. Less than two weeks after Stanford's historic victory, teams from the University of Washington and Ellensburg State Normal School took to the court. Two years after that, the University of Nevada and Oakland's Mills College joined the intercollegiate fray. By then, women's basketball had become a serious pursuit, as the Nevada students learned when they met Berkeley in a physical game that, according to Mabel Craft, "would have crushed into fine powder those Dresden china shepherdesses who had the honor to be their grandmothers."[27]

"Fourteen to one was the tune to which the Berkeley co-eds literally and figuratively wiped up the floor of Odd Fellows' Hall yesterday with their guests from Nevada," Craft reported. "It is not a polite way to treat visitors, but almost anything goes in basket-ball." Craft also took the opportunity for a dig at Berkeley's less successful male athletes, who had recently voted to deny the female players varsity letters. "The athletic girls from the Berkeley hills proved that if the young men can seldom win at anything, the girls at least are capable of upholding the college honor," she noted. Craft well understood the double standard operating. In 1892, she had graduated first in her Berkeley class. The school's academic medal, however, was given only to men. Although the runner-up refused to accept the honor and stated Craft should have it, the administration had declined to break precedent, and the medal went unawarded.[28]

Far from discouraged by the loss, the Nevada players fought back. The next spring the school hired Stanford assistant coach Ada Edwards, who had refereed the 1896 contest, to coach the team. Edwards was hired for a month, and she coached two additional weeks at her own expense. The work paid off. The Nevada players put up a far more respectable performance against Berkeley, losing 7–3. A few days later, they defeated Stanford, 3–2. Edwards was rehired the next year.[29]

Such competitive enthusiasm stirred a degree of controversy, emphasizing that the battle against ideas of female frailty was far from won. In 1899 Stanford's faculty athletic committee voiced its dismay at the contests and abolished women's intercollegiate competition "for the purpose of guarding the health of the individual player." The move, however, had limited effect. When rumor of the decision reached the University of Nevada, students responded with a spirited assertion: "Let the girls play basket-ball if they want to. Encourage and assist them in every possible manner, and if the misguided professors of Stanford University should say 'Nay, nay . . .' we shall call them a lot of bald-headed, long-whiskered, cross-eyed old billy goats. So there!"[30]

Stanford's players promptly organized an independent "Palo Alto" club and kept competing, maintaining the series with their Berkeley neighbors and traveling to Reno that May. When the Stanford administration relented in 1904, Stanford became part of the Coast Basketball League, which included Mills College, Berkeley, Reno and the San Jose Normal Teacher's College.[31]

THE SAME YEAR THAT STANFORD PLAYERS STEPPED BACK INTO THE fray, another group of young western women set their sights even higher. Women's basketball had become a popular activity at Montana's Fort Shaw Government Industrial Indian Boarding School, which belonged to a network of Native American schools established around the country near the end of the nineteenth century. In May 1903, Fort Shaw superintendent F.C. Campbell had been invited to send a delegation to spend five months at the Model Indian School at the 1904 St. Louis World's Fair. He chose to send the women's basketball team.[32]

The choice was not surprising. Boarding schools such as Fort Shaw had grown out of the nineteenth century's wholesale assault on Native American autonomy and traditions. They had been designed to both educate and "civilize" young Native Americans, teaching them the skills and outlooks deemed suitable for "modern" life. Team sports, which showcased virtues such as teamwork, discipline and determination,

Team from the Fort Shaw Indian Industrial School, champions of the World's Fair, St. Louis, Missouri, 1904. COURTESY OF THE MISSOURI HISTORICAL SOCIETY, ST. LOUIS.

gave students a dramatic way to show that they could master such a curriculum. The most famous Native American sports team, the Carlisle Indian football squad from Pennsylvania's Carlisle Indian Industrial School, had garnered national admiration in the 1890s when it played and sometimes defeated the nation's top college teams. Fort Shaw's basketball players thus had the potential to drive home points not only about the abilities of women, but those of Native Americans as well.[33]

The Fort Shaw team set out for St. Louis in June 1904, playing a series of exhibition games along the route of their two-week train trip. They spent five months at the Model Indian School, putting on dance and choral recitals, demonstrating crafts and giving basketball exhibitions twice a week. The assumptions of white supremacy that lay behind both the boarding school concept and the fair's "exhibition" of Native Americans made theirs a problematic endeavor. But within those constraints, the players' abilities shone. They became a highly popular attraction. At the end of the fair, when basketball enthusiasts arranged a series of games with an all-star lineup of St. Louis players, they made their larger point with style. "To the great surprise of several hundred spectators," the St. Louis Post-Dispatch observed of the first game, the Fort Shaw players proved "more active, more accurate and cooler than their opponents." Fort Shaw took the game, 24–2. After winning a rematch, the team was named champion of the World's Fair.[34]

DESPITE THE WEST'S SUCCESSES, HOWEVER, INTENSIVE COMPETItion would prove an exception for women's college basketball. At the turn of the century, men's college athletics was rapidly becoming a major feature of the nation's sporting landscape. Men's varsities would see enormous growth in the twentieth century, developing highly competitive leagues, explosive budgets and ever-larger audiences. Women's college sports would take a different path.

Professional physical educators such as Clelia Mosher and Senda Berenson had mounted a forceful challenge to the assumptions of frailty and helplessness that so constrained middle-class women in the nineteenth century. They also promoted female independence, encouraging their students to focus their ambitions on professional careers rather than simply on making a good marriage. But they still held women to a distinctly female standard of conduct. Though Clelia Mosher poured enormous zeal into her efforts to prove women the physical equals of men, she also stated, "We cannot make a man into a woman or a woman into a man," continuing, "I will go still further and say that we do not even wish to do so."[35]

For decades, women's basketball would embody a distinctly female philosophy, as female physical educators shaped a version of the game designed both to promote female strength and to reinforce the era's classically "feminine" traits of modesty, gentility and order. Basketball, Senda Berenson explained, taught women "physical and moral courage." She also maintained that "Brute strength physical combat is not essential for women."[36]

As they worked to balance strength with gentility, physical educators turned to the shifting terrain of basketball's rules. In the first years of its existence, basketball was a highly malleable sport. The thirteen rules James Naismith drew up in 1891 gave the game its basic structure, but most of the details still had to be worked out. Naismith had not specified the number of players on each team. Foul shots were not devised until 1894, and the dribble was not widely used until 1896. As with present-day play, the rules that banned tripping, holding and other forms of roughness were open to interpretation.[37]

According to Victorian philosophy, which cast women as passive and gentle, women's games should have been calm and orderly, no matter what the rules. But Berenson, who had struggled to control her own fiery temper, knew better. She also received a convincing demonstration during some of Smith's early games, in which vigorous competition produced its share of turned ankles, fingernail scratches and pulled hair.

Berenson responded by creating a set of women's rules. She divided the court into three equal sections and assigned each player to one. Forwards played under a team's home basket, centers roamed the middle section and guards patrolled the opposing team's goal. Teams could have anywhere from five to ten players, but no one could venture outside her assigned section. As dribbling developed, it sped up the men's game, but

Berenson forbade her players to dribble more than three times per possession. She also banned physical contact of any kind. Such rules, she explained, allowed women to develop qualities such as "alertness, accuracy, coolness and presence of mind under trying circumstances," while minimizing rough play. The result, one observer later noted, "was a slow almost stately game with careful passing and deliberate shot selection from an almost statuelike pose."[38]

In New Orleans, physical educator Clara Baer designed a game with even more restrictions. Baer started with nine-player teams, then divided her court into nine sections, with one player from each team assigned to each section. Players could not dribble and could shoot only with one hand. No player was allowed to move unless the ball was in the air, and any player who fell down was charged with a foul. Her goal, Baer later wrote, was to "effect the maximum of physical development with the minimum of risk," to "induce more headwork," and to "develop

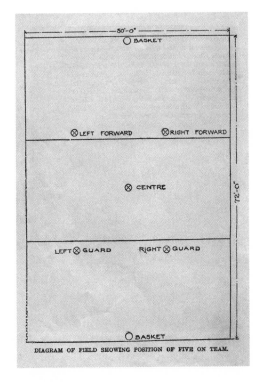

Diagram of three-division court, published in Spalding's Official Basketball Guide for Women, 1913. COURTESY OF THE SMITH COLLEGE ARCHIVES, SMITH COLLEGE.

gracefulness, which, though too often sadly lacking, is a valuable asset for girls at the growing age."[39]

Baer published her regulations in 1895, calling the game Basquette. Berenson did not circulate a detailed set of her rules until some years later, and many early teams used Baer's nine-player game.[40] In 1899, however, Berenson was chosen to edit the first set of "official" women's rules, published by Spalding's Athletic Library as "Basket Ball for Women." Though Baer continued to publish versions of her game, the three-division court took hold, and adaptations of Berenson's rules would remain the official women's regulations until the 1930s, when they were replaced by a two-division court and a six-player game.

Female physical educators also moved to rein in the varsity competition that had aroused so much enthusiasm at Stanford and elsewhere. In their minds, both men's and women's varsity sports encouraged overly intense emotions and too easily distracted students from the less exciting work of daily training. At Stanford, female students were only allowed to play varsity basketball after completing a year of physical education training, and Clelia Mosher banned games with Berkeley for several years because the students seemed to care more about beating their long-time rival than about exercise, cooperation or good sportsmanship. Other educators never allowed intercollegiate competition at all. By the 1920s, only a tiny handful of four-year colleges played women's intercollegiate games.[41]

In place of varsity games, physical educators designed the "play day," an institution that would define female physical education for the next half-century. Play days involved intercampus visits by groups of physical education students. Sometimes they included only two schools, sometimes more. Rather than pitting one school against another, organizers often chose teams that deliberately mixed players from the different institutions. The ensuing games were played for fun, rather than to win, and they were often followed by teas or dances.

"We invited the entire basketball group from Chapel Hill to be our guests at a party and game," a North Carolina educator wrote in a typical play day description. "You understand that I put the PARTY first and the game second as that is the way we wanted it. . . . Each girl who had come out for basketball in each school had an opportunity to play at some time in the game." The party consisted of refreshments and a dance. "The game lasted three quarters of an hour and the dance lasted two hours. We hardly remember what the score was—because it was by far not our first interest. Everyone had a good time. . . ."[42]

Modesty became another important theme. In an era obsessed with female sexual propriety, any activity that focused on women's bodies could spark criticism and suspicion. Mabel Lee, a Boston Normal graduate who became one of the nation's foremost physical educators, was fond of telling the story of her first formal exercise class, organized by her Iowa high school principal in the basement of a local church. The class proved short-lived as "such a buzzing started about town (on the premise that it was improper for girls to engage in such activities and with a man teacher at that, and of all things in a basement room at the church without a chaperone) that some mothers had their daughters withdraw." Other critics objected to the blousy trousers—called "bloomers"—that became standard physical education apparel in the 1880s.[43]

Administrators moved quickly to shield their students from such critiques. Marion Stevens Hood, a turn-of-the-century student at the all-female State Normal School in Greensboro, North Carolina, later recalled the care with which students prepared for the bloomer-clad walk from their dormitory rooms to the school's gymnasium. "After players put on their 'gym' suits . . . they must put on long black stockings, a top skirt which had a way of hanging down behind, and throw a coat around the shoulders," she explained. "The rear effect of the whole outfit reminded one of a rooster's tail feathers in wet weather, but we were nothing if not sticklers to the strictest sense of modesty."[44]

Many physical educators also went a step further, explicitly barring male spectators from games and classes. In 1902, when Atlanta University women played an exhibition game, only female students and teachers were permitted to attend, much to the dismay of their male peers. "Those who were present were pleased with the game," the student magazine politely reported. "Miss Greenough is an excellent instructor and the girls are apt pupils. They have learned readily because they enjoy it. We await the next game with much eagerness as it will, perhaps, be open to a larger number."[45]

Such bans sometimes caused more problems than they solved. In 1907, when Charlotte's Elizabeth and Presbyterian schools met for an intercollegiate game, the contest took on a carnival air, as binocular-toting young men scaled the roofs around the fields to catch a glimpse of the action, and were then chased down by police officers and arrested. Similar curiosity surfaced at the Stanford–Berkeley contest. Although men were barred from the audience, Mabel Craft reported, throughout the game the "windows were black with faces." Once the novelty wore off, however, most teams were able to play in peace.[46]

These careful efforts to shape a distinctly female game deflected many potential critics. But they could not fully obscure the revolution that women's sports represented. Even the most adroit physical educa-

Charlotte News *cartoon depicting the stir caused by the first women's inter-collegiate game in Charlotte, North Carolina, 1907.* COURTESY OF THE ROBINSON-SPANGLER CAROLINA ROOM, PUBLIC LIBRARY OF CHARLOTTE AND MECKLENBURG COUNTY.

tor could do little to combat her most fundamental challenge—the idea that sports was a strictly masculine preserve. Like other women's rights activists, physical educators found that their claims on independence and physical confidence were frequently viewed not as expanding the bounds of womanhood but as invading territory that belonged to men.

Such tensions were particularly evident at coeducational schools, where men and women came into closest contact. At times, athletics could become an excuse to restrict the very presence of women at such schools. Stanford, where the student body had celebrated the 1896 victory with such enthusiasm, offered one example. The school's charter had limited female enrollment to five hundred students. In 1899, as the student body expanded, Stanford trustees began to discuss raising that cap—a proposal that sparked considerable controversy. Some opponents of increasing female enrollment devoted particular attention to the supposed effects of female students on men's athletics. They claimed that women distracted men from sports by encouraging too much flirting, and that "the women put the standard of scholarship so high that the men cannot reach it and at the same time give proper attention to athletics."[47]

Efforts to expand women's sporting activities provoked their own complaints. At most institutions, men were accustomed to having the run of the gymnasium and other athletic facilities, and were often reluctant to share the space with women. When Mabel Lee was hired to teach physical education at Beloit College in Wisconsin, she ran into precisely this problem. When she arrived, the college's female students were not allowed to use the swimming pool, located "in the one building the men felt should be their exclusive domain."[48] It took a full semester of negotiation to get the pool opened to women, and then for a meager total of four hours a week.

Shortly afterward, Lee recounted, the student paper reported the apparently apocalyptic results. "Cancellation of the proposed interclass swimming meet was announced Thursday by Coach E.J. Osgood," the article ran. "The reason given for the action was that the meet would interfere with the use of the tank by the women of the college. Since the tank has been put at the complete disposal of the women's athletic department, any aquatic hopes the men might have cherished have been shattered, according to Coach Osgood."[49]

Such sharp distinctions between men's and women's activities—and, by extension, between male and female nature—would plague female athletes throughout the ensuing century. As at Beloit College, women's efforts to participate in existing athletic institutions would often be cast as a zero-sum activity, in which gains for women inevitably meant losses for men. Perhaps more significantly, the association between sports and masculinity meant that women who pursued athletic excellence often found their womanhood called into question. Sports-minded women might simply have been described as "healthy" or "athletic." Rather, they were often referred to as "mannish."[50]

FACED WITH THESE CHALLENGES, FEMALE PHYSICAL EDUCATORS focused on distinguishing themselves from their male colleagues and charting their own paths. At schools across the country, they built all-female departments and facilities where women could pursue sporting activities in a carefully controlled environment, without interference from competitors or critics. Their intelligence, energy and independence were well suited to this task. Many physical educators became savvy administrators who learned to negotiate the twists and turns of academic bureaucracies, and to carve out space for themselves and their students. They banded together in several state and national associations that came to wield considerable influence over educational policy. Their stress on the differences between men's and women's athletics became a key source of autonomy, as well as power. When Anna Hiss designed the women's gymnasium at the University of Texas, for example, she famously made the basketball court slightly shorter than a standard men's court. On one level, her decision suggested that women had less stamina than men. On another, it ensured that no men's team would ever usurp the women's space.[51]

With such efforts, physical educators built women's college sports into a separate and often powerful realm, one that ran by its own rules and where women were wholly in charge. But it was also a carefully defined realm, marked by a philosophy that still bore the stamp of Victorian ideals. While assumptions of female frailty had been banished, many other Victorian traits remained. Physical educators encouraged young women to be strong, but not overly forceful. They taught self-discipline, self-reliance and teamwork, but deliberately downplayed competition. They supported basketball, but held most games in private, emphasizing long-held virtues of modesty and restraint. It would require a different group of women to break out of that mold.

SECTION II

GRASSROOTS RISE
AND DECLINE

1920–1960

· 2 ·

High School Girls Spur the Sport

In the spring of 1920, the girls' basketball team from Iowa's Correctionville High School boarded an overnight train for Drake University in Des Moines. The team could not afford a sleeping car, so players napped in their seats. Enthusiasm ran high. In three seasons of play, they had compiled a record of 69–0, and won an invitation to Iowa's first-ever girls' state high school championship.

If Iowans had any doubts about their daughters' strength or stamina, the tournament schedule failed to reflect them. Correctionville played five games in two days, and "the only place to rest was in the dressing room on wrestling pads on the floor." The team played three games on the final day, and one went into overtime. Players got a half-hour break between the semifinal and the final. But in the final contest, Correctionville beat the squad from Nevada High School, 11–4, and was crowned Iowa's first girls' high school champion.

"I think perhaps the thing that I remember most about it was how tired we all were," team member Ona May Wilkin Breckenridge recalled thirty years later. "It was fun though. I'd do it again and I don't believe any of us suffered any ill effects from it, either."[1]

THE CORRECTIONVILLE PLAYERS WERE FAR FROM ALONE IN THEIR excitement. Girls' high school basketball teams sprang up throughout the country in the 1920s, embodying a view of women that differed markedly from the cautious decorum encouraged by college-based physical educators. Physical educators had fashioned their game from the cultural conventions of the nation's middle classes, where womanly ideals were governed by the ladylike refinement epitomized by country clubs, afternoon teas and charity endeavors. Elsewhere in the country, however, many women lived lives far removed from teacups and tennis courts. In rural communities, factory towns and working-class urban neighborhoods, women held down physically demanding jobs, shouldered responsibility for family support and walked the streets without the benefit of male protection. For many of these women, gentility was a luxury and female fortitude a given. Athletic competition seemed like fun, a fine place to channel youthful energy.

Iowa high school star Sarah Alien
Longchamp, Ida Grove, Iowa.
REPRODUCED, WITH PERMISSION,
FROM THE COLLECTIONS OF
THE IOWA WOMEN'S ARCHIVES,
UNIVERSITY OF IOWA LIBRARY.

This female sporting enthusiasm touched many lives. A handful of eager competitors—most notably the extraordinary Babe Didrikson—garnered national renown. Far more young women played their hearts out in local communities, performing for family and neighbors. In Iowa, girls' high school basketball became a state obsession. Elsewhere, eager players formed leagues and teams—sometimes battling physical educators for the right to compete. The Amateur Athletic Union (AAU) began to organize a national infrastructure for the women's game. "Basketball is the subject from morning until night; every one talks of it," one high school newspaper reported. Whenever a group of girls gathered together, the writer noted, "you can guess they are talking about basket ball."[2]

As well as drawing on local views of female strength, young women's competitive enthusiasm gained energy from shifts in the prevailing winds of national culture, which laid new emphasis on female accomplishment. In August of 1920, women finally won the right to vote, setting off celebrations around the nation. Women were joining in the nation's booming factory economy and were filling growing numbers of positions as sales clerks, telephone operators and secretaries. Newspapers and magazines regaled their readers with pictures of young city girls called "flappers," who bobbed their hair, stayed up all night at dances and wore thin, fashionable dresses that barely reached below their knees. Other women undertook even more daring endeavors. In the early 1920s, Bessie Coleman was feted throughout black America for her skill at the controls of an airplane. A few years later, Amelia Earhart won national fame as the first woman to fly across the Atlantic. For young women in the nineteenth century, ideas of proper womanhood had been governed by modesty and self-restraint. By the 1920s, the emphasis was on a vibrant, adventuresome personality, as well as a flirtatous brand of sexual appeal.

Female athletes personified many of these trends. French tennis star Suzanne Lenglen floated across the court in gauzy silk attire, dazzling observers with her wardrobe and winning match after match with her relentless play. In 1920, the United States sent its first official female delegation—a group of swimmers and divers—to the Olympic Games in

Antwerp, Belgium. In 1926, nineteen-year-old swimmer Gertrude Ederle slathered herself with grease and set out to swim from France to England across the icy, twenty-one-mile-wide English Channel. Only five men had accomplished the feat, and the fastest of them had taken more than sixteen hours. Despite strong winds and swells, Ederle waded onto British sand after only fourteen hours and thirty-one minutes, beating the record by almost two hours.[3]

The young women who came of age in the 1920s and 1930s delighted in such exploits, which were splashed across front pages, touted on radio broadcasts and displayed in movie-theater newsreels. In Beaumont, Texas, Mildred "Babe" Didrikson, who would become one of the nation's first female basketball stars, listened eagerly as her father read newspaper accounts of the 1928 Olympics, the first to include women's track and field. "It sounded like the greatest thing in the world to me," she wrote in her autobiography. "I started in training for the Olympics right then and there."[4]

Like many aspiring young athletes, Babe Didrikson grew up in a world far removed from the genteel surroundings of women's college campuses. Beaumont was a port city and an oil town—the Texas oil boom had started in 1901 when "black gold" started gushing from a test well at nearby Spindletop. The economic boom that followed filled the city with families whose female members were no strangers to physical labor. Many had come to the city from nearby farms, where women commonly plowed fields, hauled wood, picked cotton, killed chickens and drew water by hand. In Beaumont, women worked at a range of demanding occupations, including factory labor and domestic work. When times were hard in the Didrikson family, Babe's mother took in laundry, and Babe joined her in the arduous task of scrubbing, rinsing and hanging. "Little as I was, I'd wear my knuckles down scrubbing on that wash board," she wrote. She took her first factory jobs while still in junior high school, working in a fig-packing plant and a potato sack factory.[5]

Didrikson was athletic from the start. From a young age, she ran the streets of Beaumont with her brothers and sisters, playing pranks, joining in ball games and searching for new adventures. She ripped dresses, beat up boys and bragged about her accomplishments to anyone who would listen. She soon became known as the toughest kid on her block—boy or girl—and when teams were chosen for baseball, foot races, marbles or anything else, she was usually the first picked. She played more with boys than girls—"Girls did not play games that interested me," she later explained—and was always looking for new challenges.[6]

"Once they were building a new house in the neighborhood, and we were playing follow-the-leader there," she recalled. "Just the framework of the house was up—the studs and the flat rafters. I led the kids in climbing all over there. There was a sand pile alongside the house. I jumped into it from the top of the house. There was a sliver of wood in the sand pile, and it went right into the side of my leg. I still have the scar. . . ." As soon as she was bandaged up, she headed back out. "I started up to the top of the house again, and missed my step, and came down on my side with a terrible thump. My whole leg was skinned and bruised. I'd have got a whipping for sure after messing myself up a second time like that, if they hadn't found when I got home that I had three cracked ribs."[7]

Didrikson's parents, who had arrived in Texas from Norway in 1908, often struggled to make ends meet. Still, they supported the athletic endeavors of their five children, girls as well as boys. Her father built a makeshift weightlifting machine out of a broomstick, using a flatiron at each end for weights. Inspired by their yearly circus trips, the brothers and sisters filled the backyard chinaberry tree with swings and trapezes, and practiced daredevil stunts. Neighbors also indulged Didrikson's efforts. When she decided she wanted to become an Olympic hurdler, she began to jump her neighbors' front-yard hedges for practice. When her initial runs were cut short by one family's hedge, which was trimmed higher than her head, she confronted the obstacle straight-on. "I asked Mr. King if he'd mind cutting his hedge down to where the rest of them were, and he did it," she explained. In the 1932 Olympics, her running and jumping skills would win her worldwide acclaim. But she would get her real athletic start through basketball.[8]

BY THE TIME DIDRIKSON ENTERED BEAUMONT HIGH SCHOOL IN 1928, girls' basketball had become an institution in communities across

Team from Winchester Avenue High School, Monroe, North Carolina. COURTESY OF ROSA RUSHING.

the nation. Neither men's nor women's basketball had much presence on the national sporting scene, which was dominated by sports such as baseball, college football, golf and tennis. But for most young American women, basketball was the sport of choice. Rural and small-town high schools, which often lacked enough funds or players for football teams, seized on basketball as a cheaper but equally exciting alternative, providing teams for both boys and girls. In urban areas, gymnasiums built by churches, schools, businesses and YMCAs offered perfect venues for the sport. And since balls and rims could be easily improvised, anyone could play.

"Back then, we didn't have goals or basketballs," recalled Doris Coleman, who grew up in rural Longview, Louisiana. "So I got an old foot tub, and the ball just would fit in the bottom of it. I nailed it on a tree, a pecan tree. That's what I shot at for years. All my spare time, my mother and daddy would find me out there shooting basketball. They knew exactly where I was at all times."

Basketball's popularity would live on in the thousands of period photographs that made their way into scrapbooks, school annuals and historical societies as icons of community life. The game reached across boundaries of race, class and region, drawing in rural and urban, immigrant and native born, whites, Asians, Hispanics, Native Americans and African Americans. In towns and cities across the country, these young women proudly donned their uniforms, arranged themselves around a ball and posed for a local photographer. Some draped their arms around each other and smiled. Others gazed straight and serious into the lens. Some wore long, bulky bloomers; some sported knee-length versions. A few—if the coach was daring and the community receptive—dressed in shorts. No matter how they looked or what they wore, they laid claim to a public status that women rarely enjoyed. "Back then a girl, the only time she got her name in the paper was when she was born, when she got married, and when she died," recalled North Carolina high school coach Bill Bost. "That was it. When she played basketball, at least she could see her name in the paper."

Tournament participants at Rapid City Indian School, Rapid City, South Dakota, 1929. COURTESY OF THE NATIONAL ARCHIVES–CENTRAL PLAINS REGION, KANSAS CITY, MISSOURI.

Players themselves had started many of these teams. In 1920, the year that women gained the right to vote, Charlotte, North Carolina's Central High School sponsored a basketball team for boys, but none for girls. One day the principal found his office full of young women, who informed him that he was looking at the school's new basketball team. "We had played together, we were friends," recalled team member Mary Dalton. "So we just decided we wanted to have a basketball team and we said: 'We'll be it.' " Beneath their yearbook picture, the new team proudly announced: "Man's age has been heretofore, but now woman's age is coming in, not only in politics but in athletics."[9]

The 1923 girls' team at Tipton High School in Tipton County, Indiana, described their play with similar delight. That year, "the first time in the history of the school we have had 'woman's rights' in basketball," the team's record of eight wins and two losses was better than any boys' squad had ever achieved, team members noted in their yearbook. As they celebrated those accomplishments, they offered a pointed rebuttal to the skeptics they had encountered, most notably their principal. "Mr. Leap, who is a typical man thought the girls wouldn't make such a hit, so he wanted only a few games scheduled," they wrote, "but when the 'few' were won, he desired more and more, and thus our participants play on and on, greater than the unconquerable Achilles, with only two defeats to their glorious record."[10]

The confidence that rang through the players' statements underscored the links that advocates of women's rights had drawn between physical activity and women's broader social aspirations. As women's basketball expanded, players would find it an empowering experience in many ways.

Alline Banks was "just a little redheaded, freckle-faced gal" living with her parents and three brothers on a farm in Tennessee when she discovered the athletic gift that would eventually make her the best player in the country. "I was about seven or eight," she recalled. "I was playing against the boys at school, on a dirt court. And I come to find out I could hold my own with them. I remember that. Then each morning I was there. On the old dirt court against the boys, before school." Banks had a protective father who disapproved of bloomers and did not want her to play. But she loved to compete, and with her mother's support threw herself wholesale into the game. "I have no sisters, there were all brothers, and I had to fight to hold my own," she continued. "I would love to outdo my brothers or anyone else that I played against. I wanted to be better. I was very competitive. And I had to score more points than anyone else."

At Charlotte's Central High, player Elizabeth Newitt stretched her managerial skills as well as her muscles. Like Babe Didrikson, Newitt was no stranger to hardship. She was only fourteen when her father, a railroad engineer, was killed in an accident, leaving an ailing widow and several children. "I had to learn to keep house, cook and manage money," Newitt recalled. When she became basketball team manager in 1923, she applied the same determination to that task. "I had a lot of ambition for us to grow and to be active and to be very much like the boys," she explained. "So I set out to have a lot of games, give it a lot of publicity, make a lot of money. Which we did. We had headlines in the paper, big headlines when we would have a game. We drew a big crowd. And we made a lot of money. I bought the uniforms for the girls. Had enough money to buy uniforms for the boys on the football team. And I just made money right and left."

The uniforms that Newitt purchased made a statement of their own—Central High School players felt no need to hide behind their clothes. When shorter bloomers came into fashion, some teams kept their stockings decorously up over their knees. Central High's players rolled theirs down.

Basketball also gave new meaning to height and strength. Growing up in the black community of Durham, North Carolina, 5'10½" Missouri Arledge towered over everyone in her class, boys as well as girls, and was painfully self-conscious of her height. "I always was the last person in line, because you had to line up according to height," she recalled. "And when we had pictures made I had to be on the back row." But then the Hillside High School coach spotted her in gym class and convinced her to join the basketball team. As the team's winning record grew, Arledge's fame began to spread and she found herself "always being told how *nice* and tall you were: 'So nice and tall.' " The words were music to her ears. "That helped," she noted.

At Beaumont High School, the social scene was dominated by the

Team from Central High School, Charlotte, North Carolina, 1923. Elizabeth Newitt is third from right with bow in hair. COURTESY OF THE ROBINSON-SPANGLER CAROLINA ROOM, PUBLIC LIBRARY OF CHARLOTTE AND MECKLENBURG COUNTY.

daughters of oil executives and shipping magnates, who belonged to the country club, dressed in the latest fashions and drove to school in luxury cars. With her close-cropped hair, rough manners and homemade cotton dresses, Babe Didrikson could not compete on their terrain. But like many other young women around the country, she found that the athletic skills she had honed since childhood won her a place of honor. Her freshman year, she recalled, the coach would not let her join the team because he thought she was too small. The next year, however, he relented. "I was the high scorer from the start," she wrote. "We went to different towns to play girls at other high schools, and we beat them all. I got my first newspaper write-up—a little item headed, BEAUMONT GIRL STARS IN BASKETBALL GAME. Then it was, BEAUMONT GIRL STARS AGAIN." [11]

THIS GROWTH DID NOT PROCEED WHOLLY UNCHECKED. AS HIGH school teams proliferated, the physical educators who dominated college women's athletics watched with alarm. Not only did high school teams promote heated competition, players often performed before large, paying audiences. Crowds, profits and bared knees had delighted Elizabeth Newitt and her Central High School teammates. They appalled physical educators, who worried that schools were exploiting young women to make money and that the explosion in spectator sports was nurturing the skills of a few at the expense of the many. These women often disapproved of men's varsities as well as women's. But they aimed their reform efforts at women's sports, where they felt the greatest responsibility and saw the best chance of success.

In the early 1920s, physical educators launched a nationwide effort to promote their brand of sedate, cooperative play in high schools. Girls' basketball became their major target. As they pressed their cause, they picked up local allies, especially at predominantly white schools in larger cities, where administrators tended to share their middle-class views of female conduct. State by state, supporters of girls' basketball found themselves having to fight to keep their teams. In places where they lost, play days and intramural sports became the norm in high schools as well as colleges.[12]

One of the most important battles took place in Iowa. Basketball's popularity had grown rapidly within the rural state, sparking the creation of the girls' state tournament in 1920. Soon afterward, the state's female physical educators struck back, criticizing the championship and calling for its abolition. In 1925, the tournament became the focus of hot debate at the annual meeting of the Iowa High School Athletic Association, which governed both girls' and boys' sports. At the end of the meeting, the members voted 259–25 to end the event.

Supporters of the game, however, would not be stopped. They believed strongly in their cause—one coach became an instant legend when he stood up and declared: "Gentlemen, if you attempt to do away with girls' basketball in Iowa, you'll be standing in the center of the track when the train runs over!" After the meeting, representatives from the twenty-five dissenting schools decided to form their own organization—the Iowa Girls' High School Athletic Union (IGHSAU). In the decades to come, the efficiency and independence of the IGHSAU would build the most vibrant girls' high school basketball program in the nation.[13]

Tellingly, all the rebels were male. Disputes over women's basketball would never be a simple matter of women versus men. Many men would continue to encourage women's play, and until the 1970s, most of the nation's highly competitive women's teams would have male coaches. The battle lines over women's sports would instead be drawn between clashing assumptions about women's capabilities and about the role that sports should play in individual development and community life.

Some opponents of women's basketball cast their arguments in terms of male and female nature, portraying competitive sports as an exclusively male arena, which young women were physically and psychologically unfit to enter. Others adopted more nuanced positions. Most physical educators were critical of the entire varsity endeavor, male or female, but tended to focus on its unsuitability for women. Other detractors emphasized the community and commercial side of sports, suggesting that young women would be unable to bring in enough gate receipts to finance their play. Still others questioned whether girls needed the lessons of competitive sports as much as boys did. In these last two arguments lay an issue that would plague women's sports into the twenty-first century—the concern that girls' teams would draw too many resources away from more deserving boys' squads. In the minds of the IGHSAU founders, this reluctance to share resources, not concerns about young women's health, was the major reason the girls' tournament was eliminated.

Supporters of girls' sports, in contrast, tended to be local principals and coaches who believed strongly in the value of organized athletics and who thought girls as well as boys should reap the benefits. G.L. Sanders, one of the IGHSAU's founders, explained his conversion to his female students' cause in a 1948 article. From 1912 to 1920, Sanders wrote, "I spent so much time with the boys . . . that I didn't pay much attention to girls' basketball. Then suddenly it dawned on me that less than half of my high school enrollment was being provided with the priv-

ilege of participation in any sort of supervised athletics. So I began encouraging the girls in my school to play the game."[14]

The IGHSAU held its first tournament in 1926. The winners, from
Hampton High School, reveled in their achievement. "Leaving overwhelming disaster in their wake, their record unblemished by defeat,
the Hampton Sextet—the demons in red—swept to a state championship," their yearbook description read. "Handling the apple with an
adroitness never seen before in girls' basketball, sacrificing personal ag-
grandizement for cooperative play yet playing colorfully and brilliantly,
battling from the initial tip-off to the final gun, pivoting, double passing,
guarding mercilessly, darting and flashing about the waxed floor like
streaks of red . . . a greater team than this has never been assembled."
Scores bore out the extravagance of the claims. In an era where games
could still be won with single-digit tallies, Hampton averaged 44 points

Team from Ida Grove High School, Iowa state champions in 1928. REPRODUCED,
WITH PERMISSION, FROM THE COLLECTIONS OF THE IOWA WOMEN'S ARCHIVES, UNIVERSITY
OF IOWA LIBRARY.

a game. In the finals of the Franklin County tournament, they had defeated Hansell 100–2.[15]

In subsequent years, girls' basketball wove itself into the fabric of Iowa life. Between 1925 and 1950, IGHSAU membership grew from twenty-five to seven hundred schools. Throughout the state, communities strove to make the most of what they had. Some teams played outdoors; others competed in "crackerbox" gymnasiums that varied widely in width and length, in which defenders could often count on low-hung ceiling rafters to help block shots. "Home-court advantage" meant not simply the support of a partisan crowd, but also knowing a court's secrets: how to tailor plays to a floor's unusual size, how to use close-set walls for unorthodox bounce passes and how best to avoid the red-hot, coal-burning stoves that often stood perilously close to the action. Most uniforms were homemade, and as the Depression set in, players in at least one town practiced in their socks, saving their precious basketball shoes for games.[16]

Travel proved its own adventure. Basketball had been invented as a winter sport because it could be played indoors. But in rural Iowa, the season's rain and snow turned dirt roads into quagmires, often eliminating the need for pregame warmups. A reporter at one early game attributed the outcome to the victorious team's ability to outlast their balky vehicles, noting, "The girls hadn't lost their pep even if they did have to walk up all the hills and push the Fords in the mud."[17]

In the first years of the IGHSAU, teams played with the three-division rules that Senda Berenson had pioneered. In 1934, however, the state switched to a new game, one that would mark U.S. women's play for almost four decades and would last in Iowa until 1993. The new rules drew a line down center court, and assigned six players to each team. Three forwards played in a team's offensive half, while three guards blocked and rebounded on the defensive end. No one could cross the center line. At first, a player could dribble only once before passing or shooting. Some time later, a second dribble was permitted.[18]

Girls' rules, which so closely mirrored shifting assessments of women's physical potential, would never have the consistency of the regulations governing the boys' game. Modifications would be introduced over the years—most notably, some schools and associations would eventually permit one or two "roving" players to play the entire court. In many states, the lack of a statewide organization governing girls' play meant that rules differed from community to community, ranging from three-division to two-division to full-court boys' rules play. But in Iowa, with its comprehensive, centralized organization, the two-division, two-dribble game became the lasting norm.[19]

In the early years, Iowa's coaches scoured their local areas for raw but promising talent, sometimes with startling results. When all-state guard Mildred Moore played her first high school game, she promptly demonstrated her potential by throwing a pass so hard it sailed right through the wall of the Hillsboro High gymnasium. In tiny Wiota, whose population hovered just above 250, and where high school enrollment topped out at 66, legendary coach J.J. O'Connor paid special attention to the Armstrong family, which boasted six daughters. Shortly after O'Connor arrived in Wiota in 1934, Maxine Armstrong recalled, "he brought a hoop and a ball out to our farm, nailed the hoop up on the barn and that's where we all started playing." Wiota made the state tournament ten times between 1940 and 1951, and won the state title in 1944 and 1945. Two of the Armstrongs would be voted into the state hall of fame.[20]

Throughout Iowa, girls' basketball became a source of community pride. "They always said, 'Coal is king,'" recalled Ethel Lira, who grew up in the coal-mining town of Numa. "But girls' basketball was queen." Many of Numa's miners were recent immigrants from Southern and Eastern Europe, and many did not speak English. But, Lira continued, "they all wanted their kids to be somebody and not to wind up working in the coal mines all their lives. So they stressed education, and they pushed their kids in sports." The determination forged by the harsh realities of coal-mining life took Numa to several state tournaments and the 1941 title. "Our girls were rough," Lira proudly recounted. "We were always known for that. They played for blood. It was always like, 'Get out of my way or I'm coming through you!'"[21]

The game got better by the year, as young women began to devote countless hours to preparing for high school stardom. In 1942, Clutier

High went undefeated and won the state championship. As the varsity was tearing through its opposition, coach John Schoenfelder explained, "the fifth grade girls were trying their luck on outdoor baskets. With overcoats, stocking caps, overshoes and mittens keeping out the severe cold, they were laying the foundation for our future teams. Before school, at recess, at noon, and after school, they were outside trying to hit the basket."[22]

"Take a tour through the country and you'll find an old tire rim nailed to the side of a building," Schoenfelder continued. "These are never rusty. They are kept polished by a constant rain of shots from an aspiring girl and one or two neighbor girls or boys."

The girls' state tournament, which became one of Iowa's most beloved institutions, was a key factor in the game's remarkable growth. The tournament gave every season a focus and became an enduring measure of success. As time went on and memories built up, it offered players and communities the chance to join a storied athletic tradition, connecting to the classic tales of triumph and heartbreak, obstacle and opportunity, hard work and courage that lifted sports beyond mere physical enjoyment. Just making it to the sixteen-team draw was an achievement, and whole towns emptied out to follow their teams to the action. When Hansell High took the title in 1940, *Life* magazine reported that there "wasn't a hall in town big enough to hold the crowds who turned out to greet the team." A few years later, when Wellsburg won it all, the school bus carrying the players home was followed by a six-mile line of cars. In 1947, the tournament sold 40,000 tickets, and fans were turned away.[23]

ALTHOUGH FEW PLACES IN THE COUNTRY COULD MATCH IOWA'S support, women's basketball drew fans almost everywhere. Even in areas where school authorities conspired to limit their opportunities, women found other ways to play the game they loved. In urban centers, where physical educators held greatest sway, young women found alternate sponsors, including churches, employers, athletic clubs and ethnic organizations. In the early 1920s, Chicagoans could follow teams whose sponsors included the Jewish Peoples' Institute, Olivet Baptist Church, the Mid-City Athletic Club and the travel-trunk manufacturer Taylor

Trunks. Paced by national black tennis champion Isadore Channels and managed by track star Sol Butler, the independent Romas (also called the Roamers) were considered the best black team in the country in the 1920s. In the 1930s, Los Angeles was home to teams such as the all-black Athena Athletic Club, the Chinese-American Mei Wah and Lo Wah teams, the Sunfreeze Ice Cream Company team, the *California Eagle*–sponsored Eaglettes and the Queen Esther Japanese. City competition was often heated, recalled Lo Wah player Dorothy Hom, and as well as having fun the players "learned survival." The Lo Wah players were small—their coach referred to them as his "chihuahuas." But they were quick and determined. "You were there to win, and that was the only thing on our minds," Hom said.[24]

Such efforts got a major boost in 1923, when the Amateur Athletic Union (AAU) decided to begin sponsoring competitive women's sports. Founded in 1888, the AAU had become the dominant governing body in American sports and had developed a national infrastructure that would

Chinese American women's basketball team, Seattle, Washington, 1938. COURTESY OF THE MUSEUM OF HISTORY & INDUSTRY, SEATTLE.

serve women well. The AAU held its first national women's basketball championship in Pasadena, California, in 1926. AMAZONS HERE FROM ALL OVER COUNTRY, the *Los Angeles Times* announced. The tournament was won by the home team, the Pasadena Athletic Club. It was held again in 1929 and thereafter was an annual event. From the 1920s to the 1970s, the AAU champion was broadly acknowledged as the nation's best women's team.[25]

In those early years, many of the most talented AAU teams were sponsored by business enterprises, which nurtured a thriving culture of industrial athletics from the 1910s into the 1950s. The idea of company-sponsored athletics had been born in the early 1900s, when labor experts claimed that company teams would inspire worker loyalty while teaching the discipline, teamwork and competitive spirit of the industrial age. W.M. Grier, president of the Southern Textile Athletic Association, summed up those sentiments in 1929. "Players have come to realize that it is teamwork that counts in the end, and they have coordinated their effort on the basketball court and in their daily tasks," he remarked. "They realize to become efficient they must know their job, and must be able to get along with their associates and know how to accomplish the best results by working with them."[26]

Team sponsorship had other benefits as well. As the popularity of women's basketball grew, businesses also began to see women's teams as savvy advertising, an appealing way to get their name into the public eye. A proliferating number of "business colleges," which trained young women in filing, typing and shorthand, saw basketball as an ideal way to recruit students, and many fielded teams. Iowa boasted two of the best: the Des Moines–based American Institute of Business and the Davenport-based American Institute of Commerce, which would win two AAU national championships in the 1940s. A wide range of other sponsors emerged. In Dallas, teams and tournaments were sponsored by Sanger Department Store, Franklin Motor Car, Sonoco Oil, Employers Casualty Insurance and Piggly Wiggly Groceries, among others. As the sport's profile rose, teams began to scour the country for talented players.[27]

Babe Didrikson moved into this world in 1930, her senior year at

Team from the American Institute of Business, Des Moines, Iowa, 1934. REPRO-
DUCED, WITH PERMISSION, FROM THE COLLECTIONS OF THE IOWA WOMEN'S ARCHIVES,
UNIVERSITY OF IOWA LIBRARY.

Beaumont High. As she told it, the Beaumont team had just finished a
game in Houston when insurance executive Melvin J. McCombs came
up to her "and asked if I'd like to play on a real big-time team." Mc-
Combs worked for Employers Casualty in Dallas, which sponsored a
team called the Golden Cyclones. He offered Didrikson a job with the
company and a chance to play for the Cyclones. She jumped at the opportunity. Only a few weeks later, she had decided to postpone her final
high school semester and was standing with her father at the Beaumont
railroad station, waiting for the overnight train to Dallas. "You never saw
anybody more excited than I was that night," she later wrote. "Here I
was, just a little old high-school girl, wanting to be a big athlete. And
now I was getting a chance. . . ."[28]

As Didrikson quickly learned, life as an industrial athlete was far
from luxurious. AAU rules barred professional players, and most team
members held down jobs, usually in the sponsoring firm. Players got
time off for travel, less often for games or practice. Finding the right job

fit was not always easy, recalled Eckie Jordan, who competed for the Hanes Hosiery plant in Winston-Salem, North Carolina. Jordan felt at home on the court, but was lost on the production line. "I started working in the seaming department . . . but I didn't stay on that seaming job any time. That's when you still had seams, and I never did sew a straight one and so a year later I was in the office."[29] Although Didrikson arrived in Dallas not knowing how to type, she was assigned a clerical position and she learned on the job. She lived in the same neighborhood as the other team members and, like them, ate at the house of the team's assistant coach, paying fifteen cents for breakfast and thirty-five cents for dinner.[30]

McCombs promoted the Cyclones with style. By the time Didrikson joined the team, he had recruited eight All-Americans. The year after she got there, he took the players out of bloomers and blouses and put them into shorts and sleeveless tops, a controversial move that nonetheless improved play and boosted audiences. Didrikson also did her part, making an immediate impact on the national basketball scene. Shortly after she joined the team, the Cyclones traveled to Wichita, Kansas, for the AAU national tournament. Although they lost to their hometown rival, the three-time champion Sonoco Oilers, Didrikson was named to the All-American team. The next year, when the tournament was held in Dallas, she scored 106 points, and the Cyclones claimed the title.[31]

By then, Didrikson was setting her sights even higher. Although basketball was fun, it was not yet a major sport on the national or international scene. As a result, when the Cyclones' season ended, she began to train for the more high-profile realm of track and field. "After dinner I'd go out in my tennis shoes and run," she recalled. "They had a hill on Haines Street that went down to a lake. I'd run all the way down there, and then I'd jog all the way back up. I'd jog my legs real high, and work my arms high, to get them in shape. Of course, they were already about as hard as they could be, but I thought they had to be better."[32]

In 1932, McCombs settled on another publicity-minded endeavor—sending Didrikson to the national AAU track and field meet as a one-woman team. The gamble paid off handsomely. In a single afternoon she competed in eight events and won six of them, including the shot put, the javelin throw, the 80-meter hurdles and the broad jump. At the end of the day, she had single-handedly amassed more points than any other team, winning the national title for Employers Casualty and widespread acclaim for herself. She followed that achievement with a remarkable performance at the 1932 Los Angeles Olympics, where she won the javelin and the 80-meter hurdles and was second in the high jump. (In a typical effort to "protect" women from too much exertion, Olympic regulations allowed them to enter only three events.)[33]

DIDRIKSON'S WELL-PUBLICIZED ACHIEVEMENTS UNDERSCORED women's athletic abilities. But reactions to her fame revealed persisting discomfort with female athletic skill in many segments of American society. For her, as for many other athletes, the shifts in womanly ideals that marked the 1920s proved a double-edged sword. In the Victorian era, when womanhood had been defined in terms of moral propriety, women had been hampered by corsets, long skirts and an insistence on genteel behavior. The new emphasis on sexual appeal gave young

Babe Didrikson, Brooklyn, New York, 1933. COURTESY OF THE LIBRARY OF CONGRESS.

women more leeway in dress and movement. But it set other, equally demanding standards that judged women by how attractive they appeared to men. Women who did not fit this mold—or did not seem to try—often faced ridicule or suspicion. By the mid-1930s, as homosexuality became a more open topic in American society, the "mannish athlete" was also in danger of being dubbed a "mannish lesbian," a label that brought harsh condemnation.[34]

Nowhere were such demands more evident than in the national sports media. While local sportswriters often warmly supported female athletes, sports coverage in major newspapers and national magazines was dominated by a handful of prominent male writers who often seemed far more interested in how female athletes looked than in how they played.

In "The Texas Babe," published in *Vanity Fair* in 1932, noted sportswriter Paul Gallico stuck Didrikson with the label "Muscle Moll," a phrase that conjured images of a woman focused on her own hard strength rather than on conventional feminine charm. Gallico waxed eloquent about Didrikson's athletic skill, calling her "magnificently graceful" as well as remarkably strong. But he struggled to reconcile her talent with his ideas of what women should be. "When a lady athlete can perform the feats that La Didrikson can," he wrote, "she begins to exercise a peculiar and mysterious fascination all her own." The closest comparison he could muster involved a circus sideshow. Although he did not fully understand the source of his intrigue, he continued, "It may be the same thing that keeps me lingering in front of the bearded lady and Airy Fairy Lillian, the Albino girl, or Mirzah, the snake charmer."[35]

Didrikson's tremendous skill, he went on to suggest, had not made her happy, largely because it held no attraction for men. "She knows she is not pretty, that she cannot compete with other girls in the very ancient and honored sport of man-trapping," he wrote. "She uses no cosmetics, creams or powders. But she competes with girls, fiercely and hungrily, at everything else." Gallico expanded on his views of sports and femininity in a later article, where he opined, "It is a lady's business to look beautiful, and there are hardly any sports in which she seems able to do it."[36] This focus on appearance was echoed by Avery Brundage, longtime president of the U.S. Olympic Committee. "I am fed up to the ears with women as track and field competitors," Brundage remarked at the 1936 Olympics. "Their charms sink to less than zero."[37]

Such pointed criticism would prove difficult to ignore. The term "Muscle Moll" became a convenient symbol for the idea of a hardened, "mannish" and thoroughly unacceptable female athlete, who stood no chance of finding a husband or living a "normal" life. In some physical education classes, signs admonished students: DON'T BE A MUSCLE MOLL. Increasingly, women in sports felt the need to demonstrate both their femininity and their interest in men through boyfriends, stylish dress or talk about marriage and children. Despite their focus on gentility, physical educators found that their decision to pursue sports-related careers put them under particular pressure to avoid the "mannish" stereotype. "My mother used to cry when I played softball," one woman later recalled. "She'd say, 'I just don't want you to grow up to be like Babe Didrikson.'"[38]

Still, the ability of national media to define female sporting experience remained limited. During the 1920s and 1930s, Americans read newspapers and magazines, visited movie theaters and listened to the radio. But in those pre-television days, mass-market media had far less influence than it would later wield. And in those communities that embraced girls' basketball, the sport had grown into a formidable institution. The players of the 1920s and 1930s had not freed themselves from the full panoply of constraints that bound women's actions. But they had accomplished a great deal. They had proven that women could compete at a high level. They had fashioned leagues, tournaments and other institutions that nurtured the talents of many aspiring athletes. Most important, they had given young women the opportunity to act, to express themselves and to develop in new ways.

Like most players of this era, Elizabeth Newitt ended her competitive basketball career in high school. But she carried the lessons she had learned throughout her life. In subsequent decades, she became one of North Carolina's most respected citizens, playing active roles in state and local education, as well as in Democratic politics. In 1992, seventy years after she had been named manager of the Central High School team, she described basketball's effects on her in vivid detail.

"Well, the thing of it is, it's teamwork," she explained. "And excellence. For instance [our] coach, Dick Kirkpatrick. We would get two free throws for a foul. And in one of the games that we played, I missed one. I was awfully good at shooting. And that one aggravated him so, that he made me stand up and shoot one hundred baskets in practice. So you emphasized excellence. And you learned to coordinate, and I knew exactly where the other forward would be. She knew where I would be. We knew how to communicate and get the ball to each other. And work with the center that would roam the field. You're not only competing against the other team, but you're developing a wonderful, wonderful teamwork. And support system. So it's teaching you character in many ways. . . . A lot of women need courses in being assertive. I think that is one of the greatest needs that we have. And I do think that basketball brings that out."

She concluded by offering a final tribute to the team and to the coach who had believed in them. "He wanted us to be every bit as good as the boys' team," she said. "And to tell you the truth, we were fantastic."

·3·

Black Women Embrace the Game

Helen "Midge" Davis stepped to the foul line at Philadelphia's New Broadway Athletic Club and sized up a crucial shot. It was the first of April 1932; the clock showed fifteen seconds left. The stakes were high: the winner would take a hard-fought, five-game series and be crowned the best black women's team in the country. Davis's squad, the newspaper-sponsored Philadelphia Tribunes, trailed the defending champion Germantown Hornets by one point.

If Davis felt the pressure, however, she did not show it. As "everyone held their breath," wrote *Philadelphia Tribune* reporter Randy Dixon, "she calmly toed the mark . . . and sank the shot." Her effort turned the tide. The game went into overtime, and the Tribunes scored eight unanswered points to take the crown. The crowd exploded.

"It was fully ten minutes before order could be restored," Dixon continued. "The cash customers fanned to fever heat by the ardor and closeness of combat gave outlet to all kinds of riotous impulses. They stood on chairs and hollered. Others hoisted members of the winning team upon their shoulders and paraded them around the hall. They jigged and danced, and readers believe me, they were justified. It was just that kind of a game."[1]

AS WOMEN'S BASKETBALL SPREAD ACROSS THE COUNTRY, IT MET with particular enthusiasm in African American communities. Young black women formed teams, worked out strategies, clashed with parents over uniforms and delighted in the sight of watching perfect shots fall through the hoop. The game quickly became an institution at African American high schools, and community teams like the Hornets and the Tribunes drew large, supportive crowds. Basketball also spread to historically black colleges, where women were forging an expansive sense of womanhood suited to the broad range of challenges faced by African American communities during the Jim Crow era. While physical educators at white schools fashioned athletic programs that meshed seamlessly with ladylike ideals of gentility and order, students at black colleges often stepped beyond those bounds. Nowhere was this clearer than in basketball. "We were ladies," recalled Bennett College star Ruth Glover. "We just played basketball like boys."[2]

This early heyday of black women's basketball did not draw the attention it deserved. The strict lines of Jim Crow meant that black women

Livingstone College team, Salisbury, North Carolina, 1934. COURTESY OF THE HERITAGE HALL ARCHIVES AND RESEARCH CENTER, LIVINGSTONE COLLEGE.

had little chance to play outside African American communities. Apart from scattered articles in black newspapers and college publications, few records were kept. Even among African Americans, memories of the era's female stars would fade with startling rapidity, overshadowed by the more dramatic exploits of the racial pioneers of the 1940s and 1950s. But like so many institutions of the Jim Crow era, women's basketball had long-lasting effects on black Americans, setting an inspiring example of black women's capabilities and nurturing a group of women who would devote their lives to their communities.

Philadelphia became an especially vibrant center for black women's basketball, as seen in the enthusiasm that greeted the Tribunes–Hornets series. The sport took off in 1931, when the newly organized Hornets, sponsored by Germantown's black YWCA, went 22–1 and claimed the black national championship. One of the city's best-known players, Inez "Pat" Patterson, then persuaded the *Tribune* to sponsor a rival team for 1932. The Hornets and the Tribunes spent that winter traveling up and down the eastern seaboard, meeting challenges from black colleges, athletic clubs, churches and YWCAs, as well as from a handful of white women's teams and at least one men's squad. Their play sparked so much enthusiasm that their games often outdrew those played by the *Tribune*'s male squad, teams from nearby Lincoln University and even the professional Harlem Renaissance team.[3]

The game also sported a bright new star. Although Germantown center Ora Washington stood only about 5'7", she was a superb athlete—powerfully built, with broad shoulders and sharply defined muscles as well as lightning speed, a fearsome work ethic and unmatched competitive zeal. She was the reigning national black tennis champion, and from the moment she stepped onto a basketball court, sportswriters heralded her as the best female cager they had ever seen. Her performance in the 1932 series did not disappoint. In the first contest, with the Hornets down by five, she took charge of the game, executing "a foul goal, then a left-handed stab on the run, and another heart-winger made on the left side of the basket over her left shoulder." She had sparked a fifth-game rally, which brought the Hornets within seconds of the championship, with an "awe-provoking" shot from well past half-court. When the

Tribune's Randy Dixon picked the year's all-star team, he called her "the greatest girl player of the age."[4]

"Ora can do everything required of a basketball player," Dixon wrote. "She passes and shoots with either hand. She is a ball hawk. She has stamina and speed that make many male players blush with envy. And despite . . . elaborate defenses especially mapped out to stop her she has averaged 16 points per game with a high total of 38 points in one game."

Otto Briggs, who managed the Tribunes, knew a good thing when he saw it. Briggs had been a longtime star outfielder on Philadelphia's most successful Negro League baseball team, and after retiring he had become an energetic entrepreneur, using his athletic fame and his position as the *Tribune*'s circulation manager to launch business endeavors that included a men's basketball team and a roller-skating rink, as well as the female Tribunes. In the fall of 1932, when basketball season opened, Ora Washington had exchanged her Hornets jersey for a Tribunes uniform. She already dominated black women's tennis, once inspiring the *Chicago Defender* to remark: "Her superiority is so evident that her competitors are frequently beaten before the first ball crosses the net."[5] Basketball would only build that reputation. The Tribunes were the best black team in the country for more than a decade, and Washington became the first black female athlete hailed as a major national sensation.

"No one who ever saw her play could forget her," one fan recalled, "nor could anyone who met her."[6]

WHEN ORA WASHINGTON ARRIVED IN PHILADELPHIA IN THE LATE 1910s, she had little inkling of the fame that lay ahead. Born just before the turn of the century, she grew up the fifth of nine children on a farm in rural Caroline County, Virginia, about seventy-five miles south of Washington, D.C. She attended a tiny, two-room school, and in the sparsely populated countryside, community baseball teams were the only form of organized athletics. The nation had seen a bare handful of black sports greats, many of whom had been barred from mainstream competition or—like boxing legend Jack Johnson—hounded out of the

Philadelphia Tribunes, Philadelphia, Pennsylvania, 1938. Ora Washington is standing, third from right. COURTESY OF THE *PHILADELPHIA TRIBUNE.*

country. The Negro Leagues were in their infancy. There had never been a national black female star.

The Washingtons were a large and close family, and unlike most black farmers they owned their own land. Still, they faced their share of struggles. In 1908, when Ora was nine, her mother Laura died in child-birth, leaving eight daughters and a newborn son. Her father, James "Tommy" Washington, supplemented the farm income with work as a house plasterer, but such jobs were scarce. At the time of the 1910 census, he had been out of work for months and the family farm had been mortgaged. The promising era of Reconstruction had come to a crashing end, and black Virginians faced not only agricultural depression but the threat of racial violence and the hardening lines of Jim Crow segregation.[7]

Like many of their peers, the Washingtons began to look north for opportunity. Ora's aunt Mattie was the first to go. She headed to Philadelphia, where the rail lines ran. She married, settled and then sent for her nieces. On one now-forgotten morning in the 1910s, Ora traveled by wagon to the nearby community of Milford, Virginia, where she boarded a northbound train. In January of 1920, just days before her twenty-first birthday, a Philadelphia census taker found her working as a live-in servant in a home on Springfield Avenue.[8]

Washington and her family found no racial Eden. Philadelphia's African Americans were generally confined to the bottom rungs of the economic ladder. Men worked mainly as laborers and women almost exclusively as maids or housekeepers. The sheer numbers of new arrivals crowded black neighborhoods to bursting, overwhelmed social services and heightened both racial tensions and racial violence. Still, obstacles were balanced by opportunities. Although jobs paid poorly, there were plenty of them. Philadelphia offered better schools, more social services and some relief from the day-to-day indignities of Jim Crow. And as in black communities across the country, the city's African Americans responded to an increasingly hostile racial climate by turning inward, building a rich range of social and cultural institutions.[9]

Southern migrants proved avid entrepreneurs, and the city's African American neighborhoods were soon dotted with restaurants, beauty parlors and barbershops, as well as churches and jazz clubs. A black-owned bank, the Citizens and Southern, became one of Philadelphia's most stable financial institutions. Cultural life blossomed as well. The city's black theaters showcased nationally renowned performers such as Bessie Smith, Duke Ellington, Louis Armstrong and Marian Anderson. At the Royal Grand movie palace, lucky moviegoers could sometimes find jazz great Fats Waller manning the organ. Throughout the 1910s and 1920s, Philadelphia's wealthiest black businessman was theater owner John T. Gibson, whose successes allowed him to maintain both a city house and a suburban estate, and to travel in a red Pierce Arrow with a white chauffeur.[10]

Migration also proved a boon to black sports, providing talented players and thousands of new spectators. On Saturdays, black Philadelphians could catch the streetcar to the outskirts of town to watch the local Hilldale baseball team take on the nation's best Negro League squads. High schools and colleges began to expand their sports facilities, fielding a broader range of teams. Philadelphia became a regular stop for the era's many barnstorming professional squads. Black churches, YMCAs and other organizations all expanded their athletic offerings. In the up-and-coming suburb of Germantown, the recently opened black YWCA was especially proud of its newly laid tennis courts.[11]

It was at the Y that Washington found her calling. Like many young working women, she joined the institution soon after arriving in the city. Then, sometime in the mid-1920s, her older sister Georgia died of tuberculosis back in Virginia. Seeing Ora's abiding grief, a sympathetic Y instructor suggested she distract herself by trying tennis.[12]

Her first lesson must have been an event. She was in her mid-twenties, a plain, light-skinned woman with big hands and a square jaw. The awe she would later inspire makes it clear that she possessed extraordinary physical ability—the kind of speed and strength and touch essential to athletic greatness. No doubt that would have shown. The mental force that would plague a generation of opponents may also have been evident.

"She was so strong," recalled Amaleta Moore, whose sister played with Washington years later. "She was intimidating. The way she looked at you: 'You've got no business in my way.'" Relatives described Washington as a hardworking, no-nonsense individual who was always looking out for family members but who also possessed a fierce competitive instinct. Nephew Lewis Hill recalled her as a kind-hearted person, a "doll-baby," but added that "if you made her mad, you had a tiger on your hands."

Washington took to the game immediately. By 1925, she had upset the reigning national singles champion, Chicago's Isadore Channels, and teamed with fellow Philadelphian Lula Ballard to win the national American Tennis Association doubles title, a crown she would hold for twelve straight years. In 1929, she broke through to the singles championship, the first of eight national titles. Not one to rest on her laurels, she began her basketball career the next fall.[13]

Throughout the 1930s, Washington and the Tribunes were an integral part of Philadelphia's vibrant black sporting scene, playing most of their home games at the Catherine Street YWCA. During the team's season, which opened in November and continued into April, Otto

Briggs arranged dozens of games. Following the successful formula of male professional teams, he often scheduled dances or other entertainment to follow a contest. Players earned small salaries and worked at other jobs to make ends meet.

Playing with full-court men's rules, the Tribunes raised black women's basketball to a new level. Bennett College player Ruth Glover played against the team in 1934 and spoke of them with unabashed admiration. "They just had it all together," she said. "They could dribble and keep the ball and make fast moves in to the basket which you couldn't stop." The team received regular coverage in the national black press, and spectators flocked eagerly to their games, sometimes packing in so tight that officials had to rope off the playing floor. By 1934, Briggs was so confident of his team's drawing power that he scheduled an extended tour of the South and Midwest, with an eye toward profit as well as promotion.[14]

25c Start saving 25c now so you can attend on Thanksgiving Nite the TRIBUNE Girls big opening **25c**

BASKETBALL Game and DANCE

Thursday Evening, Nov. 24th—Y. W. C. A. 1605 Catherine St.

OTTO BRIGGS'   THEY SATISFY

Tribune Girls vs. Bridgeton Omega Girls

National Colored Champions   Formerly Nesco Comets

Don't miss seeing ORA WASHINGTON and INEZ PATTERSON in action. They are two of the greatest girl players in the world. They make you forget the Depression.

Music: Jenning's Orchestra, Philadelphia's Latest Sensation They are Considered the Peppiest Orchestra this Side of Hades.

25c Preliminary 8:15. Come out early. Bring the family. **25c**
ADMISSION 25 CENTS.

Advertisement for Philadelphia Tribunes, 1932. COURTESY OF THE *PHILADELPHIA TRIBUNE.*

As with many female entertainers, the Tribunes' popularity rested on a combination of talent and sexual appeal. Ora Washington bowed to few feminine conventions—both her appearance and her game were frequently described as "masculine"—and she built her stellar reputation solely on the quality of her play. Other players, however, fit conventional molds more neatly. A 1933 advertisement promised "Girls! Beautiful Girls! And How They Can Play!" In 1934, when the Tribunes played a three-game series against Bennett College in Greensboro, North Carolina, they opened the first game dressed in red and white, their sleeveless tops cut low in back, and their socks chosen to match. At halftime they changed into a second set of uniforms, these gold and purple. The outfits read "Tribune" in script on the front and had no numbers—a touch that conveniently threw the referees off guard.[15]

The game had been booked in Greensboro's spacious city arena, where black teams rarely played, and more than a thousand fans showed up to see what a local newspaper called "the fastest girls' team in the world," paced by "the indomitable, internationally famed and stellar performer, Ora Washington." Washington scored 13 points as the Tribunes triumphed, 31–22.[16]

Washington's intensity set the tone for the team. "She was one of those strong players," Ruth Glover explained. "She wasn't a huge person, or very tall. But she was so fast. And see, they fed her the ball. . . . The team was built up around her." Relying more on power than on grace, Washington pressed her way to the basket with a mental and physical force that often took opponents aback. Bennett center Lucille Townsend would never forget the moment when she confronted Washington for the first time. As the two faced off in the center circle, Townsend heard a whispered admonition: "Don't outjump me." She ignored the warning at her peril. "I never saw her when she hit me, but she did it so quick it would knock the breath out of me, and I doubled over," Townsend explained. "She could hit, and she told me that she had played a set of tennis on her knees and won it."

THE BENNETT–TRIBUNES SERIES MARKED ANOTHER TREND IN BLACK women's sports—the blossoming of black college and high school ball.

Growing up at the turn of the century, Ora Washington first came to basketball when she was in her twenties and built her career from scratch. Teachers in her two-room schoolhouse had struggled to pay for books and desks, let alone athletics. Caroline County's only black high school lay so far away that students from her community who wanted to go past the sixth grade had to move to the county seat or head north. By the 1920s, however, many southern states had been prodded into expanding their black high school systems, which gave African American students far greater academic and athletic opportunities. The 1910s and 1920s also saw a playground building boom that brought basketball hoops to communities around the country, further encouraging the game.[17]

In Albany, Georgia, future Tuskegee Institute star Alice Coachman grew up with a passion for running and jumping. "If Mama wanted someone to go to the store," she recalled, "she wouldn't call anybody but me because she said 'Alice could go and come right back.' " She soon discovered the pleasures of the local playground, and it became a second home. "Most of my friends were those boys down there," she said. "They would bet me that they could beat me high jumping and I'd say 'No you can't.' And then when I would go down there and they'd be playing ball, each one of them wanted me on their side. I was a pretty good competitor." On Sundays, she took advantage of breaks between church events to squeeze in a few extra minutes of play. "It was a known fact that you had to be in Sunday School and you had to go to church," she explained. "But between that time I would jump over that fence and go right on there playing with those boys."[18]

Coachman's parents disapproved of her athletic endeavors. "You'll get yourself hurt!" she recalled them telling her. "They would say it all the time." But school coaches were delighted. A teacher first noticed Coachman's talent when she was in the fifth grade. She soon found herself playing basketball and running track on the teams at Madison High School.

In Siler City, North Carolina, Ruth Glover had a similar experience. She grew up playing with her brothers in the family yard, shooting baskets at a hoop nailed to a tree. During most of her childhood, the only girls' basketball team in town was at all-white Siler City High School. But the year she entered high school, the all-black Chatham County Training School had opened a new building, one of hundreds of new black school buildings built across North Carolina in the 1920s and 1930s. The new building included a combination auditorium/gymnasium and when a teacher organized the school's first girls' squad, Glover signed right up. Her career was temporarily derailed when her father objected to the team's uniforms—specifically their shorts. But he relented when she agreed to keep a skirt waiting at courtside. "I had to put a skirt on soon as that game was over!" she recalled, laughing. "Cover up. We didn't have cover-ups, but I had to have a skirt."

By the 1930s, members of black high school squads could also dream of college stardom. The 1920s had proved a golden era for historically black colleges, as economic growth, strengthening racial pride and an influx of eager, restless students all brought a heightened sense of possibility to black campuses. A new generation of ambitious faculty members drew on this energy to expand their schools' intellectual, social and cultural activities, as well as their athletic programs. Some black schools, most notably Howard, Spelman and Fisk, followed the lead of white colleges and instituted noncompetitive physical education programs. But many others stepped beyond those bounds and began to field women's varsity teams.[19]

Greensboro's Bennett College took particular pride in its squad, considered one of the best in the country in the 1930s. Graduates of the private, all-female Methodist school were famed for their refined taste and manners, and they were often dubbed the Bennett Belles. But the many social, political and economic challenges faced by African American communities meant that black women were used to engaging in an unusually broad range of activities, and neither administrators nor students saw contradictions between competitive sports and ladylike refinement. Rather, they pursued a flexible philosophy that allowed women to be competitive and assertive on the court, while restrained and proper off of it.[20]

Although Bennett had no formal recruiting program, a network of loyal alumnae and supportive Methodists stayed on the lookout for tal-

Bennett College team, Greensboro, North Carolina, 1934. Lucille Townsend is at left; Ruth Glover is third from left. COURTESY OF THE GREENSBORO HISTORICAL MUSEUM.

ented players, and the school found ways to help out promising recruits. One of Bennett's finest players, Almeda Clavon, came from Detroit, where she had caught the eye of school supporters. Ruth Glover's high school coach, Zenobia Bost, was also on the hunt for good recruits. Bost took a particular interest in the redheaded girl with the uncanny feel for the basket and convinced her alma mater to find Glover a campus job—a welcome financial boost for a family working to send ten children to college. In the fall of 1933, Glover enrolled at Bennett and made the varsity team. In her four years of play, Bennett would lose only one college game.

Bennett faculty carefully guarded their school's reputation as the "Vassar of the South," and demanded excellence in every realm of college life. Sports was no exception. Bennett students observed study hours from seven to nine every night, and basketball practice started after that, running from nine until eleven. On Saturdays, coach William Trent often arranged for his players to scrimmage against the boys' team from nearby Dudley High School. He set strict standards for discipline and effort. "If you in any way showed any sign of not following instructions, and so forth, he would bench you," Glover recalled. "He would call you off that team and sit you down for a while. Until you would straighten yourself out."

The hard work produced players who were disciplined and determined. As Glover made clear, Bennett's players considered themselves ladies, able to handle tea parties, business meetings or charity endeavors with grace and tact. But when challenged, they stood up for themselves. When, for example, Ora Washington warned Lucille Townsend about outjumping her, Townsend replied: "I'm in here to play just like you," and took the consequences.

THE COMBINATION OF LADYLIKE GRACE AND STRENUOUS ENDEAVOR meshed neatly with the broader goals black colleges set for their students. Ever mindful of the need to combat racial stereotypes, black administrators held young women to the highest standards of conduct through strict rules that covered almost every aspect of their dress, manners and activities. As one of ten children, Alice Coachman recalled, she had been able to sidestep many ladylike conventions, because "Mama didn't have time to tell us about all these little things." When she reached Tuskegee, however, things were different. "Tuskegee kind of came up under the old tradition of 'ladies had to sit a certain way,'" she explained. "I had to sit straight up, head up, hair had to be groomed at all times. Your body had to be groomed. . . . You had to have on stockings and shoes at all times."[21]

Even as they promoted social graces, however, faculty and administrators knew their students would need more than manners to make a difference in an often-hostile world. Rather than simply nurturing the talents of individuals, they sought to imbue their students with a strong sense of community responsibility, encouraging them to direct their abilities to meeting the many needs of the nation's African American communities. Interest in ladylike refinement in no way superseded the importance of accomplishment. Bennett president David Jones, Ruth Glover recalled, made no secret of his determination "to groom young ladies that could get out there and prove a point. That you could do well, go back home and help your community to grow." Teammate Amaleta

Moore agreed. "The whole idea was to go and contribute to the community where you lived," she said. "You were training for a given profession so that you could go back and contribute." Amid the obstacles raised by poverty and discrimination, pursuing such endeavors required economic savvy, political skill and organizational ability, as well as energy, creative thinking, determination and confidence.[22]

Female college students pursued these skills in a wide range of arenas, and sports rarely dominated even the most talented athletes' lives. But it could be a particularly powerful experience, especially in terms of confidence. "It involves your emotions," Moore explained. "And it involves your will to win." Moore met her first challenge as soon as she stepped onto a Bennett basketball court. Like most black schools of the time, Bennett's women played with full-court men's rules. During four years of high school basketball in the integrated school system of Cape May, New Jersey, Moore had played on a three-division court. In the initial days of practice, she recalled, "My tongue was hanging out." But she stuck with it and made the team.

Moore found her niche as a defensive specialist. "I played guard," she explained. "I had long arms—I was a good-sized girl. . . . So my interest was in keeping the forward from shooting. And that I would do. As Bill Trent used to tell me: 'Go in there Amie and stop her.' . . . And I enjoyed it. I used to get down and put my hands on my knees and get a squat stance. And they'd hit me—I didn't move."

Her most memorable moment came the night she stopped Shaw star Frazier Creecy, a hard-nosed, wily player. "She would dance like she was going that way, and you looked and she was going around this way," Moore recalled. "She would throw the other guards off—they couldn't keep up with her." If someone did get between her and the basket, "she came with that hair flying . . . she'd come straight for you." One night, when Creecy was tearing up the floor, Bennett coach William Trent turned to Moore and told her to do something. As Moore trotted to the court, she was determined to succeed. "I said: 'I will brace myself and let her come,'" she explained. "And I stood there like this and she dribbled straight at me. She hit me, and I didn't move. She fell back on the court—you heard her bones crack when she hit the floor—and they took

Bennett College team, Greensboro, North Carolina, 1936–37. Amaleta Moore is third from left, defending. COURTESY OF THE BENNETT COLLEGE ARCHIVES.

her off on the stretcher. . . . I didn't hit her or anything. I just stood there, but I braced myself first, because I knew she was going to do it. I said: 'She'll never run over me.' "[23]

Ruth Glover, in contrast, was a shooter who regularly hit the basket from half-court and who impressed the Philadelphia Tribunes' coach so much during the Bennett–Tribunes series that he tried to convince her to leave school and join the Tribunes on the spot. "I could tell exactly when that ball left my hand whether it was the right shot or not, whether it was going or not," she explained. "It's a feel that you just have. . . . There's an inner voice, if you just take time to listen to it, you know." She recalled hearing that voice with special clarity during one game against Shaw. "They were ahead," she recounted. "And one of our forwards shot, to make a basket. I knew it wasn't going in. So I cut in, got the ball and put it in myself. You get that kind of little inner feeling, you know, from that. So I started kind of listening to the inner voice. I didn't always listen. But it helped me to start."

Glover had arrived at Bennett as "a little country girl," intimidated by her new surroundings. "I was a little shy at first," she explained. "A little shy and withdrawn. I was not an outgoing person." Her basketball successes, she continued, "gave me some confidence in myself. That I could accomplish. And even the president would make you feel good. I know when I would return to campus in the fall, he'd say: 'Oh, we're going to have some basketball this year!' Things like that. . . . He liked to kind of push girls, you know what I mean. He was behind you in whatever you wanted to do. He would follow you through, and was enthusiastic about all of those things. . . . That helped you to get confidence in yourself."

As well as nurturing individual strengths, basketball also played a key role in players' understanding of community. This sense of community was one of the most significant components of college life, Moore emphasized. "You felt a sense of worth, and a feeling of security," she said. "You learned something about the value of support from your community, from other people. . . . So that you don't have this blown-up idea that you're so important. . . . You have that support and you support [others] in the same way."

Although basketball players enjoyed special status at Bennett, drawing large, supportive crowds and seeing reports of their games in national publications such as the *Chicago Defender* and the *Baltimore Afro-American,* they were constantly reminded that with such privilege came responsibility. "You really had the feeling that you were representing the student body," Moore said. "Because they certainly cheered us on. And you felt that if you didn't win, you were letting them down as well as being disappointed yourself. So I think that sense of responsibility to a larger group was an important aspect. The relationships you develop. You develop these same kinds of relationships with other groups that you work with in the community after you get out of school."

BY THE TIME GLOVER AND MOORE SUITED UP FOR BENNETT, AFRICAN American sports had also begun to take on a new layer of significance— as a racial proving ground. Since the Civil War, black leaders had looked to sports as a promising arena for disproving racial stereotypes through dramatic demonstrations of courage, determination and sheer ability. In the 1930s, these possibilities seemed brighter than ever, as a new generation of athletes stepped onto the national and international stage. In 1932, the Harlem Renaissance captured the nation's professional basketball title over a field of mostly all-white teams. In 1936, sprinter Jesse Owens became the toast of the country after winning four gold medals at the Berlin Olympics. Boxer Joe Louis was making his way through the heavyweight boxing ranks, headed for the world title. As black men began to make inroads into national sporting institutions, the door seemed open for black women as well.[24]

This philosophy was especially evident at Alabama's Tuskegee Institute, where athletic director Cleveland Abbott used the financial foundation laid by Booker T. Washington to build an athletic powerhouse with clear racial goals and a strong focus on women's sports. Abbott, who became the Tuskegee athletic director in 1923, had seen athletics' racial possibilities firsthand. He had grown up in South Dakota, where a small group of former slaves had homesteaded land following the Civil War. Athletics had been his ticket to success. After an outstanding high school sports career, he enrolled in nearby South Dakota State College. Though he was one of only a handful of African Americans at the school, he captained the basketball team, anchored the relay team and lettered in two other sports. Along the way, it became clear that sports not only built up individuals but had the power to demonstrate, as Tuskegee hurdler Leila Perry put it: "That all people are the same. . . . You are as good as anybody else and you can do what anybody else can do."

Female athletes played a key role in Abbott's plans. Babe Didrikson had not been the only American eagerly following the pioneering female track exploits of the 1928 Olympic Games—Cleveland Abbott was watching as well. The Olympic reports fired Didrikson's dream of individual glory. Abbott set himself a broader goal. In 1927, he had started the Tuskegee Carnival, a two-day track and field competition that drew African American male stars from high schools and colleges around the South. The spring after the Olympics, he added women's events and began to build a female track team.

As Abbott lured a bevy of exceptionally talented athletes to the

Tuskegee University team, Tuskegee, Alabama, 1944–45. Alice Coachman is second row, center. Lillie Purifoy is first row, second from right. Lesper Givens is back row, second from right. COURTESY OF THE TUSKEGEE UNIVERSITY ARCHIVES.

Tuskegee campus, the basketball team took off. Most of Abbott's track recruits had grown up playing basketball, and they brought remarkable athleticism to the court. When Alice Coachman arrived at the school in 1939, the whole first string consisted of national-caliber track athletes. "They were so fast," she recalled. "They'd move the ball. . . . There just was no way for anybody to win. Not with those fast girls on there." Coachman was a high jumper, and she put her skills to good use on the boards. "I was what you may call the rebounder," she explained. "Every time the ball would go to the backboard it was mine."[25]

With players such as Coachman, national hurdling champion Lillie Purifoy and sprinter Lesper Givens, other teams could often do little besides stand and watch. "When I went up, really it was right there," Coachman continued. "All I had to do—when I went up to get the ball, I just threw the ball with one hand over to Lillie. And she threw it over to Lesper on the other end. Two points. There was never hesitation about the ball. You went up for the ball, you got it and it was gone. You didn't need any dribbling at all. That's how we won a lot of the games." The Southern Intercollegiate Athletic Conference crowned a women's basketball champion as well as a men's, and Tuskegee was a perennial titleholder throughout the 1930s and 1940s.

Young women fortunate enough to enter this charmed athletic circle found Tuskegee a buoyant, almost magical place. Abbott combed the South for talented young women and treated them like his own daughters. "If we didn't have the money, we'd just tell him, and it was taken care of," Coachman recalled. "If we didn't have soap, it was taken care of. . . . We could talk to coach about anything. He would keep up with you every month, just like your mama. And he'd tell you. 'You all right? You all right this month?' "

On sunny days, team members rubbed their legs with peanut oil made by Tuskegee chemist George Washington Carver and lay out behind the gym together. Many black women avoided the sun, seeking to keep their skin as light as possible. But Abbott believed that sun was good for muscles, and the players had fond memories of those afternoons. "We used to rub with that peanut oil, and go down there and lay on the ground. Let the sun bake us," Lula Hymes explained. "You talk about some pretty brown," Coachman noted, pointing out that the team got plenty of attention from male visitors. "The fellows wanted to see how we looked. Because they heard that we had knots in our legs. And they were so surprised, when they looked at us. Mmmmm."

"We had a good time out there," Leila Perry echoed. "Lay out there talking and whatnot. Those were good days. You'd be tired . . . but they were enjoyable."

As they practiced, worked and talked, they pushed each other to new competitive heights. In high school, Hymes recalled, her confidence often faltered. "When I would do something wrong, I would cry," she said. "I used to think I couldn't." But as soon as she got to Tuskegee: "I was told never say you can't do a thing. . . . There were three of us, used to run together in high school, and we came to Tuskegee together. And one of the girls used to beat me. And a friend told me, 'Never say you can't do it, Lu.' And I guess that's why I pushed so hard, started running so hard." Two years later, when Coachman arrived at the school,

Tuskegee University players, Tuskegee, Alabama, 1938. Lula Hymes is bottom row, center. COURTESY OF THE TUSKEGEE UNIVERSITY ARCHIVES.

Hymes took the teenaged star under her wing, working to instill her with "the winning mind," as Coachman put it. "They always pushed you to win."

And win they did. Cleveland Abbott had calculated well. Tuskegee's men's teams faced stiff recruiting competition from far wealthier white schools, who were happy to welcome a talented black athlete or two. But none of those schools sponsored women's sports. In 1937, led by the speedy Lula Hymes, the Tuskegee women captured the national AAU track title. Tuskegee would win the AAU championship in ten of the next eleven years, before ceding its dominance to another black team, the Tigerbelles of Tennessee State. The outbreak of World War II meant that no Olympics were held in 1940 or 1944. But in the first postwar Olympics, held in London in 1948, Alice Coachman took the high jump gold medal. She was the only American woman to win a track and field gold that year, and the first woman of African descent to win a medal of any kind.[26]

The basketball team did not have the same chance to shine. National AAU track meets admitted black athletes and black teams. But the women's basketball tournament was, by all accounts, less open. From the 1930s through the 1960s, AAU competition was dominated by teams from the segregation-minded South, a circumstance that heightened the potential for racial conflict and put pressure on the tournament organizers. As a result, wrote longtime participant George Sherman, black entries were not encouraged. On the rare occasion that a black team qualified, he continued, it "was placed in the bracket against the strongest northern team available" and "the officials received strong hints from the powers that be as to how they would like the game called."[27] One year when the Tuskegee team was especially good, Alice Coachman overheard Cleveland Abbott remark, "This team here would go to the finals at the national basketball tournament." But that wasn't in the cards. As far as Tuskegee was concerned, the tournament "wasn't open to the blacks."

Basketball also lacked track's international stage, further reducing its significance. Coachman loved the game. "To get that ball off that backboard, knowing that nobody else could jump that high. That was thrilling," she said. She also excelled at it. "I was just as good in basketball [as track]," she said. "If things were as they are now, I probably would be at some university going with the Olympic team in basketball."[28] But because basketball was not an Olympic sport, track took precedence. Coachman became known for her high jumping, not her rebounding.

Other black female athletes faced similar obstacles. True to her competitive spirit, Ora Washington wanted badly to play Helen Wills Moody, the white women's tennis champion and national athletic sensation. But the United States Lawn Tennis Association did not admit African Americans to major tournaments, and Wills had little to gain from playing an unofficial match against a black challenger. In the 1950s, Althea Gibson would break the tennis color line and prove herself the best female player in the world. But that was twenty years in the future. Ora Washington never got her chance.[29]

Even those female athletes who had the chance to demonstrate their worth drew limited attention, simply because Americans as a whole followed few women's sports. When Joe Louis battled his way to the world heavyweight boxing crown, every fight was carried on the radio, and his exploits garnered front-page headlines in newspapers around the country. When Lula Hymes went flying down the track in front of all of her competitors, she was celebrated in black newspapers. In white publications, she might get a line or two, but rarely more.

But although the accomplishments of black female athletes had limited effects on the country's racial hierarchy, they meant a great deal to African Americans, serving as unmistakable, emotionally satisfying proof that the lowly social and economic status to which blacks were confined resulted from white prejudice and not from blacks' own shortcomings. Athletic triumphs over whites carried a special sweetness. One year, Ruth Glover remembered, coaches scheduled a game between the women's teams from Siler City's black and white high schools. Glover's team won. The victory meant a great deal. "I'll have to be honest—I was glad we won," she explained. "Because being in a small town, I had experienced a lot of segregation and so forth. . . . I had experienced all of those things. So it was a thrill, kind of, to beat them." While most whites paid little heed to the remarkable string of championships won by Tuskegee's track women, African Americans cherished them. "Kids on the campus loved you and respected you," Leila Perry noted. "And they thought you were the greatest. . . . I think that a whole lot of people looked up to Tuskegee women."

The dual meanings of athletic travel illustrated the ways young women moved between the parallel worlds that they inhabited, one hostile and resistant, one nurturing and affirming. Travel took young women beyond the protective embrace of their campuses and into a world peppered with "white" and "colored" signs, in which they were often barred from restaurants, hotels and bathrooms. When Tuskegee's track team traveled to far-off meets, Alice Coachman recalled, the bus often stopped for bathroom breaks, and "the girls would go on one side of the road, and the boys would go on the other side." That the Tuskegee women were the best women's track team in the country meant little to a restaurant or gas station owner determined to maintain the color line. But such obstacles could not stop them from soaking up everything they could.

"Coach Abbott was the type of person where if there was anything historical on our route to those meets, he would stop and let us go around and see," Coachman explained. "Like to the Alamo, out in Texas. . . . Out to Mt. Vernon—all the historical places."[30] And a little went a long way. In 1939, Abbott took the team to the New York World's Fair and gave Coachman two dollars to spend. "I thought I was rich," she said with a smile. "I was walking around there with two dollars in my pocket and a navy-blue dress on. I was somebody. . . . I thought I was something."

ALL THESE WOMEN BELONGED TO AN ERA IN WHICH COUNTLESS African Americans did much with little. Using the resources they had at hand, they built lives and institutions that enriched their communities and helped prepare subsequent generations for their own struggles. Athletics helped black women cultivate the capabilities to negotiate a segregated world, as well as inspire others with their achievements. Whether it was Frazier Creecy rushing headlong to the basket, Amaleta Moore standing firmly in her way, Ruth Glover launching a perfect, half-court shot, or Alice Coachman pulling down rebound after rebound, black women's basketball embodied the energy and skill these women brought to a broad range of endeavors. Ora Washington captured that spirit in a simple description of her play. "I didn't believe in long warm-ups," she once said. "I'd rather play from scratch and warm up as I went along. . . . Courage and determination were the biggest assets I had."[31]

·4·

Crowning National Champions

It was the 1951 Amateur Athletic Union championship, and on the floor of the Dallas Fairgrounds arena Eckie Jordan could do no wrong. The speedy point guard pressed up the court, moving as fast and far as the two-dribble rule allowed, passing right and then left. Her Hanes Hosiery squad had lost in the semifinals two years in a row but was finally playing for the national championship. As she ran and passed and shot, it all seemed easy. The Hosiery Girls triumphed, 50–34, in a "wonderful exhibition of basketball." The 5'2" Jordan was named the tournament's most valuable player.[1]

The Hanes Hosiery Girls, based in Winston-Salem, North Carolina, belonged to an elite group of amateur and professional teams that lifted American women's basketball to new heights in the years just after World War II. While physical educators' noncompetitive philosophy still governed women's sports in many sections of the country, many communities supported women's competition, and a quarter-century of avid play had produced an exceptionally skilled generation of athletes, whose talents had been nurtured from an early age. These women were some of the greatest to ever play the game, stars such as Alline Banks, Eckie Jordan, Missouri Arledge, Hazel Walker and the astonishing Nera White,

Eckie Jordan chases the ball in a game with Iowa Wesleyan College. COURTESY OF
ECKIE JORDAN.

perhaps the greatest player of all time. Their stories testify to the passion
women felt for basketball and the skills they brought to the game.

"It meant an awful lot to me," explained Margaret Sexton, a Tennessee native who played on five national championship teams. "We
gave up meals—I mean you didn't have time to eat. A lot of times after
work you just ride the bus and go to practice or whatever and it was
really wonderful."

EVERY YEAR, TOP TEAMS DESCENDED ON THE AAU NATIONAL TOUR-
nament for the most heated competition of the era. By the 1940s, the
tournament had grown into a gala affair, complete with opening ceremonies, a free-throw contest, numerous community events and—in a
nod to feminine convention—a beauty pageant that crowned a tournament queen from among the competitors. The event brought together a
polyglot of teams with colorful names such as the Hosiery Girls, the

Arkansas Motor Coaches, the Vultee Bomberettes and the Wayland Flying Queens. The AAU tournament champion was widely considered the nation's top women's team, and members of the all-tournament squad were the women's All-Americans. The tournament's most valuable player was the toast of women's basketball for the next year.[2]

Throughout most of the 1940s, that honor belonged to Alline Banks, a tall, slim redheaded whiz who loved the spotlight and the ball. "I had to score more points than anyone else," the Tennessee farm girl once explained, and she rarely slacked her pace. In high school, she became known as the "point a minute girl" for her high scoring average. In three consecutive AAU tournaments she singlehandedly scored more points than all her team's opponents put together. She carried three different teams to national titles, winning eleven All-American designations and seven MVP awards. Basketball was her life. "We played practically every night somewhere," she recalled. "We went all over Tennessee. I [once]

Alline Banks, front left, and Margaret Sexton, front right, anticipate a rebound at the AAU tournament. COURTESY OF THE WOMEN'S BASKETBALL HALL OF FAME.

played two games in a day. We played in St. Louis, and I played, sat down and drank a Coke, and got out there and played another game."[3]

The versatility of her play amazed onlookers. "On the basketball court she follows no set plan, has no particular style of shooting," one reporter wrote. "Just gets the ball into the basket with whatever type shot comes into her mind as she gets ready to make it. . . . If she has a 'specialty' shot it's a wheeling, pivoting affair from the neighborhood of the foul circle, made while going away from the basket—and away from her guard."[4] Even injury did little to stop her. One day, when she was playing a game in Pittsburgh, she got knocked down and kneed. "Before I got back to the hotel, I couldn't move my right arm," she explained. "So the doctor came to see me, and he said, 'You can't play with that arm.'" She disagreed, and the next night convinced the doctor to tape her right arm to her side, leaving her hand free to hold the ball. "He taped me tight, all around my body," she continued. "Well, I got to shooting, and everything I shot went in. I could shoot with either arm, I could go each way. Come to foul shots, I made all of them. And the crowd was roaring. . . ."

Hot on Banks's heels was Margaret Sexton, who had become the nation's most feared guard. Sexton went at the game with an intensity that made her an AAU legend. "Everyone wants to see the ball go in the hoop, but keeping them from doing that is exciting, too," she once said. "I didn't want anybody to shoot a basket over me, I'll tell you that. . . . If you participate in sports, you know, it's who gets there first and you get knocked down and you get up and go ahead."

Banks and Sexton reached the peak of their sport in 1943 while playing for the Vultee Bomberettes, which represented Nashville's Vultee Aircraft Corporation. The timing was no accident. The mass mobilization of male soldiers to fight in World War II transformed both women's work and women's sports. War production plants recruited female employees with a campaign that drew previously unthinkable comparisons between men's and women's work—cutting out steel aircraft parts, one advertisement claimed, was not much different from slicing a cake. In Nashville, Vultee Aircraft began hiring women to drill, grind and rivet. Women leaped at the positions, which paid much more than most women's jobs. Vultee's popularity became the perfect excuse to draw on

*AAU tournament program,
1955.* COURTESY OF THE
WOMEN'S BASKETBALL
HALL OF FAME.

a deep pool of Tennessee basketball talent to build a championship team. Banks and Sexton joined the firm, as did Mary Jane Marshall, Doris Weems and several other talented players. Two years later, in 1944, the Bomberettes took the AAU title. They repeated in 1945.[5]

When the war ended, Vultee ramped down production, fired most of its female workers and disbanded the Bomberettes. But women's basketball carried on. The Bomberettes were not ready to quit—"We were clicking," Banks observed. They found another sponsor, a beer distributor called Cook's, and won their third straight national championship while representing Goldblume Beer.[6] Elsewhere, the end of war did not mean the end of factory teams. Plenty of women had labored in factories before the war, and plenty stayed on the job once the conflict ended. Even as Vultee left the sport, other firms stepped in. The most successful of these would be Hanes Hosiery. If the Vultee Bomberettes had been the quintessential wartime team, the Hanes Hosiery Girls, whose sponsor manufactured nylon hose, embodied the postwar consumer spirit.

Hanes sat near the heart of the southern textile region, where women's basketball had a long and distinguished history. Textile mills had always relied heavily on female labor, and mills began sponsoring women's teams as early as the 1900s. In 1920, the Southern Textile Association Basketball Tournament, featuring both men's and women's play, began a long run as one of the top amateur events in the nation. By 1940, the Hanes teams were so popular that Hanes president James Weeks built a two thousand-seat gym, which regularly filled with cheering fans. "It gave everybody in the company something to talk about and look forward to," longtime player Eunies Futch explained. "Back then, that was the thing to do—to go watch the Hanes Hosiery boys and girls play."[7]

At first, Hanes management paid more attention to the men's team. But the women quickly showed their potential. While men's industrial teams were losing ground to an expanding college game, the dearth of women's college play meant that a women's AAU squad could still aspire to be the best team in the country. By 1947, Hanes had resolved to build a national championship squad, designed to boost employee spirit and push the company's wares. With the war at an end, and Americans immersed in the concerns of peacetime, a group of trim, athletic women seemed an ideal advertisement for the company's most famous product—nylon stockings. Hanes made the most of them. The team played an extensive schedule of exhibitions, league games and local clinics, and players were required to always look their best when off the floor. At the start of a big tournament each team member received her own box of freshly manufactured hose.

Like most AAU teams, Hanes had a male coach, Virgil Yow, who had cut his teeth coaching men's basketball and applied what he had learned to the women's game. The gap between men's and women's rules was not as wide as it once had been. Although AAU rules still used a two-division, six-player game, in 1936 rulemakers had introduced a roving player. Under the rover system, when a team switched from defense to offense, whoever was handling the ball could cross the line, as could the player defending her. Closer guarding was also allowed, and by 1947 players could dribble two times per possession. The shifts sped up the game. Many teams adopted the newly popular fast break, and defenders had to stay on their toes, as no one knew which guard would cross the line on any given play. Using four players on offense, rather than the men's five, made for a more open game in which post players had plenty of elbow room. As well as devising fast-break plays, Virgil Yow instituted a conditioning program and a "test and measurement" system, in which new players took as many as 10,000 shots from a carefully regulated array of court positions.[8]

Hanes fielded a broad list of All-Americans, including Tennessean Jimmie Vaughn and Arkansas phenomenon Lurlyne Greer, who would win three straight national MVP awards. But at the heart of the team was a pair of mismatched players known as the "two E's," who would be best friends for the rest of their lives. "Big E" was Eunies "Eunie" Futch, who came from Jacksonville, Florida, and stood 6'2". While some tall players were lured to basketball by coaches eager to take advantage of their height, Eunie had loved the game since childhood. "I can remember going to the playground . . . and I couldn't get the basketball up to the goal," she once said. "But I kept on, and I guess one of my biggest thrills was when I could finally get it through. I practically lived on the playground." Although Jacksonville's high schools did not field girls' teams, she played for several years on local AAU squads. Virgil Yow first spotted her when she was a high school sophomore, and kept after her until she was old enough to join his team. "I graduated Wednesday night, January 15, 1947," she recalled. "I caught a Greyhound bus Friday night."

"Little E" was Eckie Jordan, who had grown up "teething a basketball" in the textile town of Pelzer, South Carolina. Six of the seven Jordan children played the game, and in the evenings "we would sit in the kitchen and go over the ball games and Daddy would talk about things we were doing wrong and had to improve on." Her mother was equally enthusiastic. On game days, "I never had to wash the dishes and she was always ready to go." In 1944, her senior year of high school, Jordan led tiny Pelzer High to the South Carolina state championship. In 1948, she headed to Winston-Salem to try out for Virgil Yow. Although she barely topped five feet, her ballhandling skills carried the day. "Coach thought

I was too short to play," she noted decades later, "but I proved him wrong." In 1951, her MVP title underscored her point. "Eckie Jordan was the real star of the tournament," Yow reported. "She got, by far, the biggest ovation of any player when she went out onto the floor." Hanes would win again in 1952 and 1953.[9]

By the mid-1950s, however, times were changing in women's basketball. The generation of teams and stars that had sparked the postwar renaissance were passing from the scene. Alline Banks and Margaret Sexton had retired, and Jordan and Futch would soon join them. Hanes Hosiery would disband its team in 1954. New sponsors entered the arena, and a new generation of players began to make their mark.

One of the most dramatic changes came in 1955, the year a black college team was invited to the tournament for the first time. Philander Smith College, a small Methodist school in Little Rock, Arkansas, had been fielding women's teams for decades—as early as 1918 a Philander Smith team had defeated all comers and declared itself Arkansas champion.[10] In 1955, coach Bob Green Jr. put together an especially strong team, going 19–3 and taking the South Central Athletic Conference title. By then, African Americans had begun to make some inroads into

Eckie Jordan, left, and Eunies Futch, Hanes Hosiery's "two E's."
COURTESY OF ECKIE JORDAN.

national institutions, thanks to a changing racial climate and a new set of legal precedents—most notably the Supreme Court's 1954 *Brown v. Board of Education* school desegregation decision. Trading on his team's success, Green was able to secure an AAU invitation.

The key to Philander Smith's success was Missouri Arledge, who would become the first black woman to be named a basketball All-American. The Durham, North Carolina, native was far from a typical AAU star. She did not start her basketball career until eighth grade, when the coach at Hillside High School, Carl Easterling, spotted the 5'10½" player in gym class and persuaded her to join his team. Her family didn't think much of women playing sports, and at first she only went to practice because Easterling provided a personal escort. "He would come to my class, the last class of the day and wait outside the door, take me by my hand and walk me up to the gym," she explained. "That's the only way I would stay." Finally, Easterling tired of the daily walk and tried a bribe. "If I did well, he would try to ensure that I got a scholarship to college." Although Arledge was lukewarm about basketball, she wanted

Missouri Arledge Morris at Hillside High School, Durham, North Carolina, 1952–53.
COURTESY OF MISSOURI ARLEDGE.

badly to go to college and knew her family could not afford to send her. She began to walk to practice on her own.

Arledge became a local sensation, setting record after record. Easterling pushed his players hard, and it was not unusual for the team to score 100 points a game. Spectators flocked to the contests. "The gym used to be maybe a third full of people when we started out playing," Arledge recalled. "But by the time I was a senior, the gym would be full." Easterling had no trouble keeping his promise—her senior year she had twelve scholarship offers to choose from. She picked Philander Smith for a simple reason—she wanted to travel, and the Little Rock–based school was the farthest from her home. Playing for Philander Smith required some adjustments. Easterling had taught a highly structured game, while Green emphasized a more open, run-and-gun style. But Arledge made the change, and the team prospered.

As the Philander Smith players made the long drive from Little Rock to St. Joseph, Missouri, where the AAU tournament was held, they had no idea what lay in store. St. Joseph had hosted the competition for years, and first-time participants were always dazzled by the show the town put on. The Philander Smith players were no exception. "We were just starstruck," Arledge said. "I mean just in awe. When we walked in, it was a great gym. I'd never seen a gym that big. And the teams that were there had on professional-looking uniforms. They all had on the same tennis shoes. We had tennis shoes, but we didn't have on the *same* tennis shoes. Their names were on their shirts. It was just big time."

For Philander Smith's players, however, there was an additional surprise. The South's strict segregation meant that Arledge and her teammates lived in a largely black world, and few realized that white women played the same game they did. Seeing the AAU's array of all-white teams was quite a shock. Still, the players were far from intimidated—testament to the confidence that black communities nurtured in their sportswomen. "When we got there and we saw that all the teams were white, we just thought that for sure we're going to win," Arledge recalled. "I don't know why, but we thought we were going to win the tournament because I guess we lived a sheltered life in college. We didn't see too many—well I don't remember seeing any—white girls playing basketball. All you saw were black girls playing basketball."[11]

"That's what segregation will do for you," she later added. "You just live in this little shell, and you don't know what's going on with the rest of the world. And you're just shocked when you find out there's a whole other world out there."

Although Philander Smith's players did not win the tournament, they more than held their own. It was their first trip, and one of their star guards was injured early. Still, they reached the quarterfinals, upsetting the number-four seed along the way. Everyone treated them well. Arledge played brilliantly and was named to the All-American squad.

Like many of the racial gestures undertaken in the wake of the *Brown* ruling, AAU integration proved ephemeral. It was one thing to bring in a symbolic team or individual, quite another to build a fully integrated institution. After the tournament, Arledge declined an invitation to join the national team, preferring to focus on her studies. That fall, she transferred to Tuskegee. Although Philander Smith returned to the AAU tournament in 1956, it only won a single game. The tournament periodically hosted Latin American teams—testament to that region's thriving basketball culture—as well as a handful of Native American squads. But black teams and players remained few and far between. The next black All-American, Sally Smith, would not be named until 1969.[12]

The 1955 champions, the Wayland Flying Queens from Wayland Baptist College in Plainview, Texas, represented a more lasting change. In 1954, the Queens had become the first team from a four-year college to win the national title. Wayland was part of a new trend, one of a handful of predominantly white colleges whose ties to basketball-crazy communities were proving stronger than physical educators' pressure to remain noncompetitive. In 1943, four-year Iowa Wesleyan College had established a varsity basketball team in response to demands for trained high school girls' coaches. In 1948, the Queens joined the fray.[13]

Wayland's team became renowned not only for its players' skill but for the style in which they traveled. Plainview was a small town in the middle of the vast West Texas plains, and offered few other diversions. "There wasn't a lot of social life," explained two-time All-American Kaye

Garmes. "I mean, it was a Baptist university. . . . And the gym was always open. We'd go to the gym at night and play basketball with the guys. That's how we would entertain ourselves with our dates. We'd play three-on-three or whatever." Girls' high school basketball was a beloved West Texas institution, and the prospect of a college team brought out the best in Plainview residents. The local Harvest Queen Mill agreed to donate uniforms, and the players became known as the "Harvest Queens." Town beauticians did the players' hair before big trips. The most generous gift came from alumnus Claude Hutcherson, whose Hutcherson Air Service used a fleet of small airplanes to transport passengers and cargo throughout the Great Plains region. In 1951, Hutcherson began using his four-seater Beechcraft Bonanza planes to transport the Queens to their away games, and the team became known as the Flying Queens.

The idea of playing basketball in college came as a sudden revelation to hundreds of young white women who had never dreamed of such an

The 1958 Wayland Flying Queens. COURTESY OF WAYLAND BAPTIST UNIVERSITY.

opportunity. Georgia native Patsy Neal discovered Wayland in "a three line paragraph in the bottom corner of the sports page that changed my life forever."[14] Carla Lowry, who grew up in small-town Mississippi, would never forget the moment she picked up a copy of *Parade* magazine and saw the Queens on the cover. "It said that they had won their eighty-first [game] and their third national championship. I thought: 'By God, I want to go play with those guys.' So I hopped on a bus and traveled for two days." Wearing a pair of red Converse tennis shoes, she spent the next several days scrimmaging with two dozen eager players from around the region. She could hardly believe it when coach Harley Redin offered her a scholarship. "I have always said that if I had the money, I would have paid them to let me play," she said.

On the strength of recruiting, as well as Harley Redin's coaching, the Queens built up a remarkable record. Starting in 1954, they compiled a 131-game winning streak against the top competition in the country. The streak encompassed four straight AAU championships, the first time such a feat had been accomplished. "That was probably the most significant thing in my life, to join that group and get a chance to play," Lowry explained. "It was just such fun to play with people who were so good, that you had to just be better."

The Queens' 1955 victory solidified the dominance they would maintain for most of the decade. But unbeknown to them, that tournament also held the seed of their eventual downfall. Buried at the bottom of the 1955 All-America roster was a tall, slim teenager fresh from dribbling past cow manure on her family's Tennessee farm. Nera White had built her muscles while plowing and lifting feed sacks, and honed her determination by shepherding six younger siblings through the tasks that her father—who had lost a leg to blood poisoning—could not do. While playing on her high school team, she caught the eye of H.O. Balls, owner of Nashville Business College (NBC). Balls had sponsored a team since 1923 and knew talent when he saw it. He had spotted Alline Banks and Margaret Sexton at a high school tournament, and launched them on their AAU careers. Nera White would follow in their footsteps—and beyond. By the time her career ended in 1969, the 6'1" forward had been named an All-American an unprecedented fifteen times and was widely acknowledged as the greatest woman ever to play the game. For many who were fortunate enough to see her play, even the bright stars of the 1980s and 1990s would pale in comparison. "I coached two Olympic teams and I've seen the best players in the world," observed Sue Gunter, who played with White in the 1960s, and went on to become one of the sport's most distinguished college coaches. "Nera White is the best of them all. She is the greatest of all time."[15]

In any sport, the greatest players have a superhuman touch—they seem to leap higher, float longer, see several plays ahead with the ease of breathing in and out. Nera White had that kind of magic. Her long-range set shot was "just effortless," Kaye Garmes recalled. "She was a very strong woman, and with her wrist snap, she could send the ball from about the center line. You couldn't play a zone against her, because she would step over the center line . . . and she could shoot very comfortably. I mean she could make a sham out of the three-point line."

"She just could jump higher, run faster," Gunter noted. "Great touch on the basketball. Post you up. Shoot the three as we know it now. I mean that kind of range. So what are you going to do with her? She could leave the free-throw line and float to the basket. . . . You couldn't press us. Hell, you couldn't think about pressing us because all we did was give her the ball and clear out. There was nobody going to catch her. You just couldn't do it."

Like all transcendent players, White married her skills to a profound understanding of her sport. "There is a reason why you do everything," she once explained. "For me, everything was always geared toward the final score. My job wasn't to score, it was to be a threat to score."[16] Teammates echoed those words. NBC fielded a raft of formidable competitors, including six-time All-American Doris Rogers and thirteen-time All-American Joan Crawford. White knew how to help them shine. "If she needed to score, she scored," Gunter recalled. "If she needed to be the stopper, and the defender, she did. If Crawford had the hot hand, then Nera was the assist leader that night. It's just phenomenal what she could do."

For the next decade and a half, White dominated AAU play. Still, her story was far from a fairy tale. Despite her remarkable skills, she often

Nera White with championship trophies. COURTESY OF THE WOMEN'S BASKETBALL HALL OF FAME.

struggled. Her size and strength clashed sharply with conventional views of femininity, and she often endured cutting remarks about her height, deep voice and flat chest—remarks that, she later reported, "affected me a great deal."[17] She never came to terms with fame, and she never rested on her laurels. Off the court, amid a small circle of basketball-centered friends, she was known for her generosity, and many came to rely on her encouragement and advice. Near the end of her career, she adopted a teammate's son and raised him by herself. But she was shy in public, nervous enough to throw up regularly before games, and she hated losing more than anything. Throughout her career, she let her play talk for her.

The brunt of her competitive drive fell on Wayland Baptist. From the mid-1950s through the 1960s, NBC and Wayland were the dominant forces in national women's basketball. From 1959 to 1966 no other team made it to the AAU finals. The teams' formidable skills, as well as their contrasting styles, made for a long and memorable rivalry.

Wayland coach Harley Redin understood showmanship as well as coaching, and his teams always had a glamorous air. When both the Queens and the barnstorming Harlem Globetrotters were snowed in at a Nashville hotel, Redin convinced Globetrotter star Marques Haynes to show the women some tricks, and then transformed the Queens' pregame warmups into Globetrotter-style displays of fancy dribbles, spins and passes. The Queens had several traveling outfits, and when they landed at local airports, they turned plenty of heads. "We were given these blazers and skirts," recalled Margie Hunt, a Flying Queen from 1960 to 1964. "We looked like flight attendants, really, when we walked through airports. We had black leather heels. . . . It was totally outside of anything I had ever even dreamed about." The team's play was equally dramatic. One of the best minds in the game, Redin was constantly experimenting with strategy and loved to devise new plays for tournaments, delighting in the surprises he sprung on his opponents.[18]

NBC's players, in contrast, traveled in cars, often held down full-time jobs and focused on executing a straightforward system to perfection. Coach John Head, who had succeeded Leo Long, was a "quiet disciplinarian," Sue Gunter recalled, and the team's plays consisted of two defenses, two offenses and two breaks. "That's what we worked on," Gunter continued. "We worked on it every single day. Everybody that we played knew exactly what we were going to do when we came into the gym. It wasn't a matter of scouting us. But they couldn't beat it, because of the execution."

Throughout the late 1950s, the teams played head-to-head. NBC stopped Wayland's 131-game winning streak in the semifinals of the 1958 AAU tournament and went on to the championship. Wayland came back to win again in 1959, holding Nera White to 8 points in the championship game. NBC won in 1960 and Wayland in 1961. Everyone looked forward to the matchups. "When we played Wayland, we knew we had to put out everything that we had, which we did, both teams did," Joan Crawford explained. Spectators loved the games as well, she continued, "because they knew they had two real good teams that were really going after each other to win."

By 1962, however, NBC had gained the edge. Starting that year, the

NBC national championship team, 1960. Nera White is far left; Joan Crawford is far right. Sue Gunter is center left, next to Coach John Head. COURTESY OF THE WOMEN'S BASKETBALL HALL OF FAME.

team would go on to win eight straight national titles, beating Wayland in the finals every year. NBC had two major advantages. Wayland players had to be enrolled in school, and thus were limited to four years of play. Most of NBC's players were employees rather than students and could stay on as long as they liked. Nera White and Joan Crawford played together for eleven years. "We knew almost what each other was going to do," Crawford said. "We didn't have to look or aim. A lot of times, in a fast break, I'd just throw it down to Nera, she'd just throw it down to me." And the Queens could not stop Nera White, who stymied them at every turn and won their lasting respect. Margie Hunt played on Wayland's varsity for four years and lost the championship to NBC every year. She would never forget the day she stood and took a charge from White, then got up from the floor to the whispered admonition: "Do that again . . . and I'll kill you." But as she described White's talents, her voice rang with admiration. "They think some man came up with the first finger-roll layup," she commented. "Not true. Nera White did that forever."

FROM THE 1940S INTO THE 1960S, THE AAU REPRESENTED THE PEAK of national women's competition. But it was not the only game in town. Starting in the 1930s, a number of top players left amateur ball and entered the professional realm. The most notable was Arkansas native Hazel Walker. In 1949, Walker organized a touring women's team like no one had ever seen. The team, dubbed "Hazel Walker's Arkansas Travelers," played six months a year from 1949 to 1965, often driving hundreds of miles between engagements. The Travelers played almost every night and often twice on Saturdays. They used full-court men's rules and played exclusively against men's teams. Usually, they won.

Hazel Walker had loved basketball all her life. Born in 1914, she grew up on a farm outside the tiny town of Oak Hill, Arkansas, and walked two miles to school throughout her childhood. "That was before gravel roads, and so we followed two wagon tracks," she later recalled. "I kept my knuckles callused and my thumbnail wore off shooting marbles with those boys down the wagon ruts back and forth to school." She started playing basketball in grade school, shooting a rag-filled sock at a rain-barrel hoop. As she moved up to high school, her passion grew. "My parents thought I was crazy to work so hard at basketball," she wrote. "I used to get up at five in the morning and run a mile before the school bus came. Then I'd go out to the hen house and eat two or three raw eggs, because they said that was supposed to build up your wind."[19]

Like many Arkansas residents, Walker's father was part Cherokee Indian, with ancestors among the many native people who entered mainstream society in the nineteenth century. Unlike her counterparts at Indian schools, who came from Indian-dominated communities, Walker lived a thoroughly assimilated life. But her heritage showed clearly in her dark skin, hair and eyes, and she invoked it with pride throughout her career.

Like Iowa, Tennessee and Texas, Arkansas was developing a strong high school girls' program, and Walker was one of its early stars. When she was a senior, Ashdown High School placed second in the state, and Walker was named to the all-state team. When she graduated, all she wanted to do was keep playing. She won a tuition scholarship to Tulsa Business College, in Tulsa, Oklahoma, and joined the school's team, the Tulsa Stenos. Working at a soda fountain and barely scraping by—"I didn't even have a nickel for gum"—she became one of the team's stalwarts. In 1934, the Stenos captured the AAU crown. That winter, after graduation, she married Arkansas sweetheart Gene Crutcher and settled back in Arkansas. Many players stopped competing once they married, but not Walker. Over the next few years she worked as a bookkeeper for the Arkansas State Revenue Department, and managed and played for a series of AAU teams that became mainstays of national competition. She would be named an All-American ten times.

By the end of the 1930s, she was reaching the age when most AAU players hung up their shoes. But then, in 1940, her husband was killed in a railroad accident. "I don't guess I really got over that," she wrote years later. "I just started playing ball all the harder. Basketball was my life." Her team, Little Rock's Lewis & Norwood Flyers, had won the AAU title in 1937 and 1940. They would win again in 1941. The following year, she would be the tournament MVP.

Walker was especially well known for her accurate set shot and deadly aim from the free-throw line. She was national free-throw champion six times, once sinking forty-nine of fifty throws to win the title. She could also mix it up with the best. "She'd go down the floor, and she'd plow into you," Margaret Sexton explained. "We had a girl playing guard that was pretty well stacked up . . . not real trim . . . and boy she went down that floor and she knocked this ball player of ours down. She knocked her out for a little while. She couldn't take her foul shots."

Like all great stars, Walker could also rise to the occasion. She started having trouble with shin splints in the fall of 1941, and sat out most of the season. But when the AAU tournament rolled around, she was ready. In the semifinals, the Arkansas Motor Coaches played the American Institute of Business (AIB), which had never won the tournament. "R.C. Bechtel was coaching AIB," Alline Banks recalled. "AIB was ahead by one point. And it was just seconds to play. And he just knew he had the championship won. Somebody threw Hazel the ball, she took one step over the center line and let go. Bottom of the net. R.C. Bechtel fainted dead out."

Still, there was much more to Walker than a keen eye for the basket. She impressed everyone she met not only with her skills but with her vivacious demeanor. "Hazel Walker was a personality gal," Banks said. "She was a great competitor, a great ball player and a great lady." Walker could charm anyone, and her bookkeeping experience gave her a keen sense for the bottom line. By 1946, she decided to make the precarious leap to the professional arena.

At the time, the main professional women's team was a squad called the All-American Redheads, whose players dyed their hair red as a gimmick and traveled through the country playing men's teams with men's rules. The Redheads were among dozens of mostly male barnstorming teams that crisscrossed the country in the pre-television era, when opportunities for entertainment were often few and far between. Barnstorming teams would arrive in a community and play a game against a local team, dazzling spectators with displays of skill and often spicing the experience with comic routines. The NBA's Boston Celtics sprang to life in 1915 as the "New York Celtics" and then became the "Original Celtics," playing over a hundred barnstorming games a year. The Harlem Renaissance, organized at Harlem's Renaissance Casino ballroom in 1923, was known for fast, driving play. The Harlem Globetrotters, founded in Chicago in 1926, would become famous around the world for fancy ballhandling routines and would still be going strong eight decades later.[20]

For most athletes, becoming a professional was a calculated risk. Throughout the first half of the century, most American sports were run under the "amateur ideal," which held that true athletes competed for honor, not for money. The AAU was quick to bar players seen to be profiting from their talents, as were the national tennis and golf associations. As a result, professional opportunities were few and far between, and even an athlete of Babe Didrikson's caliber and fame had to bounce from sport to sport and exhibition to exhibition to make ends meet. Still, the amateur ideal worked best for wealthy individuals who could pursue sports as a hobby. Most members of AAU teams had to work as well as play, and teams themselves came and went depending on the whims of sponsors. As a result, the Redheads were able to persuade a number of talented players, including Walker, to turn professional.

Walker, however, would not be a Redhead long. Her long career had taught her the ins and outs of managing a basketball team and after three years with the Redheads, she was ready to strike out on her own. In 1949 she quit the team to form the Arkansas Travelers. For the next sixteen years, the Travelers became a fixture in towns across the South and Midwest. Like the Redheads, they played with men's rules and scheduled games almost exclusively against men's teams. Their six-month tour was tightly packed. They would drive into town, play an evening game and then take off in the morning for the next date, which might be several hundred miles away. "It was just routine—like taking a drink of water," Walker once recalled. "We had a lot of doubleheaders.

Hazel Walker's Arkansas Travelers. Walker is at center; Francies Garroutte is third from right. COURTESY OF THE WOMEN'S BASKETBALL HALL OF FAME.

Sometimes we would play one game at seven and then drive forty miles and play again that same night. Then we had to get up and move the next day. We played eleven or twelve games a week sometimes."

For women who loved basketball, it was ideal. "Once you make up your mind, that is all there is to it," Walker wrote Francies "Goose" Garroutte in a recruiting letter. "I guarantee you, you will be happy, satisfied, have [the] best time you ever had or will ever have, save money, and play all the basketball you want to."

Like other barnstorming teams, the Travelers exhibited showmanship as well as skill. The players had a repertoire of ballhandling tricks—Goose Garroutte got her nickname from Reece "Goose" Tatum, one of the Harlem Globetrotters' noted ballhandlers. They also developed a handful of comic, often flirtatious routines. At base, though, they were top ballplayers who kept their winning percentage high with talent, not with gimmicks. "We played it straight," Walker wrote. "We told the men to play us just like we were men. We couldn't fast break as long as they could, but we did when necessary, and we learned to conserve our energy and put it out when it counted."

The Travelers had a profound effect on young female spectators, particularly those who lived beyond the reach of the best AAU teams. As well as setting a standard to which women could aspire, they provided welcome opportunities to a number of players. Martha Evans went to school in Sisterville, West Virginia. The town's high school had no girls' basketball team, and the boys' coach ran into administrative roadblocks when he tried to put her on his squad. Then the Travelers came to Sisterville, and the coach encouraged Evans to ask Walker about trying out. After putting Evans through a brief workout, Walker told her to call as soon as she had graduated. She joined the team the next year.[21]

Although Doris Coleman was a star at Longville High School in Louisiana, her future prospects looked bleak until Walker and the Travelers came to town. "I went and left a note on her motel door and told her I was interested in playing with her," Coleman recalled. "And she got in contact with me. I rode a train all the way to Little Rock. She told me, she said, 'Doris, you're just what I've been looking for.' I was just elated. I came back home and talked it over with my parents, and they didn't want me to go, but I said I was going anyway."

Life with the Travelers offered few luxuries. In the 1950s, the team traveled in a nine-passenger DeSoto Suburban, which was crammed to the brim with players and luggage. "We were each allowed one suitcase, one ball bag and one overnight bag for our cosmetics," Evans explained. "We were so overloaded that the tires had rim cuts in them." The players had two uniforms each, and they were responsible for keeping them clean. "We would come in at night, when we'd get to a motel, and we'd wash one and hang it up and let it dry," Coleman said. "We washed everything we had on. We had an old washboard, and we'd put this washboard in the sink, and that's how we did it." As women traveling alone, they ran a degree of risk. Game receipts were often paid in cash, and the all-female group could seem an easy target for would-be robbers. "There were quite a few times that we ran into danger," Garroutte recalled. "But we handled it ourselves. We carried a gun, and we weren't afraid to use it."[22]

The Travelers also walked a narrow cultural line. Women who traveled alone were stepping outside the conventions of "respectable" society, and many people "automatically thought women traveling, they were trash," Garroutte explained. They were not prepared for women athletes, because they did not know that much about them. They played on a high school level, and that's all people knew. And automatically you had to overcome the first thing that people thought: "There are going to be a bunch of rough-looking women coming in here."[23]

The Travelers dealt with this dilemma by drawing their own lines between on-court play and off-court behavior. Even as they beat men night after night, they were careful to observe all the trappings of conventional female respectability. Walker was always poised, pleasant and impeccably dressed, the most charming woman anyone could hope to meet. Team members were required to curl their hair, wear makeup and dress in skirts or tailored slacks. They avoided any hints of sexual impropriety by never dating alone. "We had to act like ladies, and when we came out of the motel room, we had to be fully dressed," Doris Coleman recalled. "Everything had to be perfect."

JAZZY BARNSTORMERS LIKE THE TRAVELERS, ALONG WITH THE AVID competitors of the AAU, offered a dramatic demonstration of women's love for basketball. But as the Travelers' careful image-shaping showed, top female athletes still stood on shaky ground. Even as they blazed new trails in the game, most players sought to balance daring on-court moves with a strict observance of womanly convention elsewhere in their lives, gaining acceptance for assertive play by suggesting it did not challenge conventional definitions of womanhood. It was a precarious position—and one that would not hold. In the 1950s, a powerful wave of social transformation and conservative cultural retrenchment would cast it asunder, sending women's basketball into a dive from which it would take more than a decade to recover.

·5·

A Man's Game

Late in January 1961, the board of trustees at Wayland Baptist College sent shock waves through the Texas Panhandle. In unanimous accord, they voted to disband the Wayland Flying Queens. The Queens had won six AAU national championships in eight years. They were the toast of Plainview, Wayland's small, West Texas hometown. But such feats had not impressed the Southern Association of Colleges (SAC), which accredited the school. Wayland was short of funds to improve its academic programs, and an SAC committee that examined the school's budget saw no point in spending money on women's basketball. Men's basketball scholarships could stay, committee members ruled, but the women's had to go. Colleges had to be accredited to stay in business, and Wayland's trustees felt compelled to comply. Reluctantly, they voted to discontinue women's basketball "at the end of the current season."[1]

Plainview citizens were outraged, and moved quickly to defend their prized team. "Wayland shouldn't give up the ship, if at all possible," wrote Dick Kranz of the *Amarillo News*. "It would be better to keep going in hopes that more colleges will adopt intercollegiate basketball for women." Surely, Kranz continued, "there must be enough 'angels' around willing to donate a women's basketball scholarship to keep the

Queens at their present level of outstanding play." He was right. A group of businessmen, headed by Claude Hutcherson, quickly organized a booster group they called the "Kings Club," and raised the money to cover a year of scholarships—twenty-seven scholarships at $500 apiece. The funds were presented to the college in March, and the trustees promptly voted to reverse their decision.

But the stir also made it clear that not everyone viewed women's basketball with such enthusiasm. A writer for the *Plainview Daily Herald,* for example, had greeted the news with far less concern. While acknowledging the Queens' many accomplishments, Bob Hilburn flatly stated that the team "fit in no way into a properly organized college athletic department." It had simply been "a sports oddity," he continued, and "no oddity will remain in vogue forever."

In an ideal world, the improving women's play of the 1940s and 1950s would have sparked new levels of excitement about women's basketball and brought the game broad public support, expanding its appeal beyond its rural and small-town strongholds. But in reality, the opposite occurred. Starting in the mid-1950s, even as stars like Missouri Arledge and Nera White climbed toward their competitive peak, American women's basketball went into sharp decline. Audiences dropped, and teams and tournaments were eliminated. Young women who dreamed of basketball stardom found it even harder to pursue. More than a decade would pass before the sport began to recover. From the mid-1950s to the mid-1960s, the sport went through a dark age.

Spurring this startling reversal was a series of social and cultural shifts that in the 1950s worked a wholesale transformation on American society and culture. Across the country, rising incomes, increased mobility and expanding middle-class ambitions loosened ties to the local communities that had so warmly supported women's teams. The shift also gave greater weight to middle-class institutions—such as colleges, universities and accrediting committees—that set little store in female physical strength. Key developments in postwar life, most notably suburban expansion and the advent of television, were shaped by a wave of cultural conservatism that prized conformity and emphasized male-female distinctions. In sporting realms, this altered cultural climate meant that men's sporting exploits rose to new heights, while women's athletics plummeted.

For men's basketball, the end of World War II marked the start of a golden age. Before the war, baseball and football had been the nation's top male sports. But basketball was ready for a move. Starting in the 1930s, rulemakers adopted a set of changes that sped up the game. A smaller, lighter ball, fewer fouls and the elimination of the center jump once held after every basket led to fancier ballhandling and far faster play. As one enthusiast put it, "a dull, slow and unexciting game" became "a game of speed, skill and rhythm; a sport that is also an art; a game that is now filled with emotion."[2]

These improvements caught the eye of sportswriters and promoters, who saw profits in the newly dramatic game. In the mid-1930s, promoters began to schedule college contests in New York's Madison Square Garden. The large, enthusiastic audiences that gathered, along with the revenues they produced, soon prompted the formation of the nation's first national college basketball tournament—the National Invitational Tournament—in 1938. The National Collegiate Athletic Association (NCAA), which had run men's college sports since 1906, established its own national championship in 1939. Colleges across the country were soon scrambling to win a place in the national spotlight, seeking out top coaches and players and sinking money into travel and facilities. Owners of professional basketball teams made their move after World War II, banding together in 1949 to form the National Basketball Association (NBA). Showcasing former college stars such as George Mikan, Bob Cousy and Bill Russell, the NBA took the game to new heights, drawing more fans in the process.[3]

The growing popularity of men's basketball helped college and professional teams make inroads with the great arbiter of postwar sporting success—television. Commercial television broadcasting began in 1946 and rapidly transformed American entertainment. By 1960, nine out of ten American families owned television sets, and television was supplanting radio as the major focus of national popular culture. Those sports able to find a place in the network lineups won new fans and new revenues. Others saw their audiences evaporate, as fans turned to television programs or took advantage of new roads and cars to venture off to other forms of entertainment. As ties to local communities loosened, industrial teams were hit especially hard. From 1951 to 1953, the Hanes Hosiery Girls won three straight AAU titles. In 1954, citing declining attendance, Hanes disbanded the team. "All of a sudden we had competition with television," Eunies Futch later explained. "Everybody had a car. . . . You could see it coming."[4]

Both television and increased mobility prompted the growth of a national sporting culture shaped by the priorities of television networks and the national press. The shift would forever alter the landscape within which American sports teams played. By the 1960s, growing numbers of teams would seek not simply local fame but rather the broadest possible audience. Television and ticket sales pumped money into college and professional sports—revenues that would wield profound influence over the ways that schedules were arranged, teams were financed and status conferred.

Finally, athletes would be evaluated on new terms—a shift with particular significance for women. Sports had not gained its wide appeal simply through the display of physical skill. Rather, its popularity rested on the degree to which athletic exploits represented broader social values, which ranged from belief in the virtue of competition to admiration of strength, speed or selflessness. In the first half of the century, most female athletes drew their support from hometown crowds who cheered on nieces and daughters, friends and colleagues, and who championed a spectrum of female capabilities that could encompass the strength of a cotton picker, the grit of a factory line worker or the poise of a community leader. To connect to a national audience, however, a female athlete needed to embody the values of mainstream culture, displaying a form of womanhood that a broad range of spectators found pleasing to behold. In an anxiously conservative era, fitting such a bill would prove an especially difficult task.

The postwar years brought both prosperity and unease. A budding civil rights movement challenged long-established racial hierarchies. Cold War tensions prompted fears of nuclear attack from outside and set off a hunt for enemies within—a hunt whose targets rapidly expanded from Communist revolutionaries to anyone who seemed to threaten the social or political status quo. Citizens delighted in an expanding consumer culture while worrying about the materialism it promoted. Increasing mobility and rapid suburban growth drew millions of Americans out of familiar communities and into strange new worlds. In the face of such uncertain transformations, many Americans searched for stable ground.

For many, this search led to an idealized vision of middle-class family life, one which came to dominate books, movies, magazines and especially television. In this world, men and women played distinct and firmly defined roles. As in the Victorian era, men were cast as the breadwinners, those fitted to contend with the cut-throat political and economic worlds. Women were the nurturers, devoted to turning their homes into centers of warmth and stability.[5]

The women who populated these visions, with their high heels, tiny waists, full skirts and flawless hair, personified a potent new form of womanhood. They were domestic, focusing their energy on supporting husbands and children. They were erotic, working to make themselves attractive and playful companions for their husbands. They were genteel, pursuing their daily affairs with smiles, spotless outfits and practiced ease. Such ideals lay far removed from the heated, sweaty competition of top-level basketball. Within this formulation, the qualities essential to athletic success—speed, strength, aggressive determination—were cast not as human traits but as specifically masculine ones. Male athletes fit neatly into this picture. Female athletes did not.

The seeming contradiction between athletic skill and feminine convention was nothing new to female athletes. Even at their height of popularity, top-level female teams had rarely portrayed the strength and assertiveness required to play basketball "like boys" as an integral part of womanhood. Rather, most had been careful to combine on-court intensity with off-court femininity. Along with the nation's best women's basketball, the AAU tournament featured a player beauty pageant that crowned a tournament queen. The Philadelphia Tribunes team was advertised as "Girls! Beautiful Girls!" Jimmie Vaughn was both an All-American and an AAU beauty queen, and when Hanes Hosiery recruited her to Winston-Salem, the local paper noted her multifaceted appeal. "Two important additions to the national title-aspiring Hanes Hosiery Girls' basketball team were made yesterday—both coming in the same package," the copy ran. "The package was in the person of Jimmie Vaughn, her dual contributions being top-notch adeptness at doing things with a basketball and vivacious glamour—both items something at which the predominantly home-grown Hosiery lassies seldom are second best." Conventional good looks gave fans—especially men—an added reason to come out to the games, while offering the reassurance that the athletes who performed so well remained "real women."[6]

Owners, coaches and players often made specific efforts to play up femininity. Many AAU teams banned slacks and mandated lipstick. Squads that did not fit the feminine bill could find the going rough. In one AAU tournament, for example, a New Orleans team sponsored by Jax Beer apparently sparked a good deal of consternation. Although the Jax were "exciting to watch," AAU stalwart George Sherman noted, "AAU officials were disturbed that the team not only played like men, but several of the girls also looked like men!" According to AAU referees, Sherman continued, "from time to time a highly placed AAU official

Jimmie Vaughn, AAU tournament queen, 1944. COURTESY OF THE WOMEN'S BASKETBALL HALL OF FAME.

would hint strongly that it would be in the best interest of the tournament if certain teams lost." The New Orleans club was apparently one of those. "I don't know that any official actually 'cheated' the Jax team," Sherman concluded, "but they didn't lean over backwards to give them any breaks."[7]

In 1954, the AAU addressed the issue of sports and femininity directly in a "Statistical Survey of Former Women Athletes." Published in the *Amateur Athlete* magazine, the study addressed a set of telling questions that focused not only on physical abilities but on sexual appeal. "Are athletics harmful to women?" author and former track star Roxy Anderson asked. "Do they tend to make a girl lose her charm and beauty? Is it true that athletics for women result in lasting injuries and sometimes make childbirth difficult?" The answer, she assured readers, "is a big NO!" She went on to report that 91 percent of the women surveyed were married and 79 percent had children. Rather than becoming "mannish and hardened," Anderson argued, top athletes found that "the spotlight of publicity only served to make them more conscious of their appearance and manner." The magazine's editors made a point of noting that Anderson herself "looks more like a movie queen than a woman of 41. She's very feminine and loaded with personality which she credits to athletics."[8]

BALANCING TALENT AND FEMININITY CAME EASILY TO SOME PLAYers. Top athletes came in many shapes and sizes, and many of them fit quite neatly into feminine conventions, giving sportswriters the opportunity to wax eloquent over their physical charms. Jimmie Vaughn was both an All-American and a tournament queen. Alline Banks pivoted on long, slender legs and charged to the basket in a blur of auburn hair. "You're quite wrong if you think all women athletes are the muscular, mannish type," wrote a reporter who visited Banks in the mid-1940s. "Instead of the 'muscle moll' Paul Gallico used to write about in women's sports," he noted, Banks was "a stylishly slender girl who wore polish on her nails, the usual amount of other makeup, and who looks not at all like a girl who would be the world's No. 1 performer in feminine basketball." The only physical hint of her skill, the reporter concluded, was "hands that are slightly larger than usual. . . . That and a beautiful grace

Alline Banks in 1944.
COURTESY OF THE WOMEN'S
BASKETBALL HALL OF FAME.

in her step which tells you instantly she has perfect control of every muscle in her five-foot, eleven-inch, 137-pound frame."[9]

Many women also became practiced in balancing strength and charm, blunting the implications of their talent. Hazel Walker, for example, was a remarkably strong woman. "Night after night I have seen her shoot a hundred free throws in a row, first standing, then kneeling, then sitting flat on the floor, sometimes even with her back to the goal," explained one of her former players. Walker and the Travelers also beat male teams with regularity. But, another friend recalled, "the really amazing thing about it all is that she did it with such grace, style, charm, and laughter that she never offended anyone, not even the males. I'm sure she and her teammates bruised a lot of male egos on the court, but I'm also sure that those men had never seen a more beautiful or charming woman."[10]

Striking a balance between on-court intensity and off-court femininity cleared some space for female athletes. But it was a tenuous achievement. The strategy did not win support for women's athletics in and of itself. Rather, it suggested that female athletes could be acceptable *if* they also met all the requirements of conventional femininity. As a result, it did little to dislodge the idea that sports was properly a male endeavor or to stake a strong female claim to the virtues of strength, determination and assertiveness. It left athletes who did not fit feminine ideals open to attack—as when a coach at one AAU tournament asserted that Nera White was a man and demanded a physical examination to prove him wrong. It also placed female athletes at the mercy of larger social trends, with consequences that became apparent as the 1950s advanced.[11]

As the era's twin emphasis on glamour and family life narrowed standards of womanhood, sharpening distinctions between "masculine" and "feminine" activities, those women who played "like boys" found it increasingly difficult to keep one foot in both worlds. These difficulties were compounded by a related trend—growing public alarm about homosexuality. Gay men and women became a more visible part of American society in the 1950s—sometimes by choice, sometimes as targets of the era's political witchhunts. In the edgy postwar climate, where almost any hint of nonconformity was cast as a threat to social order, homosexuality sparked fear and condemnation, and alarmist rhetoric raised suspicions about women who showed any hint of masculinity. The consequences for women's sports were palpable. Athletes who were lesbians worried about exposure. Those who were not feared being tarred by suspicion. Concerns about possible connections between women's sports and lesbianism reduced enthusiasm among institutions, spectators and sometimes players themselves.[12]

Support for top-level women's basketball had always been limited to a scattering of states and communities. Not only did the unfavorable Cold War climate prevent the game from spreading, it prompted retrenchment. For many young women, the gap between sports and femininity became simply too great. "To many girls, being athletic means muscles," one prominent physical educator noted in 1962, when the new attitudes had settled firmly into place. "Having muscles means bulges and being called a tomboy. If so labeled, she believes she will lose social prestige and will rate zero with the boys." Despite all their success, even the Flying Queens could be regarded as a "sports oddity." Strong local support helped save the Queens. Other teams would not be so lucky.[13]

BLACK COLLEGE WOMEN WERE AMONG THE FIRST TO EXPERIENCE the effects of the shift. In the 1930s, many black institutions had defied the physical education philosophy that dominated white schools, instead fielding highly competitive teams bolstered by concepts of womanhood that celebrated strength and determination. But by the 1940s, college administrators were moving closer to an increasingly conservative cultural mainstream, and physical educators' arguments for fashioning distinctly female programs began to carry more weight. In school after school, varsity schedules gave way to play days and to highly femi-

Clark College physical education students, Atlanta, Georgia. COURTESY OF THE CLARK COLLEGE PHOTOGRAPHS COLLECTION, ROBERT W. WOODRUFF LIBRARY OF THE ATLANTA UNIVERSITY CENTER.

nized events such as the "Best Proportioned Figure" contest held at Atlanta's Clark College in 1951.[14]

In the fall of 1955, when Missouri Arledge transferred from Philander Smith College to Tuskegee, she found a school far different from the one that track stars Alice Coachman and Lula Hymes had attended. As in many black colleges, men's sports was on the rise. But the school's once-powerful women's basketball squad played largely "for enjoyment," and the school was rife with rumors that women's basketball had run its course. In the early 1960s, Tuskegee disbanded its team. The loss of once-mighty black college varsities was especially ironic for black women. At the precise time that a changing racial climate sparked expanding possibilities for black male athletes, black women saw their options narrow.

Girls' high school teams also suffered as physical educators across the country stepped up their campaign against competitive play. During the 1920s and 1930s, physical educators had managed to tamp down competition in a number of states. In the favorable postwar climate, they moved forcefully to extend their reach into communities that had resisted their influence. One of the most dramatic battles unfolded in North Carolina. As with many states, postwar North Carolina was home to two distinct visions of high school girls' basketball. White urban schools were dominated by play days and physical education programs. In rural areas, textile towns and African American communities, varsity programs thrived. Statewide, supporters of girls' competition held something of an edge. Most African American high schools sponsored varsity teams, and a 1951 poll of more than four hundred white high schools showed an almost even split over whether to support top-level varsity play.[15]

But the scales were about to tip. In 1950, a group of coaches made a bid to increase the statewide profile of girls' basketball, founding a well-publicized private tournament that they dubbed the girls' high school state championship. The Girls' Invitational opened to great enthusiasm, and by its second year was outdrawing the boys' state tournament. But the move also aroused opposition. Drawing on decades of carefully cultivated political contacts, the state's physical educators struck back. In 1952, the state board of education banned state championships for girls.

The decision touched off a statewide debate over girls' athletics, in which supporters and opponents wrote letters, lobbied state officials and aired their positions in the press. A public hearing held in 1952 set the battle lines. One of the tournament's founders, Robert E. "Bob" Lee, stressed the virtues of competitive athletics and called for equal treatment. If it were good or bad for the boys, he argued, "then the same thing applied to the girls." [16] Physical educators, in contrast, contended that women should not engage in high-level competition. In the end, the latter view won out. By 1954, the state tournament was dead.

The loss could not have come at a worse time. Even as elimination of the high-profile event left North Carolina girls' basketball reeling, the state's growing interest in the men's college game brought new pressures to bear. The state's major colleges were in the middle of a bid to lift North Carolina men's college basketball to the highest level of national competition. Their successes turned the game into a state obsession. The growth proved a boon to high school boys' basketball. It had the opposite effect on girls' teams. As enthusiasm for men's basketball grew, men's coaches began to cast the women's game as interfering with their endeavors. In 1951, at the height of the state tournament battle, one top male college coach publicly "blamed girls' basketball for causing a lack of interest around North Carolina in boys' play." [17] By the 1960s, recalled high school coach Bill Bost, men's coaches at some high schools were working to nudge women's teams out of their traditional place in the Friday night spotlight in favor of the boys' junior varsity. "When I first started coaching girls, they tried to do away with it," Bost explained. "Boys' coaches especially. They wanted to have a J.V. boys, and a varsity boys. And they would say: 'Well, if you want to play a girls' game, play it on Wednesday afternoon.' "

North Carolina's former female stars watched with dismay. Mildred Little Bauguess, an all-state high school guard who became a mainstay of Hanes Hosiery's championship squads, saw the change in her own family. Basketball had been her ticket to community, statewide and then national recognition. Decades after her career ended, she remained a hometown star. "Right now, I can walk downtown, and at least eight out of ten people will say: 'You're the one who played ball,' " she recalled in

1993. "This many years off, forty-some years ago. . . . 'You're the one that played ball.'" But in the early 1960s, when her two daughters reached playing age, the teams and tournaments that had showcased her talents were largely gone, and neither daughter showed an interest in her sport. "We had put the basketball goal up, and had it fixed to official height and everything else," she explained. "And all the boys in the neighborhood played, but they never played. Neither one of them."

For young women caught in the midst of the shift, the loss of opportunity was devastating. From all-black West Charlotte High School, Mary Alyce Alexander watched with dismay as the state's black colleges disbanded their varsity teams. "I could see it coming," she said. "I felt as if I were being betrayed. But what can you do? . . . I thought of myself as another Babe Didrikson Zaharias. I thought I could do anything athletically that I had the opportunity to do. But that was the missing thing, the opportunity."

Across the nation, as women's basketball teams were downplayed or disbanded, another activity rose to take their place—cheerleading. Organized cheerleading had begun in the late nineteenth century as an exclusively male activity. In the 1920s and 1930s, mixed squads were the norm. But in the postwar era cheerleading became a predominantly female enterprise, mirroring the broader cultural split between male and female activities. With its emphasis on the female figure, on wholesome good looks and on support of male teams, cheerleading fit perfectly with the womanly ideals paraded across postwar magazine pages and television screens. As men's sports teams gained greater notice, so did cheerleading squads, bolstered by public approval and by an expanding cheerleading "industry" that sought to expand the market for uniforms, pom-poms and megaphones. At many schools, a place on the cheering squad became the ultimate symbol of female success. Women's basketball, in contrast, faded from view.[18]

The set of shifts that eliminated so many women's basketball teams, elevated cheerleading to a prized female pursuit and vaulted the men's game to new heights was more than a passing fad. It transformed the meaning of American basketball. For the first half of the twentieth century, basketball was as much a woman's sport as it was a man's. Basket-

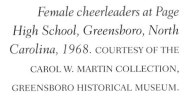

Female cheerleaders at Page High School, Greensboro, North Carolina, 1968. COURTESY OF THE CAROL W. MARTIN COLLECTION, GREENSBORO HISTORICAL MUSEUM.

ball's limits on physical contact, combined with its popularity in women's colleges, led many early observers to dub it a women's game. Not until the 1930s did male college players shake the image that they played a "sissy" sport—one that did not measure up to the more dramatic masculinity of football. Into the 1940s and early 1950s, a women's high school or industrial team could easily be more successful than its male counterpart, drawing larger audiences and basking in greater prestige. But as the 1950s drew to a close, women faced an uphill battle. The new men's rules, which stressed speed and strength, boosted the masculinity of the men's game—a connection that would only increase when slam dunks and high-flying acrobatics came into vogue in the 1970s. The rapid growth of men's college and professional basketball also created a new generation of die-hard fans who would associate the game almost exclusively with men. By the 1960s, for the first time, basketball was largely a man's game.

WOMEN'S BASKETBALL DID HOLD ITS OWN IN SOME COMMUNITIES. The visions of suburban prosperity that flooded movies and magazines lay well beyond the reach of many American families, and countless young women grew up meeting challenges far more taxing than perfect pot roasts or spotless sheets. In places where the game had sunk deep roots, it persisted and even thrived. In the Iowa countryside, high school girls played with the same verve they had always known, and the girls' state tournament—thanks to a new, savvy promoter by the name of E. Wayne Cooley—grew more popular by the year. A handful of other states, among them Arkansas, Tennessee, Mississippi and Texas, maintained strong high school programs. AAU stalwarts such as Wayland Baptist and Nashville Business College kept playing, providing a handful of post–high school opportunities.

Such successes remained profoundly local, shielded from national cultural trends but unable to influence them. Still, as women's basketball entered one of its darkest periods, they would prove enormously important. Even as many young women found their options limited to cheerleading, a fortunate few were able to keep women's basketball alive, as players and increasingly as coaches. Throughout the 1950s and 1960s, this group of dedicated women would nurture their sport's flickering flame, developing their understanding of the game and dreaming of a better day.

TITLE IX AND
COLLEGE COMPETITION

1960–1993

· 6 ·

Keeping the Flame Alive

At North Carolina's Gibsonville High School, Kay Yow lived and breathed basketball. She came from a long and proud tradition: her parents had both played on textile mill teams, and her cousin Virgil had coached the three-time AAU champion Hanes Hosiery Girls, as well as men's teams at Hanes and High Point College. Although the North Carolina girls' state high school tournament had been abolished, Yow lived in a community where local support for women's basketball still ran strong. In high school, she routinely played in front of packed stands and once scored 52 points in a game. Her senior year, she made the state's East-West all-star team.

Yet in 1960, when she graduated second in her class from Gibsonville High School, the future coaching star took the same route as most of her high school peers—she quit the sport.

Without a protest, without a whimper.

In 1960, Yow had little choice. Although basketball filled North Carolina's newspapers, radio broadcasts and television programs, most of the teams were male. In 1957, the University of North Carolina Tar Heels sparked a state and national sensation with an undefeated season and a triple-overtime national championship victory. Several state teams

Kay Yow starred at Gibsonville High School in 1960.
COURTESY OF KAY YOW.

were building national reputations. But women were largely relegated to the sidelines, serving as the cheerleaders and beauty queens that mirrored the well-groomed housewives and mothers who had become icons of American femininity. In such a world, girls didn't play basketball after high school, any more than they dreamed of becoming engineers, surgeons, CEOs or president. Unless a young woman was lucky enough to grow up in one of the scattered communities where women's basketball was still highly valued, even envisioning the possibility would have required a formidable imagination. And in the conservative, conformity-minded society of the era, that kind of daring was rare. "It was very different then, like everything else," Yow explained decades later. "I grew up in a time where people answered questions. They didn't ask questions."

But even as many women put basketball behind them, a smattering of others were fighting to stay in the game. A handful of former players—many of whom had been the first in their families to go to college—started small-scale programs within college physical education departments. Although these fledgling efforts paled beside AAU competition, their founders became some of the first women to coach the competitive game. Largely unpaid and carrying full teaching loads, these coaches scraped together funds and often paid for balls or uniforms themselves, working purely for the love of the sport.

For much of the decade, their dedicated labor brought limited results. But change was coming. By the late 1960s, the women's liberation movement began to brew, fueled by the kind of questions Kay Yow's generation had not asked. The movement pushed at the boundaries of conventional womanhood, celebrating a wide range of female abilities and launching a far-reaching expansion of women's social roles. It also inspired a push for legal equality that spilled over into sports. Basketball coaches eagerly seized the new opportunities. In 1972, when a revolutionary act of Congress transformed the landscape of women's college athletics, this determined group of women was ready to turn law into reality.

Sue Gunter was one such pioneer. Like so many avid players, she grew up on a farm outside a small, basketball-crazy town—in her case Walnut Grove, Mississippi. "About all we did was play basketball," she explained. "We laughingly now say our high school had two sports, girls' basketball and boys' basketball. We played year-round. I don't remember basketball not being in my life."

Gunter would never forget the euphoria she felt the day her father brought home something she'd been begging for—a leather basketball. "He had been to a stock sale," she remembered. "He backed up to unload the truck, and I saw this little box hanging up in the back of the truck . . . I can remember it like it was yesterday, how excited I was to have the real basketball."

Unlike Kay Yow, Gunter knew there were ways to keep playing after high school. As her high school career came to an end, she began to assess her options. One of her best high school friends, Carla Lowry, had played her way on to the Wayland College team. Gunter made the pilgrimage to Plainview for coach Harley Redin's tryouts but didn't make the scholarship cut. Undaunted, she traveled to Tennessee to try out for Nashville Business College's John Head, who was more impressed. In 1958, Gunter donned an NBC uniform.

Like many players of her era, however, Gunter set her sights higher than a factory job or a secretary's desk. She wanted to go to college. Recognizing his players' growing ambitions, NBC owner H.O. Balls had made arrangements with Nashville's Peabody College for players to enroll there if they wished. Gunter did, and the decision made for a hectic life. The NBC team practiced promptly at eight each morning. As soon as they were done, Gunter had to catch a bus back to her apartment, shower and rush off to class. But it was thrilling. She played the best basketball of her life, with the best players she had ever seen. She also developed a profound admiration for John Head's straightforward coaching method, the precision and clarity with which he taught the game. "He was a stickler for detail," she noted. "There was nothing fancy . . . his purpose was to win championships." Of the four years she played with the team, they won the national championship two years and were runners-up in the two others.

At some point during those years, Gunter junked her idea to be a journalist and decided to become a college basketball coach. It was a daring move. Few colleges had women's basketball teams, and coaches were almost never paid. But Gunter was determined to succeed. "It was something I knew I had to pursue; I couldn't just let it go," she explained. "All my life I have had a love affair with the game. It has meant more to me than anything other than my mom and dad." After she graduated from Peabody, she took a job as a physical education teacher and women's basketball coach at Middle Tennessee State University.

Meanwhile, at the University of Maryland, future coaching star Chris Weller was developing a similar determination. Like Gunter, Weller grew up immersed in sports. "I didn't like dolls, and to this day I can't sew or cook," she recalled. "I was in home economics; I was a disaster. That was the hardest class I took." She spent her childhood playing basketball with neighborhood boys. But unlike Yow or Gunter, her high school had no team to play for, no way she could cultivate her most cherished talent. "They had nothing for girls sportswise," Weller said. "I was in the National Honor Society but I didn't feel I was good at anything. There were basically three career choices for women—secretary, teacher or nurse. I picked the lesser of three evils—to be a teacher."

In 1962, however, she found the chance she had been wanting. She enrolled in the University of Maryland, which had just begun to sponsor a club-level basketball team. The club had a volunteer coach and no uniforms. They drove their own cars to games. Nonetheless, the players took their efforts seriously. "It was the real deal," Weller said. "Our coach did not believe in practicing on weekends, but I'd get the team together on Sundays and practice."

On the team, and in her physical education courses, Weller "got fired up" about women's sports: "I felt like I grew and found myself." By the time she was a senior, she was speaking out about the lack of athletic opportunities for girls as well as the lack of athletic coaching and training classes for female physical education majors.

"I remember the dean of the college was teaching a philosophy course on the value of sports," she explained. "I would argue if these values are so good, why aren't the girls having these opportunities? . . . Anything to do with athletics, the women weren't in those classes." She spent the rest of her college career fighting to open such classes to women. "We had to stand up and say, 'Look—we're participating very seriously with sports and we believe in the values of sports, too,' " she concluded. " 'If we're going to get out there and spread it to the high schools, you're not giving us the wherewithal to do it.' Finally, a year after I left, women could take the coaching and training classes."

Across the country, sports-minded women were beginning to fight similar battles. Women fortunate enough to play at schools like Wayland or Iowa Wesleyan were taken aback by the lack of opportunity outside their charmed circle and began to challenge physical educators' noncompetitive model. For Margie Hunt McDonald, playing basketball in the tiny town of Carmago, Oklahoma, had been "just like breathing." Moving on to Wayland was like a dream come true. But after she graduated and began to coach, she discovered how lucky she had been. Most women "didn't have that opportunity," she noted. "If you lived in California, forget it. You lived in Florida, forget it. New York. You're not going to be able to play. And that's when it finally hit me."

When Patsy Neal was playing high school ball in rural Georgia, she and her teammates felt they had "just as much right to get on the court as the boys did." Wayland was no different. Then she took a physical ed-ucation job at the University of Utah, where play days were the norm. Eager to keep competing, she joined an AAU team. It was nothing like she had ever experienced. "We didn't have a lot of support," she remem-bered. "We struggled to get someone to sponsor us so we would have uniforms. It was a real struggle . . . it was like going from riches to rags." Neal and her peers knew from experience that far more was possible, and they began working to spread that vision.

Across the country, the battle for funding and facilities was arduous. Winning respect for women's sports was difficult enough. Once women began asking for resources, resistance often stiffened. Focused on preparing their men's teams for rising levels of high school and college competition, most administrators showed little interest in women's sports. The idea of athletics as a male domain was deeply ingrained. It could also be a convenient excuse to focus a school's resources on men's teams, while dismissing women's sports as unimportant or suggesting that their advocates lay outside the pale of normal womanhood.

"There was nobody to help us," Gunter recalled. "Men's athletics was not going to do it. They didn't want to spend money on it. We were fight-ing so many elements. Some thought we were a bunch of girls wanting to be guys, or that we needed to go play intramurals. But the competitive nature of us as women really emerged. We *were* going to compete."

AS THE DECADE ADVANCED, A GROWING NUMBER OF PHYSICAL educators found themselves making similar resolutions. Some, like Patsy Neal and Margie Hunt McDonald, had roots in competitive pro-grams. Others had watched talented athletes chafe at the limitations of play days and sensed the extent to which avoiding competition isolated women from the foundations of postwar political and economic life. A few of these women had begun to recommend that their profession re-evaluate its philosophy. Others had gone a step further, cautiously ini-tiating limited intercollegiate play. Their efforts got a boost when the federal government became alarmed that U.S. athletes were falling be-hind the archrival Soviet Union in international sports competitions, and launched a series of efforts that urged U.S. women to take competitive sports more seriously. It also helped that the American Medical Association conveniently reversed earlier claims that women were not fit for sports and urged them to spend more time exercising. In 1966, the Division of Girls and Women's Sports, the physical educators' main national organization, created the national Commission on Intercollegiate Athletics for Women (CIAW), designed to oversee women's intercollegiate competition and organize national tournaments.[1]

Once competition began to revive, many women realized how much they had loved high-level play. Although Kay Yow had not mourned the end of her basketball career, her college years were haunted by the vague sense that "something was missing." Soon after graduation, she found out what it was. She applied for a job teaching English at Allen Jay High School, close to her hometown. School principal Doyle Early remembered her high school basketball career and made her a deal: she could have the job if she would coach Allen Jay's girls' team. Although she was reluctant at first, Yow's knack for coaching quickly became evident. Her first team went 22–3 and won the conference crown. Her teams won league titles the following two years. "I loved coaching," she noted. More important, she realized how much she had missed the game. "I came to understand that the thing that had been missing for me in college was basketball."

AS KAY YOW REDISCOVERED HER LOVE OF BASKETBALL, SHE AND HER peers were caught up in a much larger tide of social change that swept across the country in the late 1960s—one that would push open doors for women in many fields.

The press for change had started in the 1950s, when African Americans—many of them women—began to challenge the long-established system of Jim Crow segregation. By the 1960s, these challenges had sparked an open revolt against legal segregation, as African Americans across the country fought for the right to vote, to patronize public institutions and to be treated like full American citizens. Civil rights protests laid bare deep cracks in American society, exposing the country's failure to live up to its promise of democratic equality. Once begun, the process snowballed.

For future basketball coach Vivian Stringer, the social revolt hit home when she failed to make her high school cheerleading squad. Cheerleading had not been her first choice. As with so many of her peers, Stringer's early sports experience mingled determination with a maddening lack of opportunity. In the late 1950s and early 1960s, Stringer and her friend Arlene Gary were two of the best young players, male or female, in Edenborn, Pennsylvania. "We played basketball as long as I can remember," Stringer recalled. Although Stringer and Gary were the only girls on the playground court, they suffered from no lack of respect. "If we weren't the captains, we would always be the ones they picked up first," she continued. "We ran things. In fact, the guys would come to my house sometimes to help sweep the floor and do the dishes so my mom would let me go." Although Stringer's mother had never played sports and thought her daughter was wasting her time, her father was proud of her talents and encouraged her.

But like Chris Weller, Stringer had no high school team to play on, because German Township High School did not field a girls' squad. As she reached high school age, rather than refining her own skills, she found herself helping her male peers excel. She helped them work through plays on the playground and whispered advice from the sidelines of high school games. "They would look at me as they were coming off the floor, and I would say, 'You need to cut harder to the ball, follow through.' . . . With the boys who played football, I would get so frustrated because I could see where the holes were, and how the guys needed to keep their heads down, get the ball and drive harder through." It was a difficult experience. "My satisfaction was that on Saturday or Sunday they would still come down and play. . . . Sometimes these guys would walk maybe a couple of miles just to come over to the Edenborn basketball court."

As in most of the country, the closest thing Edenborn girls had to a sports team was the cheerleading squad. Although Stringer had little interest in cheerleading, she realized that it was the best way to stay close to the floor and the team. So she began to practice cheers and routines. She had always liked gymnastics and her athleticism showed. When tryout day came, she was ready.

There was, however, a catch. Stringer was one of only a handful of black students at German Township High. Stringer had little experience of racial prejudice. Edenborn was a mining town, with a mixed group of residents that included African Americans as well as immigrants of Polish and Italian descent. The men all worked together in the mines, and "when they went in that hole, they had each other's back." But although there was little overt discrimination at the school, there were unwritten rules. There had never been an African American on the cheerleading squad. Despite a stellar tryout, Stringer did not make the cut. She went home brokenhearted. "I didn't say anything," she remembered. "I kept thinking to myself: 'Maybe my hands—my fingers weren't straight, or maybe when I did my kick my toes weren't up. Maybe I didn't drop my voice low enough. Maybe I didn't smile.' I looked at myself to see what it was that I didn't do."

In earlier years, such discrimination often went unchallenged. Faced with exclusion, African Americans simply turned their backs and focused on other endeavors. But by the mid-1960s, that was less and less the case. Unbeknown to Stringer, a representative from the NAACP had been at the cheerleading tryouts. That evening, he came over to Stringer's house. "I was upstairs doing my homework, and my father called me downstairs," Stringer said. "The man said: 'Look, I just want you to know that I was so hurt you didn't make the squad. You were clearly the best cheerleader there. There's no question in my mind. Everybody knew it. Everybody in the gym knew it. And he said, 'We need you to allow us to go down and speak on your behalf.' " At first Stringer said no. She didn't want to be given anything, and she didn't want anyone "to feel I had been pushed in." But the man pressed his point. If she did not stand up, he argued, the issue would simply fester, and the next black candidate would face the same obstacle. "If it's not you, then who?" he asked. She finally agreed. The NAACP approached the school board, which then placed Stringer on the squad.

"It was rough," she recalled. "Everyone in the school knew—the NAACP's having a special meeting with the board. . . . I remember being so nervous, and not wanting to go to the first practice, and waiting until the last second so I could be there when everybody else had gone

Vivian Stringer, high school cheerleader, in 1966. COURTESY OF GERMAN-MASONTOWN PUBLIC LIBRARY, MASONTOWN, PENNSYLVANIA

in the bathroom and changed their clothes and done their little chit-chats. It was a terrible feeling. . . . You felt like an outcast. You've just got to come in with everybody else, but you feel less than that. And then I was angry with myself because I knew that I wasn't less. I was clearly qualified—I was better."

Like the physical educators who had come to see the limits of play days, Stringer now saw her community with new eyes. Though she had heard about civil rights protests, like many African Americans outside the South, she saw racism as a southern problem, not something that applied to her. Suddenly, she knew better. As she thought about the incident, she came to realize that the absence of conflict did not mean true integration. "It was one thing to be friendly and talk and keep moving and be supportive of each other, but that real kind of close thing, it wasn't there," she explained. "But I never realized that." There were also other issues. "It came [down] to things like, do you have school board members? I never had a black teacher. And no people that were cheerleaders or majorettes. But you didn't think anything of it. The big beat went on, and everything was O.K."

As people across the country began to ponder racial inequality, women's issues bubbled up as well. Countless middle-class women chafed at the limitations of suburban motherhood and felt the frustrations given voice by Betty Friedan's scathing critique, *The Feminine Mystique*, published in 1963. Within the civil rights movement, women who had spent years dissecting the workings of racial oppression began to use the analytical tools they had developed to consider the status of women. They did not like what they saw. In the fall of 1964, a group of female civil rights activists authored a landmark statement that asserted: "Assumptions of male superiority are as widespread and deep rooted . . . as the assumptions of white supremacy," and called for the start of "the slow process of changing values and ideas so that all of us gradually come to understand that this is no more a man's world than it is a white world."[2] Increasingly, groups of other women began to examine their own lives and to speak out for women's rights. The women's liberation movement had begun.

The movement was broad and varied, reflecting the depth to which assumptions about men and women were tightly woven into American society. Once women began to look around them, inequalities became painfully obvious. Women were limited to certain jobs, and often could not rent apartments or open bank accounts on their own. They were paid less for their work. Many college courses, ranging from coaching to engineering, were closed to them. At political meetings—even those focused on social issues such as civil rights—they were expected to serve coffee and stroke male egos. Leadership was men's work.

As the women's movement began, women took a range of actions. A key strategy was "consciousness raising"—discussion groups that encouraged women to examine their own lives for inequalities they had taken for granted. Activists launched legal and legislative campaigns for equal employment opportunities and equal pay, as well as an end to discriminating laws. A particularly dramatic incident in the summer of 1968 involved two hundred women who picketed the Miss America pageant to protest widespread portrayals of women as sexual objects. The protesters packed a trash can with the bras and girdles that for so many years had pressed women's bodies into the "ideal" female shape. They then set them on fire.[3]

Such defiantly "unfeminine" activity drew harsh condemnation, and many women—athletes and coaches among them—sought to distance themselves from the activists' assertive behavior. "I never wanted to be known as a women's libber," Chris Weller said. "Some of us wanted to be considered feminists; some were afraid of the word," Vivian Stringer noted. But the questions activists raised could not be ignored. "That was the time that Martin Luther King was shot, Robert Kennedy had been killed," Stringer continued. "Women were second-class citizens. It was time to question whether the country was doing the right thing."

Coaches of early women's college teams, who were doing much with almost nothing, had plenty of those questions. Players and coaches were there mainly because of their passion for the game. "Back then, the only reason to be a female college athlete was that you loved it," explained University of Texas coach Jody Conradt. "You enjoyed the closeness of the team. The camaraderie. And you played for that reason." But they knew they deserved more.[4]

Kay Yow, center, in her first college coaching job at Elon College in North Carolina.
COURTESY OF ELON UNIVERSITY.

When Stringer got her first job at historically black Cheyney State College, she spent her own money to recruit and drove her team to games in an old, highly unreliable prison bus. Intersections were a challenge, she recalled: "I'd slow down but not enough to stop because we weren't sure we were going to start again, so my assistant would crane her neck out the window and yell, 'Vivian, keep going, no one's coming.' "[5] Kay Yow took her first college job at tiny Elon College in 1971 and got by on a shoestring. "We paid for our own gas and food," she remembered. "We bought our own uniforms and ironed the numerals on." At Maryland, Chris Weller and her players pinched pennies on every travel meal. "The players said I could smell a Denny's a hundred miles away," she said.

By the late 1960s, Sue Gunter was teaching physical education and coaching at Stephen F. Austin State University in Nacogdoches, Texas. She repeatedly begged her department chair for uniforms and other basics for her team. Finally, the chair decided Gunter needed to experience the obstacles firsthand and took her to some meetings. "We started off with one of her superiors, and we went to a couple of the deans of the college, and we finally wound up in the president of the university's office," Gunter recalled. None of the administrators had any interest in spending money on the team.

"I left that building, and there were tears running down my cheeks because I was so angry," Gunter continued. "But she had made the point: 'Sue, this is what I fight every single day.' "

It was easy to be disheartened. Like civil rights activists, female coaches faced an entrenched power structure that they had little chance of changing on their own. Like their predecessors, they would need help from other quarters. Confronted with intransigent, segregationist opposition, civil rights activists had fought a two-front battle. Even as grassroots activists organized citizens into boycotts and demonstrations, other leaders worked to produce the laws and legal decisions that would bring federal clout to bear on local conflicts. Together, federal mandates and local action broke the back of segregation. Women's basketball would follow a similar path. As a grassroots women's movement spread throughout the country, a cadre of women and men began to fashion a

Sue Gunter coaching at Stephen F. Austin State, Nacogdoches, Texas.
COURTESY OF STEPHEN F. AUSTIN STATE UNIVERSITY.

revolutionary piece of legislation that would inaugurate a new era in women's sports: Title IX.

ON JUNE 23, 1972, PRESIDENT RICHARD M. NIXON SIGNED INTO LAW a massive bill entitled "The Education Amendments of 1972." One section was labeled "Title IX." The wording was simple on its face: it effectively barred educational institutions from discriminating based on gender. It would spark an athletic revolution. Though few realized it at first, the law gave women's athletics programs legal clout for the first time in U.S. history. Title IX would open doors to women throughout educational institutions—including those of gymnasiums.

Title IX did not begin as an athletic bill. Rather, it grew out of the mounting frustrations of thousands of women who found that opportunity failed to match their expanding ambitions. One of these women was Bernice "Bunny" Sandler, who discovered in 1969 that despite her doctorate in counseling, she could not find a job. She had taught part time at the University of Maryland for seven years but had not been considered for any of seven full-time faculty positions that had come open. The department, where she had also earned her degree, made no secret of the reason. One faculty member acknowledged her qualifications but said, "Let's face it. You come on too strong for a woman." Two other job rejections were equally sexist. A research executive told her he refused to hire women because they were absent too much with sick children. An employment agency counselor pronounced her "not really a professional," but "just a housewife who went back to work."[6]

Spurred by indignation and bolstered by legal research, Sandler began to gather stories of discrimination in higher education throughout the country. Working through the Women's Equity Action League (WEAL), she eventually filed a class-action suit with the U.S. Department of Labor, charging " 'an industry-wide pattern' of discrimination against women in the academic community" and asking for a broad-based investigation. After the suit was filed, several female members of

Congresswoman Martha Griffiths of Michigan, 1970. COURTESY OF THE LIBRARY OF CONGRESS.

*Congresswoman Patsy Mink
of Hawaii, 1972.* COURTESY OF THE
LIBRARY OF CONGRESS.

Congress stepped into the fray. Early in 1970, Michigan Democrat Martha Griffiths gave a landmark speech on sex discrimination in education. That summer, Edith Green, a Democrat from Oregon, introduced the first higher education bill on gender equity and held pivotal hearings on the topic. Democrat Patsy Mink of Hawaii would eventually co-author the bill.[7]

Like Sandler, these women understood discrimination all too well. Patsy Mink was a prime example. Mink's grandparents had come to Hawaii from Japan in the early 1800s to work on the islands' sugar plantations, and she had seen friends, neighbors and family members summarily arrested and interrogated following the Pearl Harbor attack. She was denied entrance to medical school because she was a woman. When she became a lawyer instead, no one in Hawaii would hire her. Realizing that the obstacles she faced required political solutions, Mink went into politics and was elected to Congress in 1965. "I didn't want to become a politician," she once said. "I wanted to be a learned professional serving the community. But they weren't hiring women just then. Not being able to get a job from anybody changed things."[8]

By the early 1970s, in contrast, equality had become the watchword of the times, and equal access to education was a popular concept. Momentum quickly built. In the Senate, Democrat Birch Bayh of Indiana seized the initiative. Bayh was the chief Senate sponsor of the Equal Rights Amendment to the Constitution, which was passed by Congress in 1972 but eventually fell three states short of ratification. He became the Senate manager of the legislation that would become Title IX. Like the male founders of the Iowa High School Girls' Athletic Union, who so strongly supported Iowa girls' basketball, Bayh described his support for the legislation as simple fairness. It gave "the women of America something that is rightfully theirs—an equal chance to attend the schools of their choice, to develop the skills they want."[9]

Having grown up a farm boy in conservative Indiana, Bayh seemed an unlikely torchbearer for women's rights. But he learned from the experience of his first wife, Marvella. "She was an all-star—a straight-A student, president of the student body, head of Girls' State in Oklahoma, president of Girls Nation, and had gotten to shake hands with President [Harry] Truman in the White House long before she met me," Bayh later explained. As her high school career drew to a close, Marvella dreamed of attending the University of Virginia. "Her application was returned," Bayh noted. " 'Women need not apply.' "

In early 1972, after several months of debate, a joint conference committee settled on the simple language that would be Title IX: "No person in the United States shall, on the basis of sex, be excluded from participation in, be denied the benefits of, or be subjected to discrimination under any education program or activity receiving Federal financial assistance. . . ."[10]

Perhaps the most fascinating aspect of Title IX's passage was the lack of attention to athletics. The legislation's profound impact on women's college sports would eventually lead many to believe it focused strictly on athletics. But at the time, athletic disparities were taken so entirely for granted that only those women directly involved in sports realized how significant they were. When Sandler and her colleagues began work on Title IX, sports was far from their minds. "We simply had no idea how bad the discrimination was," she said. Only one sports question arose during the Senate debate. Republican Peter Dominick from Colorado wanted to know if Title IX required co-ed dorms or women on football teams. Told "no" to both—exemptions were in place—Congress moved toward passage.[11]

The full Senate approved Title IX on May 22, 1972, and the House followed suit on June 8. President Nixon signed the bill June 23, and it became law July 1. The job was done with little fanfare—just as Edith Green had wanted. As the bill came down the home stretch, Sandler and other representatives of women's organizations offered to lobby for passage. But Green said no. Since the bill had no opposition, she reasoned, the less her fellow legislators knew, the better. "We were skeptical, but she was absolutely right," Sandler recalled.[12]

Nixon's signature was only the beginning. As civil rights activists knew all too well, federal laws had little meaning until someone pressed for their enforcement. And given the massive growth of men's sports, especially at the college level, creating comparable women's programs would be enormously expensive. As supporters of men's sports realized the implications Title IX held for the athletic status quo, they geared up to defend their interests. The resulting conflicts would stretch on for years.

Yet, as word of the legislation began to make its way around the country, those women who had been struggling to run basketball teams on shoestrings rejoiced. They had kept the flame of women's basketball alive through the game's darkest days. Now the future looked far brighter. When the news reached Stephen F. Austin, Sue Gunter knew immediately what it meant. Unlike the men's coach, she could not give her team scholarships. She felt Title IX would end that practice and quickly passed the word along.

"I told my kids they could be on scholarship the next year," she remembered. "They said, 'Wow, you've got to be kidding, Coach. Why?'"

"'Because of Title IX.'"

"I can't remember what I ate for dinner last night, but I can remember those kids' faces in 1972," Gunter concluded. "Title IX kick-started us. It gave us some juice to go on."

· 7 ·

The Fight for Title IX

Between 1974 and 1976, Stanford University's female basketball players got to know the athletic director's office almost as well as their own locker room. They had plenty to discuss. They wanted out of the women's gym, "so claustrophobic that our 20 fans sat on a single bench between sideline and wall," wrote team member Mariah Burton Nelson. They wanted a paid coach. They wanted real uniforms, rather than the red shorts and white T-shirts over which they tied red P.E. class-style "pinnies."

"We were angry," Burton Nelson noted. "We were persistent. We were, I'm sure, a pain in the neck."[1]

In 1972, the passage of Title IX had promised a revolution in scholastic sports. Under the new law, women were to have the same athletic opportunities as men. For aspiring female athletes such as Burton Nelson, this meant the same teams and uniforms and facilities that men had enjoyed for generations. When Stanford's program fell far short of those expectations, the Stanford players realized it was up to them to make sure those promises became reality. They made a habit of camping out at the office of athletic director Dick DiBiaso, meeting with him more than two dozen times over two years. "We just showed up without an ap-

Mariah Burton Nelson takes a shot for Stanford.
COURTESY OF MARIAH BURTON NELSON.

pointment, sat in the lobby until he agreed to see us, then listed our complaints, demands and requests," Burton Nelson said. "We got increasingly persistent. We told him Title IX had passed and that it was his job to start implementing it, that it was unfair to discriminate."

Like many young women of the times, the Stanford players felt entitled to equal treatment and were ready to fight for it. The women's liberation movement was in full swing. Women were taking up new jobs, challenging old assumptions and marching together in rallies to demand rights and respect. In 1972, singer Helen Reddy had reached the top of the pop charts with the unabashedly feminist "I Am Woman." The next year, with much of the nation watching, tennis star Billie Jean King had soundly beaten former Wimbledon champion Bobby Riggs in a highly publicized "Battle of the Sexes," demolishing the claim that women were unable to withstand the pressure of high-stakes athletic contests. Young women watched, listened and expanded their own ambitions.

"In high school, I did a project on the suffragists," Burton Nelson re-membered. "One of my male teachers pointed out that women's lib was a derogatory term, and it launched a discussion. Then at Stanford, I took every women's studies class there was. I was personally very empow-ered, and it affected my sense of entitlement as an athlete."

On a Tennessee farm, future coach Pat Summitt was building similar resolve. "Nobody in the family seemed to regard me as a girl when it came to work or playing basketball," she later wrote. "I fought hard and played hard, and I was expected to hold my own with my brothers, whether we were in the fields or in the hayloft." But she was also keenly aware that such equal opportunity was not the norm. While her brothers went to college on athletic scholarships, there were none for her. Though her mother worked as hard or harder than anyone else, when the family sat down to eat, the men came first. "At the dinner table, when my brothers would finish their tea, they'd hold up their empty glasses and rattle them," she wrote. "They wouldn't say a word. They'd just lift their glasses and shake them, until my mother served them. . . . I can still see those hands, holding up their glasses, rattling the ice. My mother waited on them. And I thought, *That isn't right.*" As she began to plan her future, one thing was clear: "I knew I wanted to make a differ-ence for women."[2]

As Stanford's players quickly learned, building up women's sports programs would prove a demanding task. It was hard enough to chal-lenge long-held ideas about women's physical abilities. Far more effort would be needed to transform institutions that had invested enormous amounts of social, political and financial capital in male sports. "Sharing money is tough," noted Donna Lopiano, who in 1974 became director of women's athletics at the University of Texas. "Opening the door and say-ing, 'Come on, play', is easier." In Title IX's early years, its supporters would spend as much time in congressional hearings and with college administrators as on the field of play. The country's best teams would come not from wealthy universities but from small schools that drew on persisting pockets of grassroots tradition. The language of Title IX was simple. Turning its promise into reality would require decades of struggle.

WHEN TITLE IX PASSED IN THE SPRING OF 1972, ITS IMPLICATIONS for athletic programs had not been spelled out. The bill's wording was broad, simply stating that neither women nor men could "be excluded from participation in, be denied the benefits of, or be subjected to discrimination under any educational programs or activities." As an extracurricular pursuit, athletics seemed at the margins of the mandate. But that impression did not last long. The bill's implications for athletics quickly became evident, and Christine Grant, the longtime women's athletic director at the University of Iowa, vividly recalled the impact. "All hell broke loose," she said.

As with any federal education law, officials in the Department of Health, Education and Welfare (HEW) were charged with drawing up the regulations that would transform words into reality. As soon as they tackled Title IX, athletics moved to center stage. First, they ruled that athletics would in fact be subject to the law's requirements. They then concluded that the best way to expand opportunity was to create women's teams. "It did not mean girls could try out for boys' teams," explained Jeffrey H. Orleans, one of HEW's civil rights lawyers. "That was not going to produce real equal opportunity, so we had to set up a way of providing separate but equal opportunity."[3]

As soon as those decisions came to light, athletic directors across the country saw the writing on the wall and mobilized for a fight. They knew that unless athletic budgets expanded to accommodate new women's teams, men's programs would get squeezed. The prospects of such increases did not look bright. The early 1970s were tight economic times, with rising oil prices, stagnant employment and spiraling inflation. In addition, the gap in funding between men's and women's sports was staggering. Many universities spent millions on men's athletics and virtually nothing on women's. Making up that disparity through budget hikes alone seemed out of the question. The National Collegiate Athletic Association (NCAA), which regulated men's intercollegiate competition, set aside a $1 million war chest and began lobbying to gut Title IX.[4]

Athletic directors were especially protective of their big-time programs, the so-called "revenue" sports of football and basketball. In the

1950s and 1960s, expanding television coverage had transformed the landscape of American college sports, raising the stakes for success. Schools successful enough to build national reputations, reach bowl games or advance to late rounds in the NCAA basketball tournament reaped the benefits of a national platform, as well as lucrative television revenues. As colleges fought fiercely for a place in this national spot-light, the money spent on recruiting, facilities, coaches' salaries and other athletic perks skyrocketed. NCAA executive director Walter Byers cast the idea of meddling with this formula in apocalyptic terms. Creating equal opportunities for women, he said, would devastate existing men's budgets. The quality of play would plummet, and spectators would lose interest. The result, he gloomily concluded, was the "possible doom of intercollegiate sports."[5]

At first, the Senate agreed. In May 1974, Senator John Tower, a Republican from Texas, proposed that football and other revenue-producing sports be excluded from Title IX coverage. The Tower Amendment promptly passed by voice vote.[6]

But women's organizations fought back. Men's "revenue" sports—mainly football and basketball—had gained their prominence in an era when women were largely barred from college competition. Exempting them from Title IX's standards would lock those old inequalities into place, institutionalizing the idea that women's sports could never be expected to carry the same weight as men's. An exemption would also have ceded authority to the marketplace, allowing money and status to take precedence over equality or education. In practical terms, removing the enormous sums spent on football and basketball from the equity equation would mean far less money for women's programs.

When the Tower Amendment passed, women leaped into action. Physical educators had just formed a new organization, the Association of Intercollegiate Athletics for Women (AIAW). The AIAW hired a tough lawyer, Margot Polivy, and launched a wide-reaching grassroots lobbying campaign—AIAW members wrote letters, sent telegrams, visited congressional representatives and testified against the amendment. They were joined by other women's groups—many focusing on sports for the first time. Until the Tower Amendment, most national women's groups had concentrated their efforts on the bread-and-butter issues of health, education and employment. But when Title IX came under attack, women's groups quickly grasped the principle at stake. The central issue was not athletics, but equality. If women settled for second-class status in the powerfully symbolic realm of sports, they would leave the field open to other "exceptions" to full equality.[7]

After months of work, the effort paid off. A joint conference committee eliminated the Tower Amendment. HEW and the congressional committee charged with reviewing the Title IX regulations took a broad view of the issue. "We had some sympathetic ears at HEW," Christine Grant explained. "I think Congress was uneasy about contemplating any kind of exemption because we were talking about educational opportunity." AIAW members rejoiced in the hard-won victory over a far more powerful opponent. "The women in AIAW were very committed to what they were doing," Grant noted. "I'm not just talking about the leadership. I'm talking about the average member. I think our volunteer system was probably the best since the Red Cross."

The final regulations were explicit about the need for athletic equality, stating: "A school must provide equal athletic opportunity for both sexes." A handful of institutions achieved exemptions, among them fraternities, sororities and "scholarships or other aid offered by colleges and universities to participants in single-sex pageants which reward the combination of personal appearance, poise and talent." Football was not among them. In measuring equality of opportunity, the regulations specified, HEW would "consider whether the selection of sports and levels of competition effectively accommodate the interests and abilities of members of both sexes." It would also look at factors that included "facilities, equipment, supplies, game and practice schedules, travel and per diem allowances, coaching (including assignment and compensation of coaches), academic tutoring, housing, dining facilities and publicity." The regulations became final on July 21, 1975, with compliance required by 1978. Women's sports programs, once scattered across a handful of schools, would become a reality across the nation.[8]

AS SCHOOLS BEGAN TO PUT TOGETHER WOMEN'S TEAMS, ASPIRING coaches were among the first to benefit. Because most coaching jobs began as part-time positions, linked to jobs in women's physical education departments, most of them went to women. In 1975, South Carolina native Judy Rose was studying for a master's degree in physical education at the University of Tennessee. "There were about thirty of us in grad school at Tennessee . . . about fifty-fifty male and female," explained Rose, who would go on to become one of the first female athletic directors of a Division I university. "And I remember the guys would walk into class—and this is toward the end of the year—and one guy would go: 'Yes! I am the new junior high football coach at such-and-such junior high school!' . . . One of the girls would walk in and she'd go, 'Guess what, guess what? . . . I'm the new women's tennis coach at the University of North Alabama!' . . . Now ours was definitely right time, right place."

But while the jobs were easier to get, they were far more challenging to handle. Most novice male coaches were hired to coach established teams or to assist more experienced coaches. Women often started from scratch, with little coaching experience. In 1974, Pat Summitt fell into the head basketball job at the University of Tennessee when the head coach unexpectedly left. "I was a twenty-two-year-old head coach, and I had four players who were twenty-one," she recalled. She dealt with the situation in the best way she knew. "I was hard on them and myself and everyone around me. I thought I had to be. I thought that's how you commanded respect."[9]

The first day of practice revealed the flaws in this single-minded approach. "I worked those prospects up and down the court, at full speed, for two solid hours," she wrote. "At the end of that, I ordered them to run a bunch of conditioning drills. I ran [them] in suicide drill after suicide drill. A group of four young ladies were running together. When they got to the end of the line, they just kept on running. They ran out the door and up the steps, and I never saw them again."

At least Summitt had players to lose. Other coaches were not so lucky. In 1975, Judy Rose was hired as the head women's basketball coach at the University of North Carolina at Charlotte. As she scurried through her new duties—like most early women's basketball coaches she was expected to teach P.E., organize intramurals and coach other sports as well—one of the first things she did was put up signs announcing an organizational meeting for the women's team. "I was so excited," she recalled.

The night of the meeting, however, few showed up. "I remember I went home to my apartment that night, and I was so depressed." One of the women who had hired her "called me at home that night, and she said: 'How did the meeting go?' " Rose continued, "And I said: 'It was awful.' And she said: 'Well, what happened?' I said: 'We only had eight people.' She said: 'That's wonderful!' And I knew I was in trouble."

Rose met with a similar response when she tried to draw spectators to her games. In one promotional effort, she wrote letters to the city's high school and junior high girls' basketball coaches, offering them free tickets to both men's and women's games. "I said: 'If you come to the women's game, I'll let you in the men's game free,' " she explained.

"I kept waiting for the replies," she said. "I never got a reply, never." She stayed perplexed until she ran into one of her supporters. "I said: 'You know I cannot believe that not one person has responded to my letter, not one.' She said: 'Who'd you send them to?' I said: 'Well, I just addressed it to "Women's Basketball Coach." ' . . . And she said: 'Uh, Judy, they don't have women's basketball in the junior high schools or the high schools in Charlotte.' I'm like: 'What?' There's nothing to recruit from. So, I mean, it was a rude awakening."

Judy Rose, first women's basketball coach at the University of North Carolina at Charlotte.
COURTESY OF JUDY ROSE.

Judy Rose was far from alone. Outside of places such as Iowa, Texas or Mississippi, female players had few opportunities and limited support. Only the most die-hard players had pressed on. Most of those had never heard of Title IX.

Indiana was a prime example. Indiana boys' high school basketball, with its renowned state tournament, was the stuff of legend. But as in many states, physical educators' pressure had largely eliminated the girls' game. In the late 1950s, when a handful of high school teachers began a cautious revival, they purposely kept a low profile. "What we would do would be to ask a neighboring school to come over to an after-school basketball game," explained Pat Roy, who would later become the director of girls' athletics for the Indiana High School Athletic Association. "We'd have a volleyball game at noon and call the whole thing 'Sports Day.' Really we were there to play basketball."[10]

"Nobody knew about it," she noted. "We weren't sure we wanted anybody to know about it because they probably would have said 'Stop.'"

The result was a culture in which young athletic women had to work hard to get respect. Twins Melissa and Melinda Miles learned this firsthand. The boys who played pickup games with them in their family's driveway could join teams as early as elementary school. The twins didn't get to play on one until the fall of 1973, their freshman year at Bloomfield High School. "Nobody thought basketball would amount to anything for us; it was just something to do as kids," Melissa explained. When she asked why boys had teams and girls didn't, her teachers replied, "This is the way it is."

"My dad would also talk about how boys are different, boys are better," she continued. "He was trying to get my goat, but in part he was trying to prepare me, that it's different for boys and girls."

The difference also came clear in the way the Miles's parents reacted to their sporting ambitions, as opposed to their brother's. "I remember asking my mom over dinner one night if I could try out for the high school basketball team," Melissa explained. "She just said, 'We'll see.' She didn't get that it was important to me. It wasn't a big deal. It was like my asking if I could join the Latin Club. But when Bill wanted to play, it was a big deal."

In upstate New York, future coach Tara VanDerveer had run into similar roadblocks. As a young girl, VanDerveer pursued basketball with a determined passion. When local boys left her out of playground pickup games, she saved up her allowance and bought the best basketball she could find. "If the boys wanted to use the ball, they had to take me with it," she noted. But she had little encouragement. "My father couldn't have been a more supportive parent," she wrote, "but even he couldn't see the point of a girl playing basketball." It was hard to blame him, she continued. "It was foolish to think I'd have a future in basketball. How could there be a future when there wasn't a present? There was no girls' basketball team in my junior high school. There was a so-called team in high school that played all of four games but held no practices. There were no women that I knew or had heard of who made their living in the sport." [11]

As soon as they got the chance, however, women showed what they could do. At Bloomfield High, the Miles twins and a handful of their friends spearheaded their team to a 67–2 record over four years, going unbeaten each regular season and winning forty-eight straight games at one point. "Once my parents saw we were good, my mom and dad jumped on the bandwagon," Melissa recalled. "They encouraged us. It was very frustrating that they had not realized how important it was to us to begin with."

Bloomfield High won the county title all four years and reached the state championship game in 1976, the first year that Indiana held a state tournament for girls. More than nine thousand fans attended the championship game, where the unbeaten Warsaw Tigers defeated previously unbeaten Bloomfield, 57–52. In 1977, the Miles twins led the team back to the semifinals, and Melissa was named to the Indiana Girls' All-Star Team. But like most high school players at the time, they had never heard of Title IX. Not until they talked to a recruiter from West Point, where they eventually enrolled, did they realize how much women's sport was about to change.

BY THE MID-1970S, IT WAS CLEAR THAT CHANGE WAS COMING. STILL, obstacles loomed. As newly hired coaches started to build programs, they had only a handful of government regulations to deploy against decades of habit and tradition. Some women found male allies at their schools. At Cheyney State, for instance, Vivian Stringer developed a fast friendship with men's basketball coach John Chaney. Stringer was hired in 1971, the year that women's college basketball scrapped the six-player women's game in favor of five-player, full-court play. The two young coaches hit it off, and began to work together on plays and strategy. "We had so many lively debates," Stringer recalled. "And so many times the players would come in the gym and we would have been working through a lunch, working with salt and pepper shakers, about 'We need to do this defensively,' and 'Here's what I would do offensively,' 'How would you handle this and that?' "

When practice time came, the men's and women's teams mingled on the floor, while Stringer and Chaney took turns lecturing on strategies and fundamentals. "We took the game called basketball as just that," Stringer explained. "Not women's basketball or men's basketball. Because of the way it was presented, the guys had ultimate respect for the women players. And the women broke their necks all the time to keep up."

When Chris Weller became the women's basketball coach at Maryland in 1975, she worked hard to convert Maryland's men's coach, the legendary Lefty Driesell, and succeeded to a point. "Finally, he understood I was just as passionate about my team as he was about his," Weller said. "At press conferences where he went first, he would end by introducing me and saying, 'Now those girls are serious.' I cringed every time he would say 'girls,' but he'd come a long way."

One day, Weller's team was stood up by a group of male players they were supposed to scrimmage in preparation for a big game against Old Dominion. Driesell stepped in, dragging his team managers with him. " 'I'll do what you need,' " she recalled him saying. "I told him I needed a tall player on the low block," she continued, "and he said, 'I can do that.' To this day I regret not having a tape of Lefty running up and down the court with his managers playing us."

Most coaches faced far greater resistance. When Tara VanDerveer enrolled in the University of Indiana in the early 1970s, she saw the situation plainly. Indiana had one of the strongest women's programs in the country. But her team's second-class status was palpable.

"It was the whole athletic system that values the men so much more than the women," VanDerveer later wrote. "The men had the gym every day from two until six o'clock, so we didn't practice until evening. There was never a thought that we could split up the prime practice times between us. Basically, it was steak for the men, hot dogs for the women." The disparity, she continued, "struck me as selfish, hoarding all the good things for themselves. I didn't really understand it. I was coming of age during the civil rights movement, and I was passionate about issues of fairness and equality. Why were blacks treated the way they were treated? Why were women treated this way?" But like Melissa Miles, VanDerveer found her complaints fell on unsympathetic ears. "No one had any answers," she concluded. "That's just the way it was." [12]

While Title IX regulations gave women some clout, they did not offer a road map to equality. In addition, the requirement that colleges pro-

University of Maryland coach Chris Weller, 1978.
COURTESY OF CHRIS WELLER.

vide opportunities that "effectively accommodate the interests and abilities of members of both sexes," contained a degree of uncertainty. If only eight women showed up at a basketball organizational meeting, did this mean they had less interest and thus required fewer resources than the men? Reluctant athletic directors, bolstered by the NCAA, seized on every ambiguity as an excuse to drag their feet. Progress was often incremental, and women's coaches carefully weighed their requests. "I didn't go in and ask for things that were outrageous, but I did ask for things," Chris Weller explained. "I wanted the things that counted, like good shoes, good equipment, a place to call home, our own locker room. . . . We didn't even have warm-ups."[13]

Like the Stanford players, Weller also wanted out of the team's second-class gym, which could hold a grand total of two dozen spectators—that was, if everyone stood up. After some stiff negotiation, she won the right to play in Cole Field House, where the men's team played. "We didn't even have our own locker room, we had to use the visitors' locker room," she said. "But I knew if we just got our foot in the door, that they weren't going to be able to get us out of there."[14]

While they battled for resources, women's coaches also began to shape the guidelines for a distinctive form of competition. Leaders of the AIAW, which governed women's sport the way the NCAA governed men's, were determined to chart a path that departed from the trail men had blazed, avoiding the academic and recruiting scandals that plagued the male athletic model. They were well suited to the task. Women such as Katherine Ley and Carol Eckman were longtime physical educators, strong-willed women who believed in female independence and were accustomed to putting students first. They and others like them made a powerful impression on younger coaches. "These women were so strong," Vivian Stringer recalled of her college mentors at Pennsylvania's Slippery Rock University. "They had doctorate degrees and stood up for their rights. My role models were women for once in my life." As a student at Maryland, Chris Weller noted, "I began to meet a lot of impressive women."

The first set of AIAW regulations, drawn up in 1972, signaled the organization's resolve to put education first. The regulations prohibited scholarships, placed limits on recruiting and emphasized that a female athlete was a student first and an athlete second. "It was the main focus of every delegate assembly," Iowa's Christine Grant recalled of the AIAW annual conventions. "Any proposal for change was always looked at from the educational perspective. I headed a committee on recruiting. The rules said you could watch talent but couldn't talk to the athlete. It worked, and worked well. It protected the student-athlete from harassment."

As they laid down guidelines for programs and recruiting, AIAW members also began to shape the rules for bona fide national championships. Carol Eckman, the women's basketball coach at West Chester State in Philadelphia, had gotten the ball rolling in 1969, when she organized the first national invitational tournament ever held in women's college basketball. The tournament brought together fifteen teams, each of which paid $25 to cover the cost of officials and awards. Competition was only one of the goals. A health and physical education professor, Eckman saw a tournament as a place for the sport's supporters to

Carol Eckman, founder of the first national invitational in women's college basketball.
COURTESY OF WEST CHESTER STATE SPORTS INFORMATION.

meet one another and trade information. "This was a time when women's game results were printed on the society page in some newspapers," Tara VanDerveer remembered. "Travel schedules were limited, so most teams had never seen their counterparts from across the country." The host West Chester Ramlettes, starring a future coach named Marian Washington, took the inaugural title. Invitational competitions were held the next two years as well—the 1970 title was won by Cal State Fullerton and the 1971 crown by the Mississippi College for Women, coached by former Nashville Business College star Jill Upton. The AIAW took on tournament duties in 1972, instituting a series of regional playoffs that led to a national tournament.[15]

IN CONTRAST TO THE MEN'S GAME, WHICH WAS DRIVEN BY THE DEEP pockets of major universities, these early women's events had a distinctly small-school flavor. The scholarships, facilities and recruiting budgets that would eventually allow large institutions to dominate play were not yet in place. Rather, success turned on a recruiting base in a region that had retained a tradition of competition and the choice of a coach who could groom homegrown talent into championship material.

The winners of the first AIAW-sponsored championship, the Mighty Macs from Immaculata College, were a perfect example of this combination. With nuns banging buckets in the stands during games, the Catholic women's college was an improbable champion even for that early era. In 1972, Immaculata had no gym—its beloved fieldhouse had burned in 1967, and there had been no money to replace it. Instead, the team practiced in the basement of a convent for novice nuns where the walls came right up to the out-of-bounds lines. Part-time coach Cathy Rush had been hired for the grand sum of $450 a year. But Immaculata was located just outside of Philadelphia, where Catholic institutions had resisted national trends and nurtured a flourishing girls' basketball culture. Immaculata had fielded teams since the 1940s, drawing most of its players from working-class Catholic neighborhoods and developing squads whose tough, aggressive play reflected the hours players had spent competing on Philadelphia's streets and playgrounds, as well as in Catholic Youth Organization leagues.[16]

*Immaculata guard Marianne
Crawford drives to the basket.*
ROBERT HALVEY COLLECTION
OF THE PHILADELPHIA
ARCHDIOCESAN ARCHIVES,
COURTESY OF IMMACULATA
UNIVERSITY.

In 1972, point guard Marianne Crawford could pass and dribble with the best, once dazzling a local sportswriter so completely that he announced: "If there is a better guard in Philadelphia than Marianne Crawford, it's a boy, and if so, I want to see them go one-on-one."[17] Post player Rene Muth was tough under the boards, as was center Theresa Shank. Theresa was "light years ahead of her time," Cathy Rush once noted. "Six feet tall, and if anybody pressed us, she would bring the ball up. She was quick, an excellent athlete. She could jump and shoot. The whole package."[18] Most team members came from working-class families and, like generations of their predecessors, had enrolled in Immaculata because it was nearby, Catholic and cheap. Shank, a high school star, had planned to attend school out of state. But when she was a senior, her family's home burned to the ground. "I was the last one out of the house," Shank later recalled. "All I had left was the pair of yellow pajamas on my back . . . everyone was devastated. I made the decision to go to Immaculata. It's not what I wanted to do, but what I needed to do."[19]

Cathy Rush, who had been hired in 1970, proved herself more than worthy of such players. Rush was a Baptist, not a Catholic, but she had loved sports all her life. She was also married to an NBA referee, which gave her a front-row view of developments in the men's game. She thoroughly researched opponents and constantly tried out new techniques, molding the Macs into a team marked by a fast-breaking offense and pressure defense.[20]

As with many other women's college teams in the early to mid-1970s, the Mighty Macs had to focus on much more than their play. The players washed their own uniforms at times and carpooled to regular-season games. Leading the caravan, Rush earned the nickname, "Queen of the U-turn" from her players. When the team qualified for the 1972 national tournament, players scrambled to sell pencils and toothbrushes to finance the trip. "I have enough toothbrushes to last for three lifetimes,"

Player Theresa Shank (left), coach Cathy Rush (center, blonde) and other Immac-ulata players receive congratulations after winning the 1972 national title. ROBERT HALVEY COLLECTION OF THE PHILADELPHIA ARCHDIOCESAN ARCHIVES, COURTESY OF IM-MACULATA UNIVERSITY.

Sister Marian William Hoben once recalled. "They looked like little kid toothbrushes. They weren't even full-sized." Still, three players had to miss the tournament because of cost, and those who went flew standby to take advantage of half-price fares.[21]

Immaculata had not set its sights on national renown. The team did not even know about the national championship until halfway through the 1971–72 season. Several years later, when staying competitive at a national level began to require a greater investment of time and resources, Immaculata would decide such efforts conflicted with its larger educational mission and would drop from the national scene. But in the early 1970s, a little went a long way. The AIAW had set up regional tournaments that fed into a national tournament draw, and Rush got the team admitted to the mid-Atlantic competition. In the regional finals, Immaculata lost badly to rival West Chester State, 70–38. But the second-place finish won them a bid to the national tournament, in Normal, Illinois. The Mighty Macs regrouped, and Rush reworked her strategy. Immaculata played through to the final and then avenged their loss, beating West Chester, 52–48. The team that had flown standby to Illinois returned to Philadelphia in the first-class section, deplaning to a thunderous reception.[22]

IMMACULATA RULED WOMEN'S COLLEGE BASKETBALL FOR TWO MORE years, going undefeated in the 1972–73 season and taking the national title in both 1973 and 1974. In the spring of 1975, however, they finally met their match.

The 1975 national championship in Harrisonburg, Virginia, was a memorable event on several counts, not the least of which was noise. The Mighty Macs had always drawn strength from a large and loyal following, which distinguished itself in the stands by beating galvanized buckets with drumsticks. In 1975, however, the fans of Delta State, from the small town of Cleveland, Mississippi, were not to be outdone. They headed out to local hardware stores, bought wooden blocks and answered the Immaculata challenge with an equally loud rapping. Cheered by the enthusiasm but troubled by the racket, tournament organizers eventually banned all noisemakers. When the air cleared, Delta State had upset Immaculata 90–81 to win the title.[23]

Delta State's victory was especially sweet for the team's coach, Margaret Wade. She had been a member of the Delta State varsity back in 1933, the year that school administrators suddenly decided basketball was "too strenuous for young ladies" and abolished the team. It was a crushing blow. "We cried and burned our uniforms," Wade said, "but there was nothing else we could do." Wade had stuck with her sport, playing two years on a semi-professional men's team before turning to coaching. Mississippi continued to support high school girls' basketball, and Wade became one of the sport's great stars. In more than two decades of coaching, she compiled a record of 453–89–6 and took her teams to three state title games. Most of her victories came at her alma mater, Cleveland High, and she became a legendary figure throughout the state.[24]

In 1973, when Delta State president Aubrey Lucas decided to restart the women's basketball program, the first step was obvious. He asked Margaret Wade, who was teaching in the school's physical education department, to coach the team. The sixty-year-old Wade had been retired from coaching for more than a decade, and her health was fragile. She had recovered from both cancer and a nearly fatal car wreck, and she suffered from painful arthritis. But she agreed to get things started.

The other key to Delta State's success lay in an astute recruiting decision. One of the state's top high school players, center Lusia Harris, competed for Amanda Elzy High, just down the road from Cleveland in Greenwood, Mississippi. Like so many great Mississippi players, Harris had grown up on a family farm, building her muscles with her chores and honing her skills in backyard contests with brothers and sisters. Amanda Elzy always fielded top teams and Harris, who stood 6'3", was hard to miss. In the spring of 1973, she recalled, Delta State recruiter Melvin Hemphill made the drive over to Greenwood "and asked me did I want to play basketball in college."

A decade earlier, such a question would have been unthinkable. Lusia Harris was black, and Delta State was a white school. Throughout the 1950s and 1960s, Mississippi had mounted some of the country's fiercest resistance to the civil rights movement. Both Cleveland and Greenwood had been the scene of demonstrations, arrests and violence, as local African Americans began to stand up for their rights. As late as 1963, when the all-white Mississippi State men's basketball team qualified for the NCAA tournament, the staunchly segregationist governor, Ross Barnett, forbade the team to go, because participation would mean taking the court against teams that fielded black players.[25]

By the 1970s, however, blacks and whites across the South were cautiously testing a new racial order, and even Mississippians proved ready for some change. Although Lusia Harris had planned to attend historically black Alcorn State, the school fielded no women's team. Delta State's largely white campus required "a big adjustment," Harris noted, and the school offered no scholarships. But the lure of the game was enough. As she modestly put it, "I went on over and played a little ball at Delta State."

The Delta State team proved a formidable mix of restraint and resolve. Like many teams of the era, they carried on the old tradition of off-

Coach Margaret Wade flanked by her Delta State stars, 1976. Lusia Harris is second from left. COURTESY OF THE WOMEN'S BASKETBALL HALL OF FAME.

setting on-court prowess with off-court charm. According to forward Wanda Hairston, "We tried to go out and prove you could be an athlete and a lady at the same time."[26] Wade was known for her refined demeanor. "She was the type that never raised her voice," Lusia Harris noted. But like many genteel southern women, Wade was tough as nails underneath. She knew what she wanted her players to do and how to get them to do it. During games, Wade always wore a special pin under her suit jacket. "Whenever we played, she would just open that coat up, and it said, 'Give them hell.'" Harris explained. "So, you know, she would never say that, but she would just open her coat up . . . and the pin had on it, 'Give them hell.' I always remember that."

Harris was equally complex. She was a shy person, a loner who channeled her energy into playing and study. "I wanted to be able to make a living after basketball was over," she explained. "The only thing that I concentrated on was my schoolwork and playing basketball." On the court, however, she was an imposing figure: her 6'3" stature was heightened by a sizeable Afro, and she had the strength to "clean folks out from under that board," as a longtime fan noted.[27] "She could overpower people," a teammate echoed, recalling that despite defenders "hanging on her arms," Harris routinely powered up and hit her shots. Her concentration also helped her to brush off the racist comments encountered by most black athletic pioneers. "Sometimes the fans would say, you know, things in the stands," she recalled, "but my focus was to score that basket. . . . And sometimes it got to be pretty rough in the games, you know. . . . Everybody always said that I did a lot of smiling, but I had a few to say that I was pretty physical under the boards."

Mississippi had a top-notch high school girls' program, and Wade surrounded Harris with a stellar cast. In the 1976 tournament, when Harris came down with the flu, point guard Debbie Brock stepped up. Brock stood 4'11" and weighed eighty pounds—"I carry her around in my pocket," Margaret Wade joked. But she was a deft ballhandler as well as a crack shot. Backed by teammates Wanda Hairston, Cornelia Ward and Ramona Von Boeckman, she sparked the team to its second championship, defeating Immaculata once again in the title contest. As usual for Delta State, the five starters played the entire game. The same starting lineup would take the court for Delta State in the 1977 championship, defeating Louisiana State University for a third straight title.[28]

Mississipians responded with enthusiasm. In 1976, a local radio station broadcast the national tournament games to three states. The night that Delta State played a cliff-hanging semifinal, one college official reported, "They took five people to the hospital with heart attacks." After the team returned to Cleveland, students elected Lusia Harris homecoming queen. In 1977, the Lady Statesmen sold out half of their home games and made more money than the men's basketball or football teams. "Wherever we played, we had people from Cleveland and surrounding areas to travel to support the team," Harris said. "And that meant so much. . . . A lot of other places, we had more people than the home team." That same year, the Lady Statesmen received a police escort from northern Mississippi all the way to Minneapolis, where the national championship was held.[29]

AS WOMEN'S COMPETITION EXPANDED AND RIVALRIES DEVELOPED, the game began to draw more notice. On January 27, 1975, a game between Immaculata and the University of Maryland was broadcast nationwide, the first nationally televised game in women's college basketball history. A month later, women's basketball made its debut at Madison Square Garden, one of the nation's most venerated basketball facilities. More than 12,000 fans made their way into the storied arena to the strains of "I Am Woman." They were then treated to a "breathtaking game" between two of the nation's top programs—New York's Queens College and Immaculata. "Immaculata would set up and score and Queens would answer, then Immaculata would run a pattern and Queens would steal the ball and score, and so it went, nip and tuck," Queens coach Lucille Kyvallos wrote. In the end, the Mighty Macs triumphed, 65–61. Women's basketball also made another important breakthrough—snagging a long-term corporate sponsor. Throughout the postwar era, as athletic budgets grew, athletic institutions increasingly began to depend not simply on ticket and television revenues, but on corporate funding. In 1975, Kodak agreed to pay $3,000 to sponsor the first All-American women's collegiate basketball team. The next year,

Mel Greenberg, a sportswriter at the *Philadelphia Inquirer,* started the national women's college basketball poll.[30]

The sport became the focus of national attention in 1976, when a U.S. women's team competed in the Olympic Games for the first time. After decades of negotiation, women's basketball had finally become an Olympic sport—a development that would give the game an international platform and a tremendous boost. Most Americans still paid little attention to women's college basketball. But with national pride on the line, almost any Olympic sport had the chance to catch the public eye.

Internationally, U.S. women faced an uphill battle. Back in the 1950s, when the International Basketball Federation began sponsoring world championship tournaments for women, U.S. squads had won the first two titles—triumphing in Chile in 1953 and Brazil in 1957. But then other countries—most notably the Soviet Union—had surged to the fore, pouring resources into national teams even as Cold War conservatism dealt a severe blow to the American women's game. International play became something of an ordeal. International games were always played with full-court rules, and the games were especially physical. "I've often said to get ready for international ball what you ought to do is have people shoot lay-ups and take concrete, fill up a tire, and then hit them with it when they come in—swing it into them," explained Carla Lowry, who played for several national teams in the 1950s and 1960s. "I remember finishing those games and we were just totally exhausted. You had bruises and scratches all over. Nothing like anything we'd ever experienced." In 1967, at the world championships in Prague, the U.S. team went a dismal 1–6, losing by an average of 16 points per game, and coming in dead last out of eleven countries.[31]

The team that took the Olympic court in Montreal, Canada, promised a fresh start. It was full of new faces, a reflection of the changes the sport had undergone in only a few years of college play. During the 1950s and 1960s, U.S. national squads had consisted largely of the AAU's top players, most of whom came from a handful of southern states. But with the rise of college programs and the organization of the United States Olympic Committee (USOC), the AAU had ceased to play a dominant role in top-level national sports and had refocused its

The first U.S. Olympic women's basketball team, 1976. Front row (from left): Nancy Lieberman, Ann Meyers, Juliene Simpson, Sue Rojcewicz. Middle row: Gail Weldon (trainer), Cindy Brogdon, Mary Anne O'Connor, Pat Head, Billie Moore (head coach), Sue Gunter (assistant). Back row: Jeanne Rowlands (manager), Patricia Roberts, Gail Marquis, Nancy Dunkle, Lusia Harris, Charlotte Lewis. COURTESY OF USA BASKETBALL ARCHIVES.

efforts on youth programs. The Olympic basketball program was now handled by the USOC, which drew from a vastly expanded pool of talent. More than 250 women from around the country showed up for the 1976 tryouts.

Not only was the starting team racially integrated, it indicated how much the game had grown around the country. The South still held its own, fielding Pat Summitt from Tennessee, Lusia Harris from Mississippi, Cindy Brogdon and Patricia Roberts from Georgia, as well as assistant coach Sue Gunter, a native Mississippian who had pursued her coaching career in Tennessee and Texas. But California was also well represented. Head coach Billie Moore hailed from California, as did two of the players—Nancy Dunkle and rising superstar Ann Meyers. Although the team had only one midwesterner, Charlotte Lewis from

Illinois, the Northeast made a strong contribution, with Juliene Simpson from New Jersey, Mary Anne O'Connor from Connecticut, Sue Rojcewicz from Massachusetts, and Gail Marquis and Nancy Lieberman from New York.

In the weeks leading up to the Olympics, players trained as they never had before. Billie Moore knew the challenge was formidable. She and Gunter calculated that the team could not match the strength or depth of international powerhouses such as the Soviet Union, and thus focused on conditioning. "I think they thought I was going to kill them, and that was probably true," Moore recalled. She was not far off the mark. Pat Summitt later recalled that Moore was the first woman she ever met who pushed her players to their limits. Practices ran like clockwork. "She could walk into the gym and by simply looking at the clock she could tell what her team was supposed to be doing," Summitt noted. "Coach Moore challenged me every day."[32]

In Montreal, the team quickly learned it still had a long way to go. The United States lost its first game to Japan, 84–71. Against the Soviet Union, Lusia Harris scored 18 points but couldn't stop 7', 280-pound Uljana Semjonova, who camped out under the basket for soft left-handed shots, scoring 32 points in barely more than half a game. The Soviets prevailed, 112–77, and went on to win the gold medal.

Still, the United States surprised observers by defeating Canada, Bulgaria and Czechoslovakia to take second place in the round-robin competition. They got plenty of promotion on ABC's television broadcasts, prompting *Sports Illustrated* correspondent Frank Deford to remark that "It was as if the network was getting ready to replace *Charlie's Angels* with a women's basketball league." Capturing the silver medal in such a high-profile event brought the game welcome notice. "Up until then many people didn't know we had national teams playing in international competition," Juliene Simpson explained. "After the Olympics, that changed quite a bit."[33]

BACK HOME, PLAYERS AND COACHES CONTINUED TO STRUGGLE. THE NCAA was battling Title IX's requirements at every turn, stonewalling efforts to increase women's funding, continuing to lobby congressional legislators and filing lawsuits aimed at limiting the measure's reach. Some college administrations encouraged women's play; others did not. New York's Queens College had one of the best programs in the country in the 1970s. But the pleasure that coach Lucille Kyvallos took in her teams' success was "marred by a small minority of men in the Department of Physical Education who were unhappy with the attention the women's basketball program was receiving." The women's program was far more successful than the men's during those years, Kyvallos later wrote, and the situation did not sit well either with the men's coach or with other faculty members, who consistently worked to limit the women's funding. Kyvallos was far from alone in that experience.[34]

Still, women had also made great strides. By the end of the decade, sports opportunities for girls and women had soared. More than 60,000 women were playing college sports in 1976–77, twice as many as in 1971–72.[35] Basketball had grown dramatically on the high school level as well. In 1973, the year after Title IX's passage, only eight states sponsored state high school tournaments for girls. By 1977, only New York lacked a state competition. From 1972 to 1981, the number of female high school basketball players would grow more than tenfold, from approximately 400,000 to 4.5 million.[36]

Meanwhile, at Stanford, two years of sitting, talking and pressing had brought athletic director Dick DiBiaso to his female players' side. When the team started practice in the fall of 1976, the women's basketball team had uniforms, a trainer and full-time coaches—all for the first time. Head coach Dotty McCrea had assisted Cathy Rush at Immaculata, and assistant Sue Rojcewicz was fresh from playing on the U.S. Olympic team. The Stanford squad played an expanded schedule and held their home games in the 7,400-seat Maples Pavilion. Though it would still be two more seasons before the first Stanford women basketball players were on athletic scholarship, Mariah Burton Nelson and her teammates had stood up for their rights—not just under Title IX but as women. The victory was sweet. "Mission accomplished," she said.

·8·

Growing Pains

It was a cold day, and Nancy Lieberman was practicing her crossover dribble in the house. Weary of the "whock, whock, whock" of the rubber basketball hitting the linoleum, her mother warned her to stop. When she didn't, Renee Lieberman took action. "She came charging in the room with a screwdriver in her hand and punched a hole in my basketball," Nancy later wrote.[1]

Nancy began dribbling another basketball. Renee picked up the screwdriver again, and stabbed that one, too. Eventually, five deflated balls lay on the floor. At first Nancy laughed. Then she stopped. "As my supply got low," she continued, "I realized the joke was on me. She told me to get out of the house and dribble outside before she punched holes in all of them."

Renee Lieberman was not just angry about the noise. She had never liked Nancy's passion for sports. She wanted her only daughter to fix her hair, fuss with her dresses and giggle about boys. One day when Nancy was ten, Renee had pulled her out of a neighborhood football game and delivered a warning. "Honey, it's not ladylike to play sports," she chided. "Nancy, you're never going to be an athlete because it is for boys, not for girls."

*Nancy Lieberman pulls down a
rebound at Old Dominion.*
COURTESY OF OLD
DOMINION UNIVERSITY.

"Yeah," her angry daughter retorted. "I'll show you. I'll make history."[2]

Which she did. Lieberman, who grew up in Far Rockaway, Long Island, became one of the first major stars of a new era in women's basketball, displaying a brand of play that few had ever seen and taking advantage of an expanding array of opportunities. In 1976, she missed her high school graduation for the Olympic tryouts, where her aggressive style and flashy moves won her a spot on the first-ever U.S. women's team. She had the luxury of choosing among scores of college scholarship offers, the thrill of winning back-to-back national college championships, and the exhilaration of becoming a national celebrity. After college, she was courted by a handful of fledgling professional leagues and even played briefly for several men's teams. Along the way, she and a group of talented players and coaches transformed what it meant for a woman to play basketball.

But as Lieberman's confrontations with her mother made clear, seizing on these opportunities required difficult adjustments. Like many other American women, basketball players found that the new ambitions and opportunities sparked by women's liberation came with a range of dilemmas. The women's liberation movement had shaken U.S. society to its core, upending institutions, social conventions and intimate relationships. Building a new, more equal society required sometimes painful decisions about the shape that new institutions should take, the qualities a new generation of American women should embody, and the habits and ideas that needed to be left behind.

With the sport's rising profile came new challenges. Once the NCAA lost the battle to gut Title IX, the organization launched a campaign to wrest control of women's college sports away from the AIAW. Although NCAA leaders promised the game additional publicity and resources, the move intensified debate over the direction women's college sports would take, as well as who would be in charge of their development. Basketball's new push into the public eye also reawakened old tensions between athletics and femininity. As Renee Lieberman's anger at her athletic daughter showed, concepts of proper womanhood had not kept pace with the changes sparked by women's liberation. As teams and individuals worked to build an audience that would sustain their sport, they often struggled with these tensions, searching for a version of athletic womanhood that would be celebrated rather than condemned.

For a rising generation of young players, however, the new opportunities were what mattered most. These young women boasted a remarkable array of skills, and had the confidence to let them show. UCLA's Ann Meyers, who had grown up with a bevy of basketball-mad brothers, became known across the country for her crisp jump shot and versatility. Carol "Blaze" Blazejowski, from tiny Cranford, New Jersey, sparked widespread excitement by scoring 3,199 points in her career at Montclair State, finishing second only to "Pistol Pete" Maravich in all-time college scoring. That record was promptly broken by the phenomenal Lynette Woodard, who logged 3,649 points in four years at the University of Kansas.

As she worked on her game, Nancy Lieberman took as her model Muhammad Ali. The controversial boxer "represented everything I

UCLA's Ann Meyers drives past a defender. COURTESY OF UCLA SPORTS INFORMATION.

wanted to be in sports," she said. "He was bold, brash, confident, and cocky, but he backed up everything that he said he was going to do."[3] Not only did Lieberman stand up to her mother, she traveled all over New York City to find the best competition. Her search led her to Harlem, where African American competitors played some of the top ball in the city. At a time when most white New Yorkers saw Harlem as foreign, foreboding territory, Lieberman was a regular on its courts. "I wasn't afraid to go there because I wanted to play ball," she remembered. "They weren't afraid to accept me because we had a common thread. To the general public, it was, 'What is this white girl doing in Harlem by herself?' Even my mother asked, 'Honey, what's wrong with you?' "

At first, Lieberman noted, Harlem's players did not know what to make of her, "a fourteen-year-old red-headed Jewish girl taking over their game." But they quickly sensed a bond. On the court, "it didn't take long to gain their respect. We all realized we were out there for the same thing, to play ball." In the end, Lieberman's Harlem buddies dubbed her "Fire."[4]

University of Kansas star Lynette Woodard pushes the ball up the court. COURTESY OF THE KANSAS UNIVERSITY ATHLETIC CORPORATION.

When she graduated from high school in 1976, Lieberman was an extraordinary player. With an aggressive, all-around game that mirrored men's play of that era, she could hurl no-look passes, rebound with anybody and, unusual for women of that era, drive the ball to the hoop. Her expert passing earned her the nickname, "Lady Magic," after NBA great Earvin "Magic" Johnson. She also had the good fortune to be a highly visible player at a time when women's basketball scholarships were rapidly proliferating. In 1974, despite her remarkable talents, Carol Blazejowski did not receive a single scholarship offer. Ann Meyers's UCLA scholarship, awarded that same year, was the first full ride the school had ever given to a female athlete. Lieberman, in contrast, received more than a hundred offers.

As she surveyed her prospects, Lieberman's eye fell on Old Dominion in Norfolk, Virginia. Though the coastal school did not have one of the country's best-known women's programs, it was on the way up. It had made an early entry into the women's scholarship arena and placed a higher priority on women's sports than most of its peers.

Old Dominion's drive toward equality had largely been sparked by athletic director Jim Jarrett. Jarrett had imbibed his love of sports from his mother, an avid fan who "used to talk sports all the time" but had little opportunity to play herself. Later as a coach, he saw the inequities for himself. In 1970, when Jarrett took over Old Dominion's athletic department, he set about putting female students on a more equal footing with their male counterparts. One of his first decisions was to move both the men's and women's athletic programs into the institution's newly completed field house. "The original intent had been to have that for the men and leave the women in the old gym," Jarrett explained. "And one of the first things we did was say, 'Hey, look we're all moving over to the new building.' We had urinals in all the restrooms and locker rooms, and we had to deal with some of those issues, but the building was plenty big." Four years later, Old Dominion targeted women's basketball as a potential revenue-producing sport, and the school became one of the first in the nation to offer women athletic scholarships.

When Nancy Lieberman enrolled in 1976, Jarrett's vision was far from fully realized. The team traveled to away games in the "Blue Goose," an eight-door limousine with four rows of seats that Lieberman called "big and old and ugly and disgusting."[5] Remnants of the social, play-day mentality also persisted. Lieberman was shocked after one early game, when coach Pam Parsons announced, " 'We're going to go upstairs in this classroom and we're going to have milk and cookies and punch with the other team.' " Lieberman couldn't believe it. "I told her, 'I'm not going up there with them,' " she said. "I mean, I was a basketball player. I don't hang out with them. I'm not going to have cookies and milk with anybody. Me, I want to kick their ass."

But Old Dominion would not be serving milk and cookies much longer. Pam Parsons, who butted heads with the strong-willed Lieberman on many issues, left after Lieberman's first year. She was replaced by assistant coach Marianne Crawford Stanley, who had been a mainstay of Immaculata's championship teams. Stanley proved to be an inspired coach. One of three top coaches to come out of Cathy Rush's

Immaculata program—the others were Theresa Shank Grentz and Rene Muth Portland—she pursued a flexible, innovative approach to the game that allowed Lieberman to thrive. Stanley had gotten to know Lieberman when the teenager beat her out for a spot on the 1976 Olympic team, and she could relate to her headstrong star. "I remember what it was like to be a scrappy kid and be told you can't do this or that," Stanley once said. "I grew up shoveling snow off the court at home to play this game, and I bet my life she did that, too."[6]

Later, she would describe Lieberman as "probably the most tenacious ball player I've ever seen. You don't find many guards that'll rebound the way she does. You don't find many players who can completely control the tempo and complexion of the ball game as Nancy does. I don't think I've seen many people who have her confidence. You can't teach that. Nancy probably had that when she was born. She probably came out of the womb swinging."[7]

Stanley followed no set coaching system: "Individuality was very important in her scheme of things," Lieberman recalled. But she knew how to make the most of her talent, which included not only Lieberman but 6'5" Danish center Inge Nissen. In Stanley's first year, she moved Lieberman from point guard to forward to boost rebounding and cut down on team turnovers (Lieberman's teammates often couldn't handle her great passes). The next season, with an influx of more skilled players, Lieberman moved back to point guard and Old Dominion rolled to the national title. Stanley became the youngest women's basketball coach to win a national championship. She was twenty-four.[8]

Old Dominion's exciting play and the team's national success captured the imagination of Norfolk-area residents. The Lady Monarchs routinely sold out the school's 5,000-seat field house, and attendance occasionally topped 10,000 with standing-room-only crowds. "We were celebrities at Old Dominion," Lieberman would recall in 1983. "Nobody counts more in that town than a Lady Monarch."[9]

On the heels of the 1979 championship came another victory—Anne Donovan, the nation's top recruit, decided to join the team. The battle for Donovan's services further underscored the sport's growth. In 1977, Donovan's talented sister Mary had only received a handful of offers.

Old Dominion center Anne Donovan. COURTESY OF OLD DOMINION UNIVERSITY.

Two years later, as Anne neared graduation, more than 250 schools contacted her. "It was definitely an onslaught of attention," she recalled. Mary had chosen Penn State, which badly wanted Anne as well, and one day Anne picked up the phone and found herself listening to a recruiting pitch from Joe Paterno, Penn State's legendary football coach. "It cracked me up," Mary later laughed. "It drove home to me what a commodity top players had become. He never called me." Although Anne was flattered by the attention, she picked Old Dominion. In 1980, she contributed ten blocks and seventeen rebounds as the Lady Monarchs defeated the up-and-coming program at Tennessee to win their second straight national title.

EVEN AS THE GROWTH OF COLLEGE WOMEN'S PROGRAMS BROUGHT players new opportunities and new decisions, it also presented the sport's leaders with tough choices. From the start, AIAW members had wrangled with issues of programs and promotion, trying to determine how far and fast they wanted competitive play to grow. There had been disagreements. AIAW had been forced to drop its scholarship ban in 1973, when a group of Florida-based players and coaches filed a lawsuit, arguing that if men were given athletic scholarships, women were entitled to them as well. As interest in women's sports grew, and as competition increased, pressures to adopt more components of the male athletic model mounted as well.[10]

Those issues suddenly came to a head in the early 1980s with the growing interest of a rival—the powerful NCAA. Having failed in the 1970s to block the growth of women's college programs, NCAA leaders embarked on a no-holds-barred campaign to take them over. At the NCAA's 1981 annual meeting, delegates voted to schedule a set of Division I women's tournaments that would directly compete with AIAW events. When AIAW representatives objected to the move, NCAA delegates greeted them with ridicule and hissing. The objections were ignored, and the NCAA scheduled a series of 1982 championships.[11]

Across the country, schools had to decide which tournaments to enter and which organization to support. For many, deciding between the two groups was agonizing. The AIAW had played a major role in the Title IX battle and nurtured women's college sports through its hard, early years. The organization was run largely by women, and women's sports were its prime concern. The NCAA, on the other hand, was a men's organization in every way, from its leadership to its athletic priorities. Many suspected the organization did not have female athletes' best interests at heart.

But the NCAA had two things the AIAW could not hope to match: money and status. The AIAW had a $1 million budget. The NCAA, with its lucrative television contracts, had $20 million—and it promised to spend $3 million on its women's tournaments. Included in that figure were resources to put on tournament games and payments to schools that reached postseason play, helping them defray tournament expenses—something the AIAW couldn't afford.[12] "That was the only way they were going to get the women—to play to the pocketbooks of the college presidents," said 1981 AIAW president Donna Lopiano.

Despite concerns about the NCAA's motives, the organization also seemed to offer a more direct path to the funding and acclaim that top men's teams enjoyed. Many AIAW leaders still sought to chart an alternate path. But for others—as well as for many college presidents, in whose hands the final decision rested—the lure of the big time proved irresistible. In 1982, when the NCAA held its Division I tournament, almost half the country's schools chose the NCAA competition over the AIAW counterpart.[13]

The University of Texas was one of the major holdouts. Lopiano, who was also director of the Texas women's athletic department, had battled the NCAA's earlier attempts to block Title IX's implementation, and she was deeply skeptical about the scope of NCAA support for women's sports. The AIAW had "more sports for women and more [women's] television contracts than the NCAA had for five or six years," she later noted. "So going to the NCAA was going backwards, except for the funding for championship participation. I don't think there's any question in my mind that any organization with the singular concern for the development of women's sports was going to go farther and faster than being second to men's sports, which was true with the NCAA."

Pat Summitt of Tennessee disagreed. "The AIAW had been there from the beginning and allowed women an opportunity to compete," she later explained. "I almost felt like we were stabbing people in the back that had made our dreams possible at a very young age in women's sports. That bothered me because of the loyalty and dedication of AIAW. Yet, I knew realistically that the only way the sport could grow to the level we enjoy today was under the umbrella of the NCAA. That brought instant credibility to women's athletics. It gave us that name attachment; it gave us championships in a first-class arena, and we needed that. I thought that without that we may never have the opportunities to make the strides that are necessary for women to have what they have today."

In the end, eighteen of the previous year's top twenty women's basketball programs entered the NCAA tournament.[14]

The defections were the death knell for AIAW. The organization subsisted on member dues and on revenues from a handful of championship telecasts. As soon as the NCAA scheduled its own tournaments, television networks cancelled contracts to air AIAW events, sending the organization into dire financial straits. The AIAW went on with its events, and there were two basketball champions in 1982—Rutgers, coached by Theresa Shank Grentz, won the AIAW title, and Louisiana Tech took the NCAA crown. In June of that year, the AIAW closed its doors. Later, the organization filed an antitrust case against the NCAA, arguing in part that the NCAA had used its monopoly on men's sports as leverage to persuade sponsors and networks to favor NCAA events over the AIAW's. The judge who heard the case, however, did not agree, and the AIAW lost its lawsuit.[15]

AIAW'S DEMISE MARKED FAR MORE THAN THE END OF AN ORGANIZ-ing body. It closed a century of women's efforts to blaze a distinctive athletic trail. Since the 1880s, female physical educators had championed women's strength and independence. They had also raised serious questions about the drawbacks of intensive competition, noting that while growing competition in men's sports raised the level of play, a broad host of ills came with it. The AIAW embodied that philosophy. Though the organization had fought successfully for Title IX, it had purposely limited athletic recruiting, focusing on women first as students and then as athletes. Beyond that, AIAW had provided a democratic, supportive environment that encouraged women to be creative and take leadership roles, opportunities often not open to them on their own campuses. "We had all grown up together," one AIAW president said. "And I think, too, we took pride in each other. I don't think we realized the degree to which we were helping each other as women. We learned from these positions, and we were supportive of each other."[16]

While joining the NCAA promised greater funding and publicity, it meant women themselves would hold far fewer leadership positions and wield far less control over the direction of women's sports. In women's basketball, the loss of administrative control would be compounded by the declining numbers of women in head coaching jobs. By 1988, more than four of ten women's basketball head coaching jobs were held by men, compared to one in ten in 1972. In the absence of corresponding opportunities for women in men's basketball, this change meant a sharp drop in the opportunity to develop female coaching talent, and to build respect for women's abilities as leaders as well as players.[17]

In part this shift represented the growing competition sparked by the growth in salary and prestige—changes that began to attract men to the game. But it was also clear that in the newly competitive atmosphere, female coaches had to fight an uphill battle for respect. This battle surfaced in coverage of the 1985 national championship, when Marianne Stanley coached Old Dominion to its third national title, dazzling observers in the championship game. "Those who doubt that women coaches can be master strategists didn't catch Marianne Stanley's act Sunday," *Sports Illustrated* noted. For her part, Stanley pointedly remarked, "Women *can* coach this game, you know."[18]

NCAA control also underscored a fundamental shift in the nature of the women's game. Like men's college athletics, women's sports was becoming not just education but also commercial entertainment, in which success was measured not simply through the growth of individuals, but by numbers of paying customers and levels of television viewership. Some saw loss; others, opportunity. "AIAW nurtured us, but the NCAA could take us to another level," Nancy Lieberman opined years later. "They were business people, and they didn't just take us over because we were cute girls. They took us over because they had visions of what women's basketball could be today, with sellout crowds and record-breaking ratings on TV. Nineteen eighty-two was very significant for us. When we got with the NCAA, they started putting us on CBS, even if it was just for the championship game. Women's basketball is a business. It was no longer the girls' club."

But viewing women's basketball in this way raised new and daunting challenges. Building a broad audience for women's basketball would prove especially difficult, in large part because of persistent gaps between the nature of athletic prowess and prevailing views of femininity. With a century of effort, advocates of women's sports had laid to rest the notion that women were incapable of vigorous physical activity. The achievements of the women's liberation movement had gone a long way toward widespread, if sometimes grudging, acceptance of the idea that women could benefit from competitive sports and should have the right to athletic opportunities. But it was one thing to acknowledge women's right to play and quite another to embrace women's athletics with enough enthusiasm to turn on the television or get out to the games. For fans to respond in large numbers to women's teams, players would need not only to play well, but to exemplify a kind of womanhood with which large numbers of spectators could identify and that they found pleasing to watch.

This would prove an enormous challenge. Despite the advances of the women's liberation movement, mainstream ideals of American womanhood still lay far removed from the sweaty action of a basketball court. Basketball rewarded strength, determination and assertiveness— qualities prized in men but still dangerous territory for women. Many women shied away from the word "feminist" because it seemed too direct, too pushy, too openly assertive. Mainstream visions of ideal femininity still championed reticence and charm, generally leavened with a touch of glamour and a dose of flirtatious heterosexual appeal. As in the past, female basketball players would be difficult to fit into that restrictive mold.

The contradictions showed clearly in the experience of Immaculata's Mighty Macs, the first team to draw nationwide notice. The team's first set of uniforms accommodated Catholic modesty rather than assertive play. "We wore those tunics, a jumper with box pleats," coach Cathy Rush once explained. "They were wool, and you wore a blouse underneath and then bloomers. Very modest, very long and very hot." Reporters often treated the players like curiosities, peppering them with questions about clothes, hairstyles and boyfriends. At times, Theresa Shank recalled, they "seemed surprised we even combed our hair." But at the same time, many players regarded feminism uneasily. When the team heard the triumphantly feminist "I Am Woman" played before their Madison Square Garden debut, one player grumbled: "I'm not walking out to that." [19]

The challenges female players faced became even more evident with the launch of the first professional basketball league for women in the United States, the Women's Professional Basketball League (WBL). The WBL began play in 1978, seeking to capitalize on the excitement sparked by the Olympic team's silver medal and the growing enthusiasm for the women's college game. Building an audience was the league's priority from the start. While fledgling college programs were cushioned by Title IX's mandate of educational equity, the WBL's future would depend solely on the corporate sponsorships it could garner and the number of people who paid to see its teams play.

The WBL started with eight teams scattered across the country: the Iowa Cornets, New Jersey Gems, Milwaukee Does, Chicago Hustle, Minnesota Fillies, Dayton Rockettes, New York Stars and Houston Angels. The future looked bright. The first WBL game was December 9, 1978. Just under 8,000 fans made their way to the Milwaukee Arena to watch Chicago beat Milwaukee, 92–87. National media carried numerous reports on early play, and revered network anchor Walter Cronkite gave the league an on-air plug. A Chicago TV station that aired ten Chicago Hustle games attracted an average viewing audience of 140,000, twice what was expected. Several players signed endorsement contracts. Encouraged by the support, the league added six teams the next season—the Washington Metros, Philadelphia Fox, Dallas Diamonds, California Dreams, San Francisco Pioneers and New Orleans Pride.[20]

Although most salaries were small, players were delighted to have the opportunity to expand their skills and keep playing their sport. "It was hard to believe that people were going to pay me . . . to do something I loved," recalled Nancy Lieberman, who signed with the Dallas Diamonds in 1980. After a few months, her game reached new levels. "There were a lot of talented players in the league and we had some really exciting games," she wrote. "I hated to disappoint anyone, so I played hard every game and implored my teammates to do the same."[21] Between games, players pursued endless rounds of clinics and personal appearances, working to cultivate followings for their teams.

As league publicity developed, it quickly became apparent that owners were not just selling basketball. Many WBL owners did their best not only to promote their play but to link their players to mainstream feminine ideals of charm and sexual appeal. Although the league was 40 percent black, the most prominently featured stars were white. At least one team mandated makeup; another sent its players to charm school. The Milwaukee Does marketed the team with a poster that showed a fe-

The WBL's Milwaukee Does marketed their team with this image in 1978. COURTESY OF THE AIAW ARCHIVES, SPECIAL COLLECTIONS, UNIVERSITY OF MARYLAND LIBRARIES.

male deer with her tail poking provocatively through a pair of basketball shorts—an image that clearly evoked the era's paramount symbol of market-approved female sexuality, the Playboy Bunny. The New York Stars took part in a Playboy-sponsored exhibition that matched them against a team that included several actual Bunnies.[22]

Some players adopted a similar strategy. League star Molly Bolin, a product of basketball-crazy Iowa who once scored 83 points in a high school game, boasted both a formidable shooting touch and a model's looks. "For two seasons the 5'9" guard with the bouncy blonde hair has enlivened the anemic Women's Basketball League both on and off the court," a *Sports Illustrated* reporter noted in 1981, the year after Bolin shared league MVP honors with Ann Meyers. "On the court, she's a high-scoring machine. . . . Off the court? Well, suffice it to say that if beauty were a stat, Molly Bolin would be in the Hall of Fame."[23]

Bolin sought to make the most of her dual appeal, once posing in a tank top and tight shorts for a poster designed to promote the league and to make some extra money. Although the poster stirred some controversy, Bolin did not back down. "People always warned me about exploitation, like it was a dirty word," she commented. "But it's all about putting people in the seats, isn't it? You don't have to look like a man, act like one or play like one in this game. And I just wanted to show that women aren't trying to be like men. If you really want to make it when you're new, you've got to grab everything you've got and go with it."[24]

As in the past, this emphasis on femininity included efforts to conceal the fact that some of the WBL's players were lesbians. In the minds of basketball promoters, both college and professional, acknowledging that lesbians played the game would reinforce suspicions that athletic women were somehow unnatural, and thus undercut efforts to promote the sport. Though much of the groundwork for women's basketball institutions had been laid by lesbians and single women, who had the time to devote to the cause, institutions such as the WBL had no interest in acknowledging lesbians' contributions, much less the lesbians in their ranks.

Mariah Burton Nelson ran directly into this aversion in 1979, when the San Francisco Pioneers inexplicably released her. The coach blamed the quality of her play, but she thought otherwise. Only a few days earlier, she had attended San Francisco's annual Gay Pride Parade. Though simply being there did not mean she was gay, a television reporter had seen her and told her coach. The pain of being cut seared her soul. "I was devastated," she later wrote. It also presented her with a hard choice—whether to challenge the coach's decision.[25]

The cultural shifts of the 1970s had put gay Americans in a difficult bind. On one hand, gays and lesbians were becoming more visible and demanding greater respect—hence the Gay Pride Parade. In the minds of many activists, the best way to combat anti-gay prejudice was to challenge it openly. But broad-based acceptance lay decades away and being identified as gay or lesbian carried enormous consequences. As a result, Burton Nelson and other lesbian players found the era's expanding opportunities bittersweet—they were able to play, but only at the price of hiding an important part of who they were.

Burton Nelson knew that if she were going to play with another WBL team, she needed to keep her sexual orientation secret. She decided to stay quiet. "Two local feminist newspapers learned of the firing, but I refused to talk to them, fearing further repercussions," she wrote. "Though I hated the idea of being closeted, my passion for basketball temporarily won out." She left San Francisco to play briefly for the California Dreams and then for the Dallas Diamonds. But she disagreed with the Dallas owner over who should pay her moving expenses, and he fired her, describing her as "too aggressive off the court." She decided she was through with the league. "My agent soon informed me that the New Orleans team was interested," she wrote, "but I told her that I wasn't." [26]

The league itself would not last much longer. WBL owners found the first season encouraging, and expanded the league to fourteen teams. But they were a long way from financial health. Two teams folded early in the second season, and several had trouble generating enough cash to pay their players on time. Several efforts at reorganization proved destabilizing rather than profitable. After its third season, the WBL called it quits.

In part, the WBL's demise represented the risks involved in starting a professional league of any kind. But it also highlighted the particular challenges of women's sports. Throughout its short history, teams and players found themselves in a double bind. Once the novelty of professional female players wore off, criticism set in. On one hand, players were faulted for being less athletic than their male counterparts. On the other, they were widely cast as unfeminine. Many newspapers barely covered the teams at all. Although some teams became quite popular, overall enthusiasm lagged. In the first season, teams averaged only 1,200 fans per game. The average team lost $260,000. Building a profitable league would require far more time and far deeper pockets than WBL owners had. The 1980–81 season, the league's third, would also be its last. The WBL officially folded in February 1982. [27]

EVEN AS THE WBL STRUGGLED, HOWEVER, SOME COLLEGE TEAMS were meeting with far greater success, often through the old formula of combining athletic prowess with strict adherence to ladylike convention. Nowhere was this clearer than in Ruston, Louisiana, where the Lady Techsters of Louisiana Tech became the toast of the town, with home-court crowds so large and supportive that many teams refused to play there.

The La Tech team had a modest start. In the early 1970s, physical education instructor Sonja Hogg approached school president F. Jay Taylor about starting a women's basketball team. Like his counterpart at Old Dominion, Taylor was ready to support women's sports. He was aware of Title IX, knew there was local talent and had fond memories of the ex-

Louisiana Tech coach Sonja Hogg. COURTESY OF LOUISIANA TECH ATHLETIC MEDIA RELATIONS.

citement that surrounded the girls' high school games in his hometown of Gibsland, Louisiana. He soon found $5,000 to start the program and enlisted Hogg (pronounced with a long "o") as coach. She rounded up players from the student body and began to promote the team. It did not take long. "Sonja was a real live wire," Taylor said.

Much like Margaret Wade, Hogg offered a formidable mix of competitive spirit tempered with southern charm. The white-blonde coach was known for her flamboyant style, which often favored white outfits and spike heels. "I still remember when she came to recruit me," recalled three-time All-American Pam Kelly. "She pulled up in a big white Cadillac and had on a bright white fur coat and with her white hair, you couldn't miss her. She was a very flashy person, but very personable."[28]

Hogg made sure players lived up to her standards, fellow coach Leon Barmore noted. "She said to the players, 'We're going to dress like ladies, act like ladies and we'll be tough and mean on the court,' " he explained. "Miss Hogg wanted this game to be about ladies." She also paid attention to detail. At the time, most college teams carefully distinguished themselves from men's squads by adopting feminized versions of male team's names, playing as the Lady Wolfpack, Lady Volunteers, Lady Monarchs, even the incongruous Lady Gamecocks. Although La Tech's men called themselves the Bulldogs, Hogg opted for the Lady Techsters instead. Her reasoning was simple, Taylor explained. "A lady dog is a bitch."

Hogg was a master at signing players and drawing spectators. "She recruited a fan base—it was the upper end, the elderly people, and the lower end, small kids ages five through ten," Taylor said. "The kids began wearing Louisiana Tech caps and sweatshirts and brought their parents to the game." She also built interest in the team by scheduling top opponents. Taylor came up with $2,000 in appearance money to help her lure well-known Delta State to play in Ruston. Among players, she was proud of her status as the "momma away from home that every girl needs occasionally," and her warmth extended well beyond the school. Although Old Dominion and Louisiana Tech were fierce rivals, Nancy Lieberman felt closer to Hogg than to Old Dominion coach Marianne Stanley and once spent a weekend winding down at Hogg's house just weeks before the teams were to meet in the AIAW tournament.[29]

Hogg also had a clear vision of her own talents, which lay more in promotion and recruiting than in the x's and o's of coaching. In 1977, she convinced Leon Barmore to join her as assistant coach. A Ruston native who had been a star point guard first at Ruston High and then at La Tech, Barmore had built a stellar reputation coaching boys' teams at Ruston High. Years later, he would readily admit that he accepted Hogg's offer because he saw it as a stepping stone to the men's head coaching job. But like many men who were initially skeptical of the women's game, he soon learned there was far more to it than he had realized.

"The first trip I took for Miss Hogg was a scouting trip to Delta State in 1977," Barmore later explained. "I never will forget it. They had four teams playing that night in the tournament: UCLA, Montclair State, Tennessee and Delta State. I had to park about a mile from the gym, and I had to walk about a mile because of the crowd. It was a packed house—it seated probably about 4,000. I'd never seen this before in women's basketball. I saw that night something that turned me on to women's basketball. I saw a brand of basketball being played that was exciting to me. I saw Debbie Brock, a little point guard for Delta State. I saw Cindy Brogdon for Tennessee. I saw a girl named Carol Blazejowski score 44 points for Montclair State that night."[30]

The experience whetted his appetite for his job. "I went back home and started really preparing myself to help Sonja make Louisiana Tech one of the best basketball programs it could be," he said. Although Barmore would hold on to his men's basketball ambitions for a number of years, he soon joined the distinguished tradition of men who coached women's championship teams, following in the footsteps of Wayland's Harley Redin, Nashville Business College's John Head and Hanes Hosiery's Virgil Yow. He served as Hogg's assistant for five seasons, became co–head coach with her for three, then assumed the head coaching job by himself in the fall of 1985.

An emotional leader who took pride in helping lead his alma mater to the national stage, Barmore wasn't afraid to demand a lot from his female charges. He yelled, got red in the face and occasionally became so worked up that he fainted in the middle of a game. "I used to think, 'How am I ever going to play for this mean man,' " guard Angela Lawson once noted. But Barmore's focus on excellence and his proclivity for winning bred loyalty and dedication, as well as the highest winning percentage of his generation (.869). His influence also reached beyond the floor. "Next to my father, he has been the most influential man in my life," said Nell Fortner, who would go on to coach college and professional teams, and to head up the 2000 U.S. Olympic squad.[31]

In the early 1980s, the Lady Techsters firmly planted themselves on the national scene. They lost to Old Dominion in the AIAW's 1979 championship final and then again in the 1980 semifinals. In 1981, however, the Lady Techsters had their year, compiling a 34–0 record and blowing out Tennessee, 79–59, in the final game. They repeated as champs in 1982, beating Vivian Stringer's Cheyney State club, 76–62, to take the first-ever NCAA title. They won a third title in 1988. Along the way, La Tech stars like Kim Mulkey, Pam Kelly, Angela Turner and Janice Lawrence became household names in north central Louisiana.

Louisiana Tech coach Leon Barmore. COURTESY OF LOUISIANA TECH ATHLETIC MEDIA RELATIONS.

Later, Pam Gant, Teresa Weatherspoon, Vickie Johnson, Venus Lacy, Tamicha Jackson and Betty Lennox would attain similar status. The tradition of combining championships and feminine convention continued strong. "We like them to be winners on court, but nice-looking ladies off of it," Kim Mulkey noted in the fall of 1986 after becoming an assistant coach. "You don't wear raggy old jeans to class. There are some things a Lady Techster just can't do."[32]

In Ruston, the combination played remarkably well. Louisiana Tech led the nation in attendance from 1981 through 1984, drawing crowds in excess of 6,000. Fans loved the team's national fame—the first such notice the school had drawn since the heyday of its most famous alumnus, football great Terry Bradshaw. On nights when the men and women played doubleheaders, most fans would leave after the women's game. President Jay Taylor was among those who seldom missed a Lady Techster tip-off, whether at home or on the road. He was such a ubiquitous presence that he even showed up on his wedding night. "I just wanted to go to the game," he said.

·9·

Dazzling Moves, Spinning Wheels

It was Cheryl Miller's first NCAA championship game, and she took center stage. The highly heralded freshman was everywhere on the court "rebounding, shooting, stealing, scrapping and shot-blocking." She took charges, scrambled for loose balls and celebrated every score with glee. Her University of Southern California (USC) teammates were right with her. Six-foot-three twins Pam and Paula McGee loomed "like a city skyline" above their Louisiana Tech opponents. Sophomore Cynthia Cooper hit jumpers and stepped up her defense. It was a marvelous match. The lead see-sawed back and forth, and with six seconds to go USC led 69–67, with Miller at the free-throw line. She bricked the first half of a one-and-one, and La Tech rebounded. But a last-second shot bounced off the rim, and the Women of Troy were national champions.[1]

The USC players were a new force in women's basketball, the kind of team sports promoters dream of. They played a fast, exciting brand of basketball. "We just ran," recalled Paula McGee. "We were open court, and you had big players that could get down the floor. So we would play defense, rebound and run. . . . We beat people because we ran the whole floor." Cheryl Miller was skilled almost beyond comprehension, a

Cheryl Miller, University of Southern California.
COURTESY OF USC
SPORTS INFORMATION.

whirling, leaping 6'2" wonder with a remarkable shooting touch and a bright, playful personality. The McGee twins combined double-figure scoring averages with a high-style glamour that made them staples of the Los Angeles social scene. The Women of Troy were also the first national champions from a major media market, and their charismatic style, aptly managed by USC's well-heeled public relations department, brought the game a flood of publicity.[2]

USC's achievements, however, were only a beginning. Though women's basketball had made great strides, it still faced an uphill struggle for resources and respect. As so often in women's basketball history, support for the sport lagged behind the rising quality of play. The rise of the Women of Troy coincided with a profoundly conservative turn in American politics, one that slammed the brakes on moves toward equality and directly challenged the concept of women's liberation. Outside of a few hopeful exceptions, women's basketball spent much of the 1980s spinning its wheels. Not until the end of the decade, when a new set of legal and political strategies took hold, would the game gain traction again.

USC BEGAN ITS ASCENT IN THE SPRING OF 1980, WHEN PAM AND Paula McGee decided to leave their hometown of Flint, Michigan, and head for Southern California. The pair of matched, stunningly attractive and highly talented women had been a magnet for media coverage for years—by the time they reached high school, they were already so well known that at one high school track meet, fellow Michigan native and NBA great Magic Johnson came over just to meet them. Back-to-back state high school basketball championships only heightened their appeal, and scholarship offers poured in. At first, USC did not seem to have a chance. The school did not have a major program, and coach Linda Sharp could make few grand promises. But the twins liked Southern California and wanted to go somewhere they could make an immediate impact. So they signed with USC and held a press conference to announce their decision.[3]

The McGees belonged to a new trend in women's college ball, a wave of African American women moving from urban centers into the college game. As any fan of the men's game knew, basketball had long been popular in urban black communities, where it was perfectly suited to

Twins Paula (front) and Pam McGee at the University of Southern California, 1984. COURTESY OF USC SPORTS INFORMATION.

cramped playgrounds and tight budgets, and where players invested the game with an athletic dynamism rarely found in suburbs or small towns. Once colleges began recruiting female players in earnest, they began to notice the women playing in those games. Vivian Stringer spent much of the 1970s driving to communities around Philadelphia, stopping to "look on the playgrounds and see who's playing," then recruiting the competitors she liked for Cheyney State. "There was a lot of talent," she recalled. "I can honestly say I think that more adults were committed to really working with and training and helping young women. . . . There were a lot of local clubs and teams, and men and women that really just committed themselves to helping train these athletes. And there was a lot of pride."

The USC players fit that pattern. The McGees had started playing basketball in fourth grade at the urging of an elementary school coach. "He saw us, we were long and leggy," Paula recalled. "So he asked us to come out for the basketball team, and we did. And we were awful. Couldn't chew gum and walk at the same time. But he just was really talented with young people. So probably by the end of our fourth-grade year, we were pretty good." Growing up in the Watts neighborhood of Los Angeles, Cynthia Cooper begged a high school assistant coach to show her the game. The summer before her high school freshman year, Lucias Franklin "met me every day at Locke High and started teaching me the fundamentals of basketball."[4]

The McGees' freshman year, the Women of Troy reached the 1981 Final Four, losing in the semifinals to Louisiana Tech. By then, the school was becoming a magnet for other talented African Americans. The next year, Linda Sharp recruited Cooper, who had just led Locke High to California's state championship. The year after that saw the arrival of point guard Rhonda Windham, a strong-willed, two-time all-city player from New York who had no qualms about running the show. "She was a real floor leader," Cooper later wrote. "When Rhonda said she wasn't going to give you the ball, there was no point in arguing your case—you weren't getting it. If Rhonda said 'Wait until next time,' that's exactly what she meant."[5]

The fall of 1982 also marked the debut of Cheryl Miller, the most sought-after recruit in the sport's history. The 6'2" Miller had grown up playing with her brothers, including her NBA-bound younger sibling, Reggie. A national celebrity while still in high school, Cheryl played with a dazzling flair that took observers' breath away. She could soar to the hoop, dunk the ball with power and ease, and her smooth, all-around moves earned her the nickname Silk. Her energy was apparent from the moment she stepped on the USC practice floor. "You see her being so vital, so dynamic, and you want to be part of it," Pam McGee commented. Most important, she never let up in her play. "The thing I respected most about her game, was that she played with intensity," Cynthia Cooper later wrote. "She hustled and worked hard. Sometimes players with that kind of talent don't put out maximum effort, but Cheryl did."[6]

The combination could not be beat. In the 1982–83 season Miller averaged just over 20 points a game. Paula McGee put in 19, and Pam McGee 18. The team averaged nearly 86 points a game and regularly topped 100. USC's publicity department seized the moment, working hard to elevate their players from basketball stars to media personalities—female counterparts to the "Showtime" Los Angeles Lakers. They scheduled dozens of print and television interviews, promoted magazine photo spreads and landed national talk show appearances. They trumpeted the team's celebrity fans, including actor Tom Selleck, L.A. Laker Magic Johnson and even Pat Riley, the Lakers' coach. In 1984, a month before that year's national tournament, Cheryl Miller performed a show-stopping dunk at the Grammy Awards.[7]

The players' panache made the sell easy, offering a highly appealing image to spectators and sportswriters. The McGees' sophomore year, *Sports Illustrated* writer Roger Jackson composed a profile that underscored their multifaceted appeal. The article opened with University of Oregon coach Elwin Hiney, who raved about the twins' impact on the court. "To stop USC you have to stop the McGees," Hiney explained. "You have to have help on them; you can't match up with them one-on-one. Two 6'3" players with their agility and strength on the same team—you just don't find that too often." Jackson then added a few embellishments of his own, penning a telling paragraph that gave as much weight to the McGees' looks as to their skills. "Indeed, no women's team has a pair of performers who can match the McGees for sheer athletic ability," he wrote. "Each stretches 170 exquisitely proportioned pounds across her frame. Each is blessed with sprinter's speed and yet has the strength to overpower most opponents. Off the court the McGees are stylish, elegant and free of the self-consciousness that causes many tall women to slouch or forgo wearing high-heeled shoes."[8]

The McGees quickly learned that sex appeal could easily overshadow achievement. There was "this kind of cheesecake push," Paula explained. " 'They're great athletes, but they're cute.' " The sisters waged an ongoing battle to keep attention from shading into exploitation. At one photo session, they refused a celebrated photographer's request that they pose in T-shirts without bras. Their freshman year, when they graced the cover of *Jet* magazine, editors asked them to pose for the magazine's "Beauty of the Week" centerfold, which typically featured women in bikinis and provocative poses. They turned that offer down as well. Still, they had no trouble dressing up and smiling. They were proud of their looks, Paula noted, and "when you're trying to sell women's basketball . . . you sell what sells."

"We were Hollywood," she said. "If there was an adjective, we were Hollywood. We played it all the way out."

Opponents coped as best they could. When Tennessee and USC reached the finals of the 1984 NCAA tournament, for example, Tennessee fell back on the role of the disarmingly humble underdog. Publicist Debby Jennings joked that when one of the Lady Volunteers asked her about what to wear to the pregame press conference, "I told her she could wear a formal and the McGees would still knock her out of the box. . . . We're just hillbillies with bare feet." At game time, *Sports Illustrated* underscored the difference between the teams. "USC came out fired up, all high fives, hugs and fists in the air, playing up to the crowd. The Lady Vols, on the other hand, were all business, blank-faced, sedate and intense." Tennessee held the lead until the game's final six minutes, when USC, in Cheryl Miller's words, "really turned it on," shifting into high gear for a 72–61 victory.[9]

The USC players were living proof that women's basketball could aspire to the celebrity status that the men's game enjoyed. But as with their male counterparts, fame had brought the players challenges as well. The road had not been all high-fives and triumphant fists. Media coverage emphasized the team's flamboyant, playful side. But underneath the fun, "there was a lot of pain, a lot of struggle and a lot of heartache," Paula McGee noted. "You don't win two national championships back to back and not have some struggle. That's male or female. It just doesn't happen."

The players' private battles were intimately connected to their roles as racial pioneers, as well as female athletes. The USC team was the first to win the national title with an all-black starting lineup and like their male counterparts, players ran into racial stereotypes that cast them as arrogant or undisciplined. Some observers might view her and her talented brother as "cocky and arrogant," Cheryl Miller once felt the need to explain, adding "and maybe we are but only in the sense that we believe in ourselves and our talent."[10] Classes were demanding, with lofty academic standards that challenged even students who came from rigorous private schools, and who had no athletic or media commitments. The women also had to deal with the atmosphere of USC itself, a place far whiter, wealthier and more privileged than anything the players had ever known. The gap could be profoundly alienating.

"Mama drove me up to the USC campus that first morning in her beat-up Ford Pinto station wagon, the one with a broken windshield, chipped paint, wheezing engine and coughing muffler," Cynthia Cooper recalled. "I could tell right away that my classmates were on a whole different level. They were so far out of my league I considered looking for a back door to enter the dorm." Cooper went through college in a kind of culture shock. "I went where I was told, when I was told," she wrote. "I really didn't know how to enjoy myself—unless I was playing ball."[11]

Eventually, the stress of playing and publicity, of classes and relationships, took its toll. Cynthia Cooper dropped out of USC after the 1984 title and had to be persuaded to return. Paula McGee found that by her senior year, she was overwhelmed by the sense of "always having to perform. To be this commodity. . . . At the same time, we're also still trying to be full-time students, and still trying to negotiate life." Players battled to find balance and an understanding ear. The team's sudden celebrity had taken the school by surprise, and few realized how much pressure the players felt."There was nobody to say enough is enough," Paula concluded. "There was no person to take care of who we were as people." Later, Paula would go on to earn two master's degrees and start work toward a doctorate. Cynthia Cooper would become an author, coach and civic leader. But neither woman would graduate from USC.

The women coped with this range of pressures by falling back on each other. In 1983, as the media spotlight intensified and the jostling ambitions of so many stars began to create friction, the players agreed to keep any conflicts out of the media and off the court. "I think that leadership strategy is what helped us actually win," Paula said. In the end, she concluded, winning the national titles seemed a secondary accomplishment. "The real triumph for me is what I learned playing sports, and the interaction among those twelve women," she said. "Those are the fondest memories for me. That's where I got my leadership skills. And I learned how to work with women. . . . The thing that I liked about that team is that no matter what, when we crossed those black lines on that floor, we played together as a team. . . . We played as a team and accomplished the task at hand."

THE USC PLAYERS WERE FAR FROM THE ONLY ONES TO STRUGGLE IN the 1980s. Even as they braved the spotlight at the apex of their sport, others were working frantically to shore up the game's foundation. Throughout the 1970s, Title IX's supporters had withstood a wide range of efforts to undercut the legislation's impact on the federal level. But the pressure mounted in 1980, when Ronald Reagan was elected president. The election signaled a conservative political turn, driven in part by widespread uneasiness with the social changes of the 1960s and 1970s. For the next decade, this conservative reaction would stymie efforts to build women's sports programs.

Most directly, the Reagan administration put the brakes on the push toward equality that had given rise to Title IX. Rather than confront social inequities, Reagan-style conservatives tended to explain them away. If there were no women's sports teams, it was most likely because women had not wanted or needed them. For the federal government to step in with a mandate for equality was "social engineering," a misguided liberal effort to impose a false equity on institutions and society. A few months after Reagan took office, a presidential task force, headed by Vice President George Bush, began to review what the administration termed "burdensome, unnecessary or counterproductive Federal regulations." Title IX was on the list.[12]

This assault also had philosophical underpinnings that rested on old assumptions about fixed male and female natures. Most conservatives did not target all government regulations, only those whose effects they did not like. Athletic equality was unnecessary, the reasoning ran, because of fundamental differences between men and women. Well-known conservative activist Phyllis Schlafly expressed this view with particular force. Feminists, she suggested, were a group of bitter, angry women who were unable to reconcile themselves to the roles for which nature had fitted them. Rather than pressing for social change, she argued, women should cease challenging male authority, stop emulating male qualities and instead embrace their traditional place as wives and mothers. By stepping beyond these roles, she continued, women not only defied nature, they threatened the foundations of the social order. Along with many other conservatives, she laid much of the blame for social ills such as divorce and juvenile crime squarely at the feet of women who sought to widen female horizons rather than promote devotion to homes and families.[13]

Presidents have no power to eliminate laws they do not like. But they can put a damper on enforcement. Almost as soon as Reagan was elected, efforts to enforce the mandates of Title IX—as well as of a host of other programs—began to languish. The administration's public disdain for the legislation had an effect as well. For schools uninterested in supporting women's sports, such measures became a license to further drag their feet.[14]

College programs took an even larger blow in 1984, when the Supreme Court ruled that Title IX did not necessarily apply to athletics. The decision enshrined a new, conservative stance toward federal mandates that were grounded in the use of federal funds. Title IX was one such mandate. The federal government could not simply order schools to comply with anti-discrimination regulations. But it could make compliance a requirement for receiving federal money—something that in the age of student grants and loans almost no school could do without. Soon after Title IX had passed, the Department of Health, Education and Welfare (HEW), along with Congress, had concluded that if a school accepted federal funding of any kind, all the school's programs, including athletics, had to comply with federal regulations.[15]

With the encouragement of the Reagan administration, several colleges challenged the broad reach of federal legislation in the early 1980s. One such case was filed by Grove City College, a tiny Presbyterian school in Pennsylvania. Grove City argued that because the school took no federal funds beyond student grants and loans, it should not have to comply with Title IX. The case reached the U.S. Supreme Court in 1984. In a 6–3 decision, the court ruled that the legislation's language only required those programs directly benefiting from federal funding to comply with Title IX. Since athletic programs rarely got direct federal funds, they were suddenly exempt. For most women's programs, the end of federal pressure meant entering a sort of twilight zone, in which coaches of women's teams had to find ways to wring funding increases out of largely reluctant administrations.[16]

ADVOCATES OF WOMEN'S SPORTS PRESSED ON, DRIVEN BY A DEEP-seated commitment to their games and to the rights of their female students. University of Kansas coach Marian Washington was one example. "I've never been able to just focus on basketball; for me it's always been women's sports in specific and women's rights in general," Washington later said. "It's a movement. I feel we all have a responsibility to speak out." In addition to building her basketball teams, Washington founded the Kansas women's track and field program and served as women's athletic director for several years. "I wanted so badly . . . to make things happen for women's sports, in spite of any obstacles," she explained. "I was absolutely driven."[17]

Although a conservative climate hamstrung most programs, a few continued to progress, buoyed by favorable local circumstances. One of the most remarkable was the University of Texas, where a group of energetic women built a program that became the envy of the nation. Rather than contrasting competitors and ladies, the women in Austin sold their team as a straightforward symbol of female strength and excellence. The strategy worked. By the end of the 1980s, the Texas Longhorns averaged more than 7,500 spectators a game. The team earned close to half a million dollars a year—enough to pay expenses and then some. The team's fans featured some of the Lone Star State's most powerful female leaders, including future Texas governor Ann Richards and U.S. congresswoman Barbara Jordan. "Those women didn't start coming because they liked basketball," Texas coach Jody Conradt noted. "They came because they identified with the perception that women athletes are strong women. They saw the UT women's basketball team excelling where women hadn't excelled before."[18]

A calm woman who coached in a deliberate, undramatic style, Jody Conradt was not cut out for media stardom. But Texas citizens, schooled

University of Texas coach Jody Conradt. COURTESY OF UNIVERSITY OF TEXAS ATHLETICS PHOTOGRAPHY.

in the hard lessons of a frontier past, valued achievement and state pride over appearance or convention. Conradt fit that mold to perfection, with grand ambitions and the drive to realize them. "If you grow up in Texas, you develop a sense of pride early on about this state," she explained. "That pride builds confidence, a can-do attitude. . . . The perception exists that something is a little bit different, a little bit special, a little bit bigger about our state. And we are all by birth challenged to fulfill that prophecy. That goes for women as well as for men."[19]

Texas women's basketball had a long and distinguished history. Texans organized their first high school girls' tournament in 1919. During the AAU's heyday, Texas sponsored one of the strongest organizations in the country. Texas teams, including Babe Didrikson's Golden Cyclones, won the national AAU tournament five times between 1929 and 1939, and the Plainview-based Wayland Flying Queens added ten more titles between 1954 and 1975. In the 1960s, as physical educators cautiously began to sponsor college programs, Texas schools were in the forefront, often sparked by student initiative. Shortly after Wayland Baptist All-American Carla Lowry took a physical education job at the University of Texas at Arlington, she recalled, "A little girl came in and she said, 'Would you coach our basketball team?' I said: 'Do we have one?' And she said: 'We'll have one if you'll coach us.' And that's kind of the way it was in a lot of places."

In 1974, faced with Title IX's impending requirements, the University of Texas went a step further than most schools, establishing an independent women's athletics department. Donna Lopiano, who became the first women's athletics director, noted that the reason for this independence was far from altruistic—the men's athletics director simply "didn't want to have anything to do with women's sports." But as it turned out, he did the women a favor. At many schools, women's coaches had to struggle to get the attention of male-dominated athletic departments that made men's sports their priority. Lopiano and her staff could focus exclusively on supporting and promoting women's sports. "Though you had to fight for your own money and things, it gave you an independence in terms of promoting and developing your program and hiring who you wanted to hire," Lopiano recalled.

Lopiano's successes were themselves examples of the university's willingness to accept a woman who was anything but decorous and re-tiring. She had come to Austin at the age of twenty-eight, plunging into her job with a passion that sprang from the pain of her own thwarted ambitions. When Lopiano was eleven, she made the Little League baseball team in her hometown of Stamford, Connecticut. Then she was cut, because Little League rules banned girls from its teams. Although she went on to win national and international acclaim as a softball player, she would never forget how much losing her hard-won position hurt, and she was determined to give other women greater opportunities. "No question, I stayed in sport because I had been denied the chance to play Little League," she told a reporter in 1990. "I always regretted that I never got a chance to see how good I could have been at pitching a base-ball."[20]

Most women of the era still veiled their ambitions in ladylike deco-rum. When Lopiano arrived in Austin, Ann Richards advised her that the best way to get what she wanted was to "smile and act like a lady," which Lopiano termed "terrific advice." But she did not always have time for such niceties. University president Lorene Rogers initially balked at hiring such a forward woman. Others watched her almost open-mouthed. "I thought I was a passenger in a runaway car those first few years," Conradt later noted. Still, Lopiano kept her job and soon won her colleagues' respect. She became remarkably successful at sell-ing women's sports to local businesses, winning sponsors for dozens of events and endowing scholarships right and left. The academic stan-dards she set gave Texas women a national reputation not only for their fine teams but for their high graduation rate. By 1990 at least one die-hard male Texas fan was ready to declare, "I'd like to see her run the whole damn department, men and women."[21]

When Lopiano hired Conradt to coach the women's basketball team in 1976, Conradt pitched right in. Her first order of business was to schedule games against top-ten teams, so that players in her young pro-gram would experience the level of play she was trying to achieve. She was already well known in state basketball circles—she had starred for tiny Goldthwaite High School; played on a pioneering Baylor University

Donna Lopiano, University of Texas women's athletics director. COURTESY OF UNIVERSITY OF TEXAS ATHLETICS PHOTOGRAPHY.

team; and gone on to coach in high school, at Sam Houston State, and at the University of Texas at Arlington. As soon as she won the job at Austin, she began to expand those contacts, traveling widely throughout the state to market her program to the public and build relationships with high school players and coaches. After a few years, she was a familiar figure in every corner of the state, and many talented young women saw playing for the Longhorns as almost an obligation. In 1985, San Antonio's Clarissa Davis was one of the country's most highly courted high school players. She had not yet chosen a school when she watched the Longhorns suffer an agonizing Final Four defeat. She resolved to head to Austin to help out. "Watching that *hurt* me," she said.[22]

Conradt was a profoundly team-oriented coach, cultivating squads with limited star power and extraordinary depth. She also worked to teach her players lessons that girls did not typically learn. "As a coach, I have had to teach a few good but timid players to be competitive," she once explained. "It's not a pretty process and it's not particularly fun. I have to tell a player's teammates, 'Just push on her. Beat on her. Be physical with her.'" Eventually the player "reaches the point of retaliation," she noted. "Her feelings sometimes get hurt in the process. But such a player is proud of herself when she finally is able to break through and become aggressive on the court. I think it translates to life later on as well."[23]

In 1986, the focus paid off handsomely, as the team amassed a 34–0 record and captured the national championship, overwhelming USC, 97–81, in the national title game. Clarissa Davis, the tournament's most valuable player, was not even in the starting lineup. "Whether you're on the floor for the opening tip-off means very little on this team," Conradt observed. In chronicling the victory, *Sports Illustrated* reporter Austin Murphy wrote not a word about ladies, hairstyles or fingernails. "So much strength," one opposing coach lamented. "So much talent."[24]

BY THE LATE 1980S, THE PROSPECTS FOR WOMEN'S SPORTS FINALLY began to brighten at the federal level. In 1988, after a four-year struggle,

Texas player Clarissa Davis confers with coach Jody Conradt. COURTESY OF UNIVERSITY OF TEXAS ATHLETICS PHOTOGRAPHY.

Congress passed the Civil Rights Restoration Act, designed to restore the mandates struck down in the Supreme Court's Grove City decision. One of the bill's provisions explicitly stated that all school-sponsored programs, athletics included, must live up to Title IX. The move was significant. In 1972, Title IX had slid easily through Congress in part because no one realized the simple-sounding bill would spark a revolution in college sports. In 1988, however, the meaning was obvious. Rather than simply endorsing high-minded ideals about equality, Congress was explicitly promoting top-level women's play. Unlike in 1972, the vote was not unanimous. When the bill reached Ronald Reagan's desk, he vetoed it. But Congress overrode him.[25]

Reauthorizing Title IX was an important act because it once again placed crucial pressure on college administrations. As Jody Conradt herself would later put it, it was not enough simply to appeal to administrators' sense of justice. "Given my experience with Title IX, I don't think anybody's going to run out there and say, 'I want to be fair,'" she said. "It takes big things to get people's attention. People wait until they are pushed."[26]

The need for federal pressure became crystal clear in 1990, when the University of Oklahoma announced it was eliminating its women's basketball team. The team had gone through some losing years and was having trouble drawing fans. The solution, administrators determined, was to disband the team and look into starting a soccer squad instead.

Officials expressed few regrets about the team's demise. In the words of Oklahoma football coach Billy Tubbs, supporting women's basketball was "money down the drain." Women would still have intramurals, noted Oklahoma's governor, Henry Bellmon. "We have never had total equality in women's athletics, and I don't know that we ever will," he told a local paper. "They don't have the same opportunity now. There is no women's baseball or women's wrestling." He then paused a moment, pondering his words. "I guess there is women's mud wrestling," he concluded.[27]

The move sparked a storm of criticism. At the women's Final Four, coaches quickly agreed to wear red protest ribbons on their lapels "so the TV announcers would have to explain them to the viewers." The

Oklahoma state senate voted 41–6 to condemn the dismissal. The Washington-based Trial Lawyers for Public Justice, a major civil rights and public interest firm, threatened a lawsuit. The university quickly backed down, protesting that "We really didn't know that anybody cared that much about our basketball program." A week after the decision was announced, it was rescinded.[28]

Once the dust settled, Texas's Donna Lopiano offered a pointed assessment of the state of women's college sports. The picture was far from rosy. Almost two decades after the passage of Title IX, its sluggish implementation meant that the gap between men's and women's sports remained enormous. "You would hope that the O.U. debacle was an anomaly, a blight on the otherwise sane fields of college sport," Lopiano wrote. "It might even be reassuring to some to think that these are unsophisticated and uneducated 'good ol' boys' sitting around the campfire during a cattle drive playing little boys' games."[29]

Unfortunately, Lopiano continued, Oklahoma was far from an exception. While few schools had made the mistake of publicly eliminating teams, she noted, many were running "intramural programs disguised by varsity uniforms." She followed her assertion with a set of statistics. Across the country, she noted, colleges still spent over four times more on male athletes than they spent on women. Female athletes received only a third of all athletic scholarships. Coaches of women's basketball teams made less than half of what male coaches made. The latter disparity sent a telling message. At Oklahoma, for example, administrators paid "$87,000 a year to get the finest coach for their sons, and $35,000 to have a losing coach for their daughters."

Throughout the 1980s, Lopiano subsequently argued, women's coaches, players and administrators had been reluctant to forcefully challenge the athletic status quo, fearing retaliation. The situation, she continued, had worsened since the NCAA took over women's sports. "When AIAW existed, it protected all of the women in those departments because the organization protected the individuals," she told a reporter. "But now people are afraid for their jobs and their scholarships."[30]

In the early 1990s, however, coaches and players became bolder—

especially in the legal realm. The explicit reauthorization of Title IX put advocates of women's programs on a strong legal footing. Lawsuits also became a more powerful threat in 1992, when the Supreme Court ruled that a victim of intentional sex bias could sue for punitive damages under Title IX. The potential of punitive damages—designed to punish a wrongdoer rather than simply compensate a victim—vastly increased potential awards, thus making suits more attractive. At many schools, coaches and players stopped arguing and started suing.[31]

One of the first coaches to step into the legal arena was Howard University women's basketball coach Sanya Tyler. In 1991, Tyler sued the historically black school over pay and facilities. Tyler had been coaching women's basketball at Howard for eleven years and had an outstanding record. Her teams had won the league tournament six times in the previous eight years, including four straight titles from 1987 to 1990. But Howard had never given much support to women's basketball. Back in the 1930s, the first heyday of black women's college ball, Howard had stood outside the fray, a bastion of physical education philosophy. In the 1970s and 1980s, men's sports remained the university's priority, and Tyler found that her success got little or no notice. "Not only was I not rewarded for it, it was ignored," she later recalled. She was paid less than the men's coach, despite a much stronger record, and the women struggled with far fewer resources than their male counterparts.[32]

For years, Tyler lived with the situation. "I think somehow I made the same excuses that many women make when they're too embarrassed to identify with inequity," she later explained. "We somehow feel it's our fault or something we didn't do, or some accomplishment we didn't reach, or some value we didn't possess." But her perspective changed in 1990, when Howard hired a former NBA player to coach the struggling men's team, at a salary far higher than hers. When she pointed to the pay discrepancy, she recalled, "I was told that I had not played in the NBA."

The remark laid bare the assumptions that underlay the gap—assumptions that had everything to do with status and nothing to do with the work of college coaching. "I'm not building NBA players, and neither are our men," she noted. "What we're building is people who can go out and make a difference, whatever they do. . . . What was happening wasn't fair." When her complaints fell on deaf ears, she took action. "I took them to the institution I thought they respected most, and that was the court." The suit, filed under Title IX, contested the salary difference, as well as disparities in support staff, office space and practice space. In 1993, Tyler was awarded $2.4 million in damages and a promise that conditions would improve for all of women's sports at Howard. Although the award was eventually reduced to $250,000, the message was clear.[33]

Soon, many universities found themselves the targets of actual or threatened legal action. Brown University, Auburn University, Colorado State University, Colgate University and the University of Texas were among the schools that settled suits during the era. The Texas case was especially telling. Though the Texas women's basketball program was thriving, other women's sports lagged. In 1993, when seven female students launched a class-action suit, women made up only 23 percent of the school's athletes and received only 32 percent of the school's scholarships. The suit argued that Texas did not provide enough opportunities for women and asked the university to elevate four club-level women's teams to varsity status. The university settled the suit out of court, agreeing to more than double the number of women participating in varsity sports and to bring women's scholarships up to 42 percent of the total.[34]

As the legal realm came into play, basketball coaches found themselves in an especially strong position. Basketball was the only sport where women's teams could be compared one-on-one with lavishly supported men's squads. The differences were often staggering. If men's basketball teams had whirlpools and training-table meals and chartered team buses, how could the women be expected to make do with moldy showers and rented vans? If the men's coach flew around the country scouting prized recruits, how could the women's coach be limited to local talent?

Filing a lawsuit could be a risky business. In 1993, while coaching at USC, Marianne Stanley filed a suit over disparities in the men's and women's basketball programs, lost and ended up without a job. Although she was one of the best coaches in the business, with three national titles on her resume, she found herself temporarily blacklisted from the college game.[35] But other coaches benefited from the new legal climate. In 1992, when Stanford's Tara VanDerveer coached her Cardinal team to a second national championship, she was paid half of what the Stanford men's coach received. It was not hard to convince Stanford to double her pay. Andy Landers, longtime women's coach at the University of Georgia, had similar success. At the University of Oregon, the threat of a suit helped win Jody Runge a contract that included not only a salary increase but better facilities, raises for her assistants, more resources for promoting the women's team and a promise to work toward radio and television broadcasts of women's games. The next season, after an extensive promotional campaign that included the promised game broadcasts, the audience for Oregon women's basketball took a big leap upward.[36]

By the early 1990s, thanks to these courageous challenges, the sport's future was brightening. A decade earlier, USC's national championship teams had dramatically demonstrated a new kind of athleticism and the possibility of generating media excitement. Successful programs such as Texas offered a carrot to university administrators, a vision of what women's basketball could be with strong university backing. Meanwhile, legislation and lawsuits provided a stick—which most programs badly needed and which the newly installed administration of President Bill Clinton was ready to use. These developments would spark enormous change. More colleges would join the powers of the 1980s in serious support for women's basketball. A new generation of players would bring further improvements to the game. By the mid-1990s, a series of remarkable teams and moments would win the sport the broadest appeal it had ever enjoyed. Women's basketball was moving forward again.

SECTION IV

THE BIG TIME?

1993–2004

· 10 ·

Marshaling Momentum

The sellout crowd in the Georgia Dome knew it was witnessing history. Spectators watched in awe as the 1996 U.S. Olympic team pressed up and down the court, moving at breakneck speed. Passes flew tight and precise. Every shot seemed to fall. The 33,000 fans hung on every dribble, every basket, every sideways glance. When the buzzer sounded to end the game, the United States had laid waste to Brazil, 111–87, to claim the gold medal. Announcers pronounced it the best women's basketball game they'd ever seen. It was also, many thought, the most important.

"This is a great day for women's basketball," noted forward Sheryl Swoopes.

"It's the greatest feeling in the world," echoed point guard Dawn Staley. "I could stop playing basketball right now."[1]

The '96 Olympic squad was more than just a national team. It was part of a concerted effort to broaden the audience for women's basketball around the United States. The United States Olympic Committee (USOC), the NBA and a number of corporate sponsors had bankrolled a full year of practice and exhibitions for a women's Olympic team that featured a dozen of the country's best players. With two decades of serious college play under its belt, and a newly talented array of stars and teams, women's basketball seemed on the verge of achieving unprecedented popularity. The Olympic effort was designed as the final push.

Through the 1990s and into the twenty-first century, women's basketball reached further than it ever had before. Institutionally, the game gained its firmest footing yet, with college and high school programs drawing solid funding, and with the start of a new professional league. Audiences grew and television ratings rose. At the center of this expansion lay the best women's basketball anyone had ever seen, played by competitors who were faster, stronger and more skilled than almost any of their predecessors. Although enthusiasm for women's play remained far from universal, this generation elevated the game to new heights.

THE 1996 OLYMPIC VICTORY HAD ITS ROOTS IN THE GROWING POPULAR appeal of college programs, amply demonstrated in a series of dramatic national championships that showcased the strengths of the women's game. The first came in 1993, when Sheryl Swoopes of Texas

Sheryl Swoopes dribbles up court for Texas Tech. COURTESY OF TEXAS TECH ATHLETICS MEDIA RELATIONS.

Tech University mesmerized fans with a one-woman shooting exhibition in the championship game. Swoopes hailed from West Texas, where support for women's basketball ran deep, and she did the tradition proud. The sellout crowd sounded like a giant whooping crane—Swoopes! Swoopes! Swoopes!—as the lithe 6' forward swished seemingly effortless shots from all over the floor. No one could stop her. She slashed to the hoop, pulled up for jumpers, calmly sank threes, popped in free throws. Observers said she created shots like NBA great Michael Jordan. By the time the game was over, Swoopes had scored 47 points, a record for a title game. When the team returned home to Lubbock, they were greeted at a football stadium rally by 40,000 fans.[2]

The performance also brought Swoopes another women's first—a basketball shoe with her name on it. Nike's Air Swoopes shoe represented another piece in the sport's promotional puzzle, a clear sign that the corporate interests that had been so important to men's teams were now sizing up the women's game. Nike had ridden to fame as an upstart shoe company that took a chance on a player named Michael Jordan, signing him to a multimillion dollar contract in 1984, when he was a rookie in the then-struggling NBA. The gamble paid off handsomely. By the end of the decade, the NBA had become the hottest property in professional sports. Jordan's combination of acrobatic play and businesslike demeanor had made him the most famous athlete in the world, and Nike's stylish promotions had turned basketball shoes into an integral part of a fashionable wardrobe. By 1992 Phil Knight, the chairman of Nike, Inc., was widely considered the most powerful man in American sports. The growing popularity of women's basketball held out the tantalizing possibility of a new, untapped market, and new jumps in sales and profit. The Air Swoopes sneaker signaled that Nike thought the time was right.[3]

The game's momentum continued the next season when University of North Carolina (UNC) forward Charlotte Smith cut through the blur of national sports coverage with a single, remarkable shot. Just seven-tenths of a second remained in the 1994 championship game when an inbounds pass reached Smith, just beyond the three-point line. Powerhouse Louisiana Tech led UNC by two. Smith barely touched the ball, flicking it into the air. As the buzzer sounded, it swished through the net. Pandemonium erupted. The highlight tape played over and over on televisions across the country, unmistakable proof that women's basketball was a game worth watching.

But the team that really churned the waters was the University of Connecticut (UConn), which made a surprise run to the national title in 1995. The Huskies brought a new region, the Northeast, into play. They also captured the fancy of another key institution—the powerful Northeast media. As the Huskies rolled to an improbable 35–0 season, the *New York Times* treated UConn like a local team, writing stories almost every day. That decision rippled out across the country, boosting the profile of the women's game. Cable sports giant ESPN was headquartered in Connecticut and took an unusual interest in the team—especially once the National Hockey League locked out its players and suspended all its games. "It was just perfect timing, a perfect storm," explained Husky center Rebecca Lobo.[4]

Rebecca Lobo herself was a promoter's dream. Not only was she a superb player, she was a soft-spoken, articulate white woman who radiated cheerful optimism, charming almost everyone she met. The best high school center in the country in 1991, she had taken a chance in coming to UConn, an unproven program that was barely on the national radar. All that changed dramatically by the time she was a senior. On January 16, 1995, UConn hosted number one–ranked Tennessee and won what would later be seen as one of the sport's landmark games. Just over two months later, the two teams faced off again in the national finals. All the experts predicted a Tennessee win, and the Lady Volunteers led until the final two minutes. Then, on the strength of several key Lobo baskets down the stretch, UConn rallied for a 70–64 victory. After the game, Lobo was the toast of the country. Spalding designed a basketball with her signature on it, and she signed a range of other endorsement deals. She was the fresh, new face of women's basketball.[5]

TWO MONTHS AFTER THE 1995 CHAMPIONSHIP, WHEN TRYOUTS opened for the 1996 Olympic team, Sheryl Swoopes and Rebecca Lobo were both on the court, contending for a spot against dozens of the

Rebecca Lobo celebrates UConn's 1995 national title. COURTESY OF THE UNIVERSITY OF CONNECTICUT.

world's best players. The Olympic team would spend a full year training together, aiming at the 1996 Summer Games in Atlanta, Georgia. The unprecedented year of work was partly financed by the USOC, which was determined to recoup national pride—after bringing home Olympic gold in 1984 and 1988, the U.S. women had only won the bronze in 1992. But sponsors also had grander ambitions, seeking to spread the message about the improving women's game. The team came complete with a publicity staff that launched a blitz of promotions, placing players in television commercials, on talk shows, in the pages of fashion magazines and in autograph-signing sessions at local shopping malls. Games were scheduled against all the top college teams in the country, and most of the best international teams. The USOC had partnered with the NBA, which raised most of the budget from corporate sponsors such as Kraft, Champion, State Farm, Sears and Nike. "We had thoughts that this could become something much bigger for women's basketball," recalled Val Ackerman, then an NBA vice president of business affairs.[6]

Heading up the squad was Tara VanDerveer, who had made the long journey from a girlhood with no high school team to the Stanford head coaching job, where university and community support created a power-house program that won national championships in 1990 and 1992. VanDerveer lived for the ins and outs of coaching strategy and placed her faith in conditioning and hard work. She didn't care for promotional gimmicks. "I don't like being a dancing bear," she noted. She was known for her strenuous workouts, not her charm. But she was a tireless advocate for the sport, doing everything she could to demonstrate the heights of skill, teamwork and just plain excellence women could reach. "I'm always telling my Stanford players to put out their best effort every single game because somewhere out there someone is watching women's basketball for the first time," she wrote in an account of the Olympic year. "We want to give them a reason to tune in again."[7]

VanDerveer had plenty of material to work with. The women assembled for the Olympic squad were highly capable ambassadors, the most skilled group of female players Americans had ever seen. Since the United States had no women's pro league, top college stars generally

Tara VanDerveer directs Jennifer Azzi in a Stanford game. PHOTO BY ROD SEARCEY, COURTESY OF STANFORD UNIVERSITY.

played abroad after graduation, in countries such as Japan, Italy and Turkey. International ball was a tough, physical game, giving players the chance to build speed and power, and to boost their skills. Although Rebecca Lobo was widely considered one of the best college players in the country, she quickly realized that most of her teammates played "a different level of basketball." Spectators "saw women at a higher skill level and maturity," she noted. "The players were strong, fast and quick. It opened people's eyes not only to better play on the women's side but also how exciting it could be at the next level."

Off the court, the squad was testament to women's ability to surmount challenges and to the diversity of personalities that the game attracted. Nine of the twelve Olympic players were African American. Most had come from modest backgrounds, where women had no choice but to work and female strength was a given from the start. Center Lisa Leslie had grown up in working-class Los Angeles, where her mother

The 1996 U.S. Olympic women's basketball team. Front row (from left): Tara Van-Derveer (coach), Nikki McCray, Katrina McClain, Katy Steding, Carla McGhee, Sheryl Swoopes, Nancy Darsh (assistant). Back row: Ceal Barry (assistant), Ruthie Bolton, Jennifer Azzi, Venus Lacy, Rebecca Lobo, Lisa Leslie, Teresa Edwards, Dawn Staley, Marian Washington (assistant). COURTESY OF USA BASKETBALL ARCHIVES.

drove a truck. Guard Teresa Edwards's mother had raised her while laboring in the vegetable farms around Cairo, Georgia. Point guard Dawn Staley hailed from the housing projects of north Philadelphia, where her father was disabled and her mother worked tirelessly to hold a large family together. Several of the players had been among the first in their families to finish college.

Lisa Leslie, who stood 6'5", fit right into the familiar formula of toughness on the court and glamour off. Tall and elegant, with a fondness for romance novels, she spent much of her childhood poring over fashion magazines and dreaming of a modeling career. She did not start playing basketball until junior high, when a classmate begged her to come out and help the team. Like many tall girls, she found that basketball helped turn her height from a focus of teasing into a point of pride. She learned to do her hair in a style that would survive a game, and soon busied herself with sit-ups and spin moves, complementing her size with unusual quickness and a deft shooting touch.[8]

Lisa Leslie grabs a rebound
during her college career at USC.
COURTESY OF USC
SPORTS INFORMATION.

Dawn Staley could not have differed more. A 5'6" whirlwind who played both ends of the court with remarkable levels of aggression, creativity and competitiveness, Staley could rarely be bothered to wear anything more glamorous than a sweatshirt. Growing up in Philadelphia, she had been the only girl in the pick-up games at her local recreation center. She was usually the smallest player on the court, and "I was always being called a tomboy or worse," she recalled. The demanding competition helped her develop a tough skin and an inner strength, and honed both her skill and her competitive instincts. "Being so short, I wasn't able to get my shot off all the time, so I had to perfect different parts of my game," she said. "I had to learn how to dribble, I had to learn how to pass, and I had to learn how to be just tough. I mean, the guys have molded me into the player that I am today."[9]

Jennifer Azzi, in contrast, honed her game on suburban courts in the girls' basketball hotbed of east Tennessee. A bright, engaging point guard with deeply cut muscles, Azzi embodied drive and persistence. She loved basketball from the time she swished her first baskets in nursery school. As a star at Oak Ridge High School, she routinely played to packed gyms. When she ventured to Stanford to play in college, however, she faced a rude awakening. "I cried every day after practice," she recalled of her freshman year. "Our first game we had like a hundred people in the stands. The team wasn't very good at that time. I wasn't used to losing any games. It was a real struggle." Four years later, Azzi led Stanford to the 1990 national title, winning acclaim for her hustle and leadership. She was one of the last players cut from the 1992 Olympic team, but came back strong for the 1996 tryouts. "She was somebody I could count on when I needed her," VanDerveer said.[10]

The combination of grit and charm proved a captivating one, and as the year progressed, the team began to draw the widespread notice that sponsors had hoped for. It quickly became clear that media sympathies still lay with good looks and bare flesh, and accounts of on-court action regularly jostled with images featuring bikinis, sports bras and high-fashion wear. Lisa Leslie, with her model's looks and demeanor, often drew the lion's share of attention. But audiences also marveled at the players' accomplishments—especially once they began to build a remarkable winning streak. After several months of practice, the team made a grand tour of the country, taking on all the top college teams and beating most of them by 30 points or more. Players made one trip to Russia, one to China, one to Australia, playing the best squads in the world. By January of 1996, their record stood 25–0, by March, 37–0. By June it was 50–0, and both tension and anticipation had begun to mount. The team arrived at the Atlanta Olympics 52–0, with eight games left to play. They left 60–0, with gold medals draped around their necks. Women's basketball would never be the same.[11]

MOST IMPORTANT, THE OLYMPIC TEAM'S SUCCESS SET THE STAGE for a revival of women's professional basketball in the United States. Although the NBA had begun thinking about a women's league soon after the WBL folded in 1981, Val Ackerman explained, "The timing wasn't right. The NBA needed a context. That was all that was needed." Part of that context came into focus after companies began lining up to sponsor the Olympic team. "The interest of the corporations not only financially but in general convinced us there was a market here," Ackerman continued. "We were sitting on something that had the potential to be of great appeal to corporate America, particularly because our target audience was so different. We were seeing in this a way to reach women that the NBA and men's college basketball didn't have. It opens up the sport to a different base."

The prospect was tempting enough that two competing plans sprang up. The first league to hit the court was the American Basketball League (ABL), organized by a group of independent owners based in San Jose, California, and focused solely on women's basketball. The league kicked off in the fall of 1996 with franchises in Atlanta; Columbus, Ohio; Richmond, Virginia; and New England, as well as Denver, Portland, San Jose and Seattle. The next summer, in 1997, the NBA-sponsored Women's National Basketball Association (WNBA) opened its first season, fielding teams in Charlotte, Cleveland, Houston, Los Angeles, New York, Phoenix, Sacramento and Salt Lake City.

American female players, it seemed, had gone from rags to riches, forced not to play in foreign leagues but to choose between American ones. The players were eager to stay at home. "It's hell being overseas," Lisa Leslie told a reporter as she sat in an Australian hotel room, fresh from beating the Cuban national team in a pre-Olympics exhibition match. "If the game today had been for an overseas team, you would come back and you would just sit here like this and wait for the next one. You're by yourself. You think, okay, I could handle this for maybe one day, one week, but when you go six months, eight months. . . ."[12] Rather than leave the country to play, Sheryl Swoopes had taken a job as a bank teller. Rebecca Lobo remembered facing the choice of moving abroad or quitting the game. "It was a total either-or," she said. "It was my senior year in college. I was on a bus ride somewhere. I think it was February. I was daydreaming or whatever you do on bus trips, thinking, 'What am I going to do? Am I going to go overseas and play in a place where I don't speak the language and don't know anybody or am I going to stay here and try to pursue a broadcasting career?' "

In many ways, the two leagues recapitulated the battle between the AIAW and the NCAA a decade before. Should women try to chart their path with the independent ABL or cast their lot with an established men's organization? The leagues adopted divergent approaches. The ABL scheduled its games for fall and winter, the traditional basketball season. Player salaries averaged $80,000 per year, and contracts included year-round medical insurance and stock-purchase options. The league chose cities where it could build on support for strong college programs and played in small arenas to save on rent. The WNBA, in contrast, planned its games for the summer, a schedule designed to mesh with the NBA's off-season and to maximize the opportunity for TV exposure by taking advantage of the summer lull in men's college and pro sports. The league initially paid most players $30,000 to $35,000 per season and offered fewer benefits than the ABL. It placed its teams exclusively with existing NBA ownership, a strategy that locked them out of key markets such as Connecticut and Tennessee, but put them in first-class arenas.[13]

The ABL touted its independence. "We don't want to be a sideshow to the men," noted Jennifer Azzi, one of the first Olympic players to sign with the league. "It's a Whole New Ballgame," the league slogan announced. That independence, along with higher salaries, attracted a deep pool of talent. Nine of the twelve Olympians and most of the top college players signed with the ABL its first season. The league placed college heroes in their respective markets: Stanford's Jennifer Azzi started for the San Jose Lasers, UConn's Jennifer Rizzotti for the New England Blizzard and Georgia's Teresa Edwards for the Atlanta Glory. The ceremonial first game featured Azzi and San Jose defeating Edwards and Atlanta, 78–70, in front of a sellout crowd of 4,550 in San Jose. The league played a forty-game schedule from October through February and averaged more than 3,500 fans per game the first season. Led by league MVP Nikki McCray, the Columbus Quest dominated the regular season with a 31–9 record and then beat the Richmond Rage in a hard-fought five-game series for the league title. Quelling any doubts about their dominance, the Quest won the title again the following season.[14]

The WNBA tipped off in the summer of 1997, about seven months after the ABL's debut. Its main stars were three Olympic players—Sheryl Swoopes, Lisa Leslie and Rebecca Lobo—who had broken with their teammates to go with the league. Swoopes and Leslie chose the WNBA in part so they could play for teams located near their families—Swoopes in Houston and Leslie in Los Angeles. Lobo's choice revolved around which league she thought would last. "I just knew if there was going to be one group that would be able to survive, it would be the one with David Stern and the NBA's money behind it," she said.

Talentwise, the WNBA got off to a sluggish start. Although Swoopes, Leslie and Lobo were compensated well, low salaries for other players meant that the talent level was conspicuously lower than the ABL's. But the sponsoring NBA was one of the most formidable powers in sports, with marketing, sponsorship and broadcasting clout of which the ABL could only dream. And the WNBA did not stint on promotion. Shortly after the league was announced in April 1996, it lined up television deals with the high-profile networks of NBC, ESPN and female-oriented Lifetime Television. As the league's debut drew near, broadcasts of NBA games were rife with stylish ads that proclaimed "We Got Next," and a ten-page, full-color promotional piece ran in USA Today.

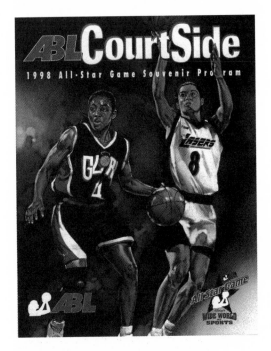

The American Basketball League featured Teresa Edwards (left) and Jennifer Azzi on this all-star program. COURTESY OF SUSAN SHACKELFORD.

Trading on the NBA's clout, the WNBA signed corporate sponsors that included Sears, Coca-Cola, McDonald's, Anheuser-Busch, General Motors, Nike and Lee Jeans. The presentation was first class: sharp uniforms, NBA arenas, lots of televised games and in-game promotions and entertainment. The effects of this promotion were evident from the start. League play opened on June 21, 1997, at the Great Western Forum in Los Angeles. Rebecca Lobo and the New York Liberty defeated Lisa Leslie and the host Los Angeles Sparks, 67–57. More than 14,000 fans attended—over three times the attendance at the ABL's debut.[15]

As the season rolled on, two surprises emerged. Fan enthusiasm far exceeded projections—teams pulled in more than twice the projected audience. And the best team in the league was paced not by one of the Olympic luminaries, but by Cynthia Cooper, whose last turn in the United States had been as a member of the powerhouse USC squads of the 1980s. Although Sheryl Swoopes had been the designated star of Cooper's Houston Comets team, she was seven months pregnant when the season began and joined the team late. Cooper, who was coming off a decade of playing in Europe, stepped up instead, aided by Kim Perrot, Wanda Guyton, Tammy Jackson and Tina Thompson, one of the few top college graduates to choose the WNBA over the ABL.

Houston's team was headed by a witty, genial Mississippian named Van Chancellor, who had spent the previous two decades coaching the women's team at the University of Mississippi. At first, Cooper noted, many team members had trouble understanding him, "especially when he'd say things like 'Go up yonder'—which meant 'go over there.'" But Chancellor knew how to get things done. "He ran a tight ship, and you were either on the boat or you weren't," she said. Partway through the season, Cooper and Chancellor determined that she should be scoring more and would need some extra leeway to do it. "Coop, play your game," she later recalled him saying. Spurred by the challenge, she began to reel off a series of extraordinary performances—a game of 30 points, then 32, then 44, then 34. When the season finale rolled around, she was the league's top scorer and MVP. Houston beat the Charlotte Sting in the semifinals, then squared off against Rebecca Lobo and New York in a one-game championship match, triumphing 65–51. Their homecoming celebration was held on the steps of Houston's city hall. Chancellor was named WNBA Coach of the Year. Although the team's success had been a surprise, it was no fluke—Houston would win again the next year, and the next.[16]

A few weeks after the WNBA championship, the ABL began its second season. The play was still top-notch and attendance remained good, jumping to an average of 4,335 per game. But investors were uneasy. Marketing lagged, in part because of competition from the WNBA. As soon as the WNBA had entered the picture in 1996, the ABL's hopes of landing Nike as a sponsor and ESPN as its main TV broadcaster had evaporated. It managed to secure sponsorships with Reebok and Phoenix Home Life Mutual Insurance, as well as a national TV contract with Fox/SportsChannel. But those deals couldn't hold a candle to the phalanx of sponsors and high-profile TV networks aligned with the WNBA.[17]

The higher profile of the WNBA, a league with decidedly lesser talent, frustrated the ABL players. "We really got little respect because we didn't have a good TV contract," said Portland Power center Sylvia Crawley, who had played on the UNC national championship team in 1994 and dazzled fans with a blindfolded dunk to win the slam-dunk competition at the 1998 ABL All-Star Game. "When I told people I played for the ABL, they would tell me just to work hard and one day I could play in the WNBA. They didn't realize the ABL had more depth and higher salaries. That was the power of the media."[18]

Although the second season went well, the ABL's future was cloudy. The league no longer had a lock on the top college talent. Of the eight All-Americans who graduated in 1998, seven went to the WNBA and only one to the ABL. The league's national TV contract dropped from thirty-six games to sixteen games on Fox, and CBS agreed to show only two games of the league's best-of-five championship series. With such poor exposure, the ABL was unable to sign more major sponsorship deals. Roughly a third of the way into the 1998–99 season, the league abruptly called it quits. On New Year's Eve, the ABL officially filed for bankruptcy, listing $10 million in debt and $500,000 in assets.[19]

Players and coaches mourned the passing of a league that put women's basketball front and center, and had tried to blaze its own trail. Still, the ABL's demise meant that talent and promotion would finally converge. Most of the ABL players were absorbed into the WNBA through the following spring's draft, bringing a shot of skill to a league brimming with exposure but shallow in talent. The mix of ABL veterans and a new crop of gifted college players brought the WNBA a new level of credibility. *Washington Post* sports columnist Sally Jenkins saw the difference at the 2002 WNBA All-Star Game, noting that the players "whose thorough likeability has been their main selling point so far, are acquiring something more to recommend them. The ponytails now have killer crossovers and the hippest out on the wing are tossing passes as snappily as their cornrows. . . . Gradually, the WNBA is becoming a game that doesn't make basketball connoisseurs shudder. In the case of this all-star game, it was a genuine pleasure."[20]

The WNBA was also becoming a magnet for top foreign players. Even though most of its salaries were lower than European leagues, the WNBA gained a reputation as the top women's pro league in the world.

"I think when you play in a country with 280 million people, and when women's basketball is one of the top sports for women—it's in high schools and colleges and it's entrenched in the culture—I think that makes for a tough league," explained Australian Carrie Graf, coach of the WNBA's Phoenix Mercury. One of the most talented imports was Aussie Lauren Jackson, who joined the WNBA in 2001. The 6'5" Jackson had established herself as a major star who could bring the ball up the court like a guard, drain three-pointers with ease and dominate play at the low post. Although she could have earned as much or more in her home country, she wanted to develop her game playing against the world's best competition. In 2003, she became the first international competitor to be named the WNBA's MVP.

Meanwhile, as more and more top U.S. college players poured into the WNBA, the league's level of play kept climbing. The youth movement's impact was unmistakable in 2003 and 2004, when teams spearheaded by recent college graduates brought home the title. The 2003 champion, the Detroit Shock, was the youngest team in the league, with an average age of just under twenty-four years. Shock forwards Swin Cash and Cheryl Ford and center Ruth Riley led the way in an especially athletic championship series. Even though his team lost, Los Angeles Sparks coach Michael Cooper reveled in the play. "I am enjoying this so much because the WNBA has gone to another level," he said at one point. "What a game!"[21] In 2004, the Seattle Storm and Connecticut Sun reprised the youth theme. Lauren Jackson and former UConn star Sue Bird, both twenty-three, led the Storm over the Connecticut Sun. The Sun featured five rookies on its roster, including starting point guard Lindsey Whalen. The league was already eight years old, and many of its original players were nearing retirement. The WNBA was becoming a young woman's game.

THE WNBA'S NEW TALENT CAME OUT OF A COLLEGE GAME THAT BE-
came better by the year, buoyed by a growing institutional base and an ever-improving crop of recruits. The college game was getting new attention of its own. Although the women's Final Four had been broadcast since the NCAA took over the tournament in 1982, its visibility sky-

The Seattle Storm won the 2004 WNBA title. COURTESY OF THE SEATTLE STORM.

rocketed with the riveting title games of 1993, 1994 and 1995. On the heels of those successes came a major commitment from ESPN to cover the 1995–96 tournament, including the Final Four, and to increase the number of tournament games it showed in coming seasons. Eventually, ESPN would televise all NCAA women's tournament games. Fans and rising players began to know and follow teams based not just on word of mouth but from what they saw on television. By 1998, the Final Four had become so popular that the NCAA instituted a lottery for would-be ticket buyers.[22]

No one epitomized the college game's achievements more completely than Pat Summitt, the legendary coach of the University of Tennessee Lady Volunteers. Summitt took charge of the Tennessee program in 1974, just two years after Title IX became law. A quarter-century later, her teams had amassed six NCAA championships, and she was widely considered one of the finest coaches in the country, male or female. As she often noted, she was no social revolutionary, creating opportunities

*University of Tennessee coach Pat
Summitt, 1999–2000 season.*
COURTESY OF THE UNIVERSITY OF
TENNESSEE LADY VOLUNTEERS
SPORTS INFORMATION.

where none existed. But she picked up the Title IX ball and took it as far as she could go, building her program into the envy of the sport and a towering example of what women were capable of achieving.

When Summitt took the Tennessee job, she was a twenty-four-year-old graduate student with a bum knee, no coaching experience and few role models. The university gave no athletic scholarships to women. Although Tennessee high schools had a long and distinguished history of support for girls' basketball, they had stubbornly refused to abandon the half-court game, handicapping her local recruits. But Summitt had been endowed with a ferocious work ethic and a razor-sharp mind, and she dedicated both to her sport's cause. She rehabilitated her knee and made the 1976 Olympic squad, coming home with new coaching ideas and two Olympic teammates—Cindy Brogdon and Patricia Roberts— who transferred to Tennessee to play for her. She took on the state high school establishment and helped push through a switch to full-court rules. She painstakingly assembled university support, tempering her zeal and hiding her frustration when the process failed to keep up with her ambitions.[23]

By the 1980s, her efforts had begun to pay off. Tennessee reached the national championship game in 1980, 1981 and 1984. In 1987, the Lady Volunteers finally broke through to the title. They repeated in 1989 and 1991. Along the way, players such as Brogdon, Roberts, Cindy Noble, Bridgette Gordon and Daedre Charles became statewide celebrities. But none eclipsed Summitt, who was headed for the highest victory total of any college basketball coach, male or female, and who became one of the most recognized and respected women in Tennessee. Anyone seeking a pillar of female strength had to look no further than Knoxville, where Summitt stalked the sidelines, coaching her team to victory after victory.

Along the way, she filled state lore with legendary stories. There was her hardscrabble childhood on a family tobacco farm, ruled over by a stern father who was far quicker with his belt than with a compliment. There was her gutsy, self-driven rehabilitation of her torn knee ligament, often considered a career-ending injury in those days. There was her decision to undertake a key recruiting trip while nine months pregnant, and the hurried flight back to Knoxville when she went into labor. There was The Stare—a penetrating gaze that related more than words. In Tennessee, she drove as fast as she wanted and never got a ticket. Her standard entrance into spacious Thompson-Boling Arena resembled that of a rock star—a solo stroll to waves of thunderous applause.

Like so many of her predecessors, Summitt often cloaked her ambitions in womanly restraint, making sure she never talked too loud or pushed too far. "There is no question that my traditional southern credentials advanced the cause of Tennessee basketball," she once explained. "I was the sort of woman that the powers-that-be were familiar with, and I appealed to them." She married in 1980, had a son in 1990 and took pride in pointing out that her coaching duties did not keep her from cooking dinner or doing laundry. She dressed impeccably, pacing the sidelines in tailored suits and heels, makeup always in place. But she also spoke with force about her efforts to expand the bounds of womanhood, challenging the idea that women should be coy or girlish. "I don't like that word, 'girl,'" she wrote in 1998. "If someone calls you a girl, what they often mean is *nice* girl. Then they tell you what games nice girls are supposed to play, and how nicely you are supposed to play them. . . . We don't have any girls on our team. We don't have any sweethearts, or babes, or junior misses, either. And I'm not Mary Poppins." The only label she wanted on her teams, she concluded, was "National Champions."[24]

To that end, she became renowned for working her teams unmercifully, scheduling long workouts and demanding practices, and riding player after player to the point of despair. "She'd put thirty minutes up on the clock, and we would run one continuous fast break drill," recalled Holly Warlick, who played for Tennessee in the late 1970s and eventually became one of Summitt's assistants. "I can remember walking out of the gym thinking, 'What have I done? My God, this woman is crazy. I literally cannot do what she wants me to. I'm not going to make it.' " The strain was psychological as well as physical, Warlick noted. "I was competitive. But man, she just about put me over the edge. It was like she punched every button in me." In the end, though, most players decided their coach knew what she was doing. "I found things in myself I didn't know I had," Daedra Charles explained. "She teaches you if you want something badly enough you can get it, but you've got to work. You go through it in her program. You go through it. But you use it the rest of your life." From season to season, Ace Clement echoed, Summitt "makes you a stronger woman." Year after year, many of the nation's top high school recruits put themselves in Summitt's hands.[25]

One of those players was Chamique Holdsclaw, a gangly 6'2" forward who arrived in Knoxville in the fall of 1995, ready to work her own magic on the sport. Holdsclaw had grown up under the watchful eye of her grandmother, June, in the Astoria Houses housing project of Queens, New York. She was the incarnation of a well-brought-up young woman: slim, shy and respectful, with a soft voice and a propensity for giggling. "My nature is not to be a pushy person," she once noted. But she had built her skills on the playgrounds of New York, where no one, male or female, was given any quarter, and where just getting on the court required guts and dedication. When she was eleven, the boys on a Police Athletic League (PAL) squad voted to bar her from the team, reasoning that "She's a girl—she stinks." When local kids formed pickup teams, the skinny girl was often left on the sidelines. "Nobody wanted to pick me," she recalled. But she kept playing, and her talent began to show. The year after she was voted off the PAL team, she went back. When the coach put her on the squad, she quickly became the leading scorer. She was soon a sought-after playground commodity. "As I got better, everybody started wanting me," she noted.[26]

By the time she reached Christ the King High School in 1991, she was known as one of the best players in the country, enchanting coaches with her all-around skills—the pull-up jumper, the three-pointer, the shot off the dribble. Perhaps most notably, she elevated the notion of hang time. "There were times when she changed position in midair," Summitt later noted. "She would move, meet an opponent, and seem to shape-shift. Suddenly, there she would be, on the *other* side of the basket, with an open shot." Although Summitt had never recruited a player from New York and doubted Holdsclaw would want to come to Knoxville, she could not let the opportunity pass. She made the trip to Queens. Chamique and June liked what they saw. The next fall, Holdsclaw was wearing Tennessee orange.[27]

Holdsclaw was notably tentative in her first college contests, still wrestling with the pull between her off-court reserve and her competitive drive. But when she came into her own, she was almost unstoppable, playing not only with breathtaking skill but with a ferocious confidence that few female players had ever displayed. "I don't think anyone has ever played the game the way she plays it," UConn coach Geno Auriemma marveled. Summitt would never forget the moment when, in the midst of a close game, she felt her shy freshman pulling on her sleeve. "Give me the ball," Holdsclaw demanded. "Give me the *ball.*" By her junior year, she held the team in the palm of her hand. "She gives everyone confidence: players, coaches, trainers, fans," Summitt observed. "You just know she's going to make it happen."[28]

In Holdsclaw's freshman year, Tennessee won its fourth national title. Her sophomore year, the team shook off a dismal 22–10 pre-tournament record and won again. But the real revolution came in 1997–98, when Holdsclaw and a handful of upperclassmen were joined by a group of remarkable freshmen—Tamika Catchings, Ace Clement,

Tennessee's Chamique Holdsclaw lays the ball in. COURTESY OF THE UNIVERSITY OF TENNESSEE LADY VOLUNTEERS SPORTS INFORMATION.

Teresa Geter and Semeka Randall. In the mysterious chemistry that makes for extraordinary teams, everything went right. Led by the "Three Meeks"—Holdsclaw, Catchings and Randall—the Lady Volunteers took women's basketball by storm. Playing with the triangle offense that had brought the Chicago Bulls three straight NBA titles, they displayed what the *New York Times*'s Jere Longman termed "an aggressive, attacking style that has redefined the women's game." The days of stationary set shots "are long gone, replaced by a thrill ride of finger rolls, turnaround jumpers, fallaways and lookaway passes," Longman rhapsodized. "Players tall enough to play center in a previous generation now deftly bring the ball up court. Behind-the-back passes and between-the-leg dribbles have become routine practice drills, not flashy ornamentation." There was no holding back. The team played, Summitt later noted, "as if they had no internal or physical boundaries."[29]

At the end of the season, Tennessee was 39–0, owned an average victory margin of 30.1 points and was celebrating a third straight national championship. Treated to a parade in Knoxville that drew a crowd four-persons deep, the team attracted a $50,000 donation and nearly doubled season ticket sales. Summitt came in for her share of acclaim. Partway through the remarkable season, *Sports Illustrated* had dubbed her the "Wizard of Knoxville" and suggested she might be the greatest college basketball coach, male or female, since UCLA's John Wooden. Her successes generated speculation that she might be the one to prove that a woman could successfully coach a top-level men's team. But she remained focused on her original goal: "redefining what young women are capable of and how they compete." Women had come a long way, she noted, but not nearly far enough.[30]

"[You] have an opportunity during your time on earth to make a difference for women," she told the *New York Times*. "What would it matter if you made a difference for men? It's not like they need it."[31]

By the spring of 1998, Tennessee's domination seemed almost unassailable. But a challenge was building. That fall, the most heralded re-

University of Connecticut coach Geno Auriemma, 2003–4 season. COURTESY OF THE UNIVERSITY OF CONNECTICUT.

cruiting class in the country belonged not to Summitt, but to Geno Auriemma at the University of Connecticut. Auriemma had taken full advantage of UConn's heralded 1995 title, using the program's newfound
fame to expand his recruiting base from the Northeast to the entire nation. His 1998 recruits—Sue Bird, Asjha Jones, Swin Cash and Tamika
Williams—would only elevate that reputation. As the century drew to a
close, UConn became the program to beat.

Geno Auriemma had come to women's basketball by a circuitous
path. He spent his childhood in a village near Naples, Italy, where his
family had no heat, no running water, no electricity, no telephone and no
car. His father came to Philadelphia in 1960 and landed a factory job. A
year later, he sent for the rest of the family, including seven-year-old
Geno. They settled with cousins in Norristown, Pennsylvania, just
northwest of Philadelphia. Geno became the only English-speaker in
his immediate family, responsible for paying bills and handling family
matters even before he reached his teens.[32]

Blessed with a shock of wavy, dark hair, a glint in his eye and the gift
of gab, Auriemma eased his way into young adulthood. "I never did
everything I possibly could to get the most out of my ability," he later
said. "I did just enough to get by." But he nursed a fierce passion for basketball. He became a point guard at Bishop Kenrick High in Norristown, and he and his friends traveled into Philadelphia whenever they
got the chance, hunting games in the city's famed pickup scene. "You
learned to play and not back down from anybody," he explained. "We
weren't going to scare anybody on the court. . . . But we loved to compete. We loved to play. We just wanted a game." He went on to play at
Montgomery County Community College and eventually earned a political science degree at West Chester State.[33]

One day, a teammate from Bishop Kenrick called and asked if he
wanted to help coach a Catholic girls' high school team. "I said, 'No
way.'" Auriemma later recalled. "'I wouldn't coach girls for all the
money in the world.' When I was at Kenrick, we wouldn't even let the
girls on the court." But his friend convinced him, and he took the part-
time job. It led to another part-time position coaching women at
Philadelphia's St. Joseph's College and then another with the boys' team
back at Kenrick High. Along the way, he made ends meet by doing con-

struction work, laboring in the mills, even working an overnight shift at a grocery store. Then he heard about a full-time opening at the University of Virginia, as an assistant to the highly respected Debbie Ryan. "Man, I don't want to go that women's route again," he remembered thinking. But he liked the school and took the job. Four years later, UConn came calling, and hired him to ratchet up its women's program.[34]

Neither UConn nor Auriemma envisioned a grand future for the female Huskies. UConn was a latecomer to the women's basketball scene. Although the school had fielded a team since the 1974–75 season, inadequate resources and lagging university commitment had left it to languish. Coaches and players fought sadly familiar battles for equipment and facilities while struggling to establish that they were serious competitors. Karen Mullins, a UConn star in the 1970s, recalled plenty of team meetings where players aired their grievances, prepared appeals for better treatment and signed petitions. When she injured her knee in her first game, she had trouble convincing doctors to operate. "They didn't want to leave a scar on the little lady's legs," she remembered. Not until female students who wanted a soccer team threatened to sue the school and the trustees went on record supporting women's sports, did the administration reluctantly give in. Figuring basketball was their best shot at developing a revenue-producing women's sport, school administrators hired Auriemma in 1985 to build the program.[35]

When Auriemma took over the team, it had posted one winning season in its eleven years of existence. It shared a locker room with the men's soccer team, played games in a decrepit campus field house and was lucky to have fifty people at a game. He won the position on his charm. UConn officials knew it would take unusual skill to attract players to a school with subpar facilities, no tradition of success and a home in the tiny town of Storrs, so small it did not even have a McDonald's. Auriemma seemed like the coach for the job. He could visit a recruit's house and "walk out the door with the family's dog in his arms," said colleague Pat Meiser-McKnett.[36]

On the court, however, the magnetic recruiter morphed into the tough, street-smart coach who pushed his players as far as they could go—and then some. Auriemma coached with a biting wit and a scrappy edge, riding his stars especially hard. "He sets us up to fail in practice every day," Sue Bird once remarked. He rarely talked about what his team's success might mean to women as a whole. He hovered at the margins of women's basketball circles, needling and picking at his colleagues, and at times complaining that many in the sport resented a male coach's success. But with players, he displayed expectations that knew no bounds. He proclaimed loudly and often that female players were capable of far more than most coaches realized. "I think expectations for a lot of kids growing up have been very low," he said in 2002. "If a girl plays bad, it's like: 'O.K., you'll get them next time. Nice try.' That's all well and good when they are 6, 7, 8, 9 years old. By the time you get to college, I'm not sure 'nice try' gets it."[37]

On the court, the sincerity that lay beneath his harsh critiques always came through in the end, and the players responded. Longtime colleague Phil Martelli once observed that if Auriemma's admirers "think it's an X's and O's thing they're mistaken. It's really about the way he handles people."[38] Rebecca Lobo concurred. "All of his players, while they are cursing him under their breath in practice, ultimately do anything he asks of them," she said. "Not a lot of coaches develop that kind of loyalty. . . . He is very, very good at understanding each player he coaches, knowing whether a player needs to be yelled at constantly or prodded along gently. He knows how to read people . . . and what buttons he needs to push."

The team's success also resonated with the public. Connecticut had few big-time sports teams, and the Huskies put on a great show. By the late 1990s, all the games were on television, thanks to an innovative arrangement in which any games not broadcast by commercial networks were picked up by a regional PBS station. Starting in December 1997, the team began a long-running string of sellouts at their home arena, 10,167-seat Gampel Pavilion. More than 16,000 fans, many with their faces painted Husky blue, routinely came to games played in the Hartford Civic Center. Enthusiasm for the game spilled over to other teams as well. The ABL's New England Blizzard had one of the best attendance records in the league. In 2002, the Mohegan Sun Indians, eager to have another draw for their casino in Uncasville, spent $10 million for a WNBA franchise, which they named the Connecticut Sun.[39]

Never did enthusiasm run higher than when Tennessee came to

town. The two teams' many strengths, combined with the coaches' contrasting personalities, made for a colorful and heated rivalry. "Everyone who badmouths women's basketball should be made to attend a Tennessee-UConn game," a UConn beat reporter once observed. Pat Summitt was the grande dame of the women's game, carrying herself with a fierce dignity. Geno Auriemma was the newcomer, a joking, needling troublemaker who once called Tennessee the Evil Empire. Their back-and-forth exchanges, which one sportswriter dubbed "The Pat and Geno Show," heightened the drama of their confrontations. And the stakes were always high. "Tennessee games were always the biggest matchups of the year," UConn star Jennifer Rizzotti noted in 2001. "No matter how much we tried to downplay it, the team that won those games usually became No. 1 in the country. . . . It was a battle for bragging rights, and there was an intensity on the court that just wasn't there with other opponents." Interest in the contests soon stretched far beyond the two schools, as the games became regular features on national television and a spark for debates among sports fans around the country.[40]

As the twenty-first century opened, UConn launched its own remarkable run. Auriemma's 1998 recruits were sophomores by the time the 2000 championship rolled around, and UConn trounced Tennessee, 71–52, to win the school's second national title. The next year the Huskies lost in the semifinals to Notre Dame, which went on to the championship. But in 2001–2, Sue Bird, Asjha Jones, Swin Cash and Tamika Williams were not only seniors but best friends, sharing an off-campus apartment and seeming to read each other's minds on the court. They played at an exceptional level, executing plays with near perfection and giving opponents little room for hope. "As good as they are," Auriemma observed, "they look to each other to get better." UConn compiled a 39–0 record, winning by an average of 35.4 points a game. The Huskies defeated the Lady Volunteers so handily in the NCAA semifinals that Pat Summitt made an unprecedented visit to their locker room after the game to congratulate them on their play. In the championship game, they beat Oklahoma, the school that almost dropped its program in 1990, 82–70. When the WNBA held that year's draft, the four UConn seniors were among the first six players chosen.[41]

Despite the loss of four such stellar competitors, UConn continued to win, largely because the starter that returned, Diana Taurasi, had become the best player in the country. A 5'11" guard with a deft, all-court shooting touch, Taurasi sported confident, fluid moves to the basket and extraordinary passing ability. But what coaches most often remarked on was her confidence "She's the most fearless player we've ever had," Auriemma noted. "Nobody looks happier out there," one reporter observed. "Nobody is harder to beat."[42]

For Taurasi, perhaps more than for any other female star before her, basketball and life seemed largely seamless. If she had any insecurities, on or off the court, she masked them with a cheerful, confident nonchalance. The person she most resembled was her coach. She and Auriemma were both children of immigrants—Taurasi's father, Mario, was from a small Italian village not far from Auriemma's hometown, and her mother Lilli was from Argentina. Coach and player were both quick with a quip, walked with a confident swagger and liked being in the public eye. Like Auriemma, Taurasi was not afraid to rock the women's basketball boat, as when she told *Sports Illustrated:* "I know this will irritate a lot of coaches, so I never said it then, but I wanted to play for a man."[43] She had chosen basketball over soccer in part because she realized Americans cared more about basketball, and more people would come to watch her play. She reveled in the UConn limelight. "People love the game, they love seeing what you can do on the court—and that's a great thing," she said.

A generation earlier, when female athletes were largely expected to be seen but not heard, her snappy, forthright style might have undercut her appeal. Instead, it was admired. She became especially popular among male fans—and not because she looked good in a bikini. "She'll rip your jugular out on the court," noted Seth Sulka, the general manager of the WNBA's Phoenix Mercury, who made Taurasi the WNBA's top pick in the spring of 2004. "I mean, she's the nicest person and has a great smile, but she'll rip your jugular out." When Nike began developing a Taurasi shoe, company officials decided to produce it in both men's and women's sizes.[44]

In the spring of 2003, UConn shocked the women's basketball world

*UConn's Diana Taurasi looks
up court, 2003–4 season.*
COURTESY OF THE UNIVERSITY
OF CONNECTICUT.

by returning to the Final Four despite the graduation of its senior stand-outs. Tennessee again loomed in the final, aiming for its seventh na-tional title. But on the strength of a remarkable Taurasi performance, UConn pulled out the victory, 73–68, to give UConn its fourth crown. The teams met again in the 2004 championship, and UConn won again, leaving the teams' national title tallies at UConn, five; Tennessee, six. The rivalry was alive and well—as was the sport. The 2004 title game drew the highest television ratings ever for an ESPN basketball game, male or female.

IN AUGUST OF 2004, JUST A FEW MONTHS AFTER UCONN PUT ITS NCAA trophy on the shelf, the latest incarnation of the U.S. women's Olympic basketball team boarded a plane for Athens, Greece. Coached by Van Chancellor, the squad was a formidable blend of pioneering vet-erans and bright-faced newcomers, all drawn from the WNBA. Once again, the stakes were high. Although the women's game had grown in popularity, it still lacked the broad appeal the men's game enjoyed. As a result, the Olympics still offered female cagers their major chance to perform before the nation as a whole. "This is all so special for us," team captain Dawn Staley explained. "It's different for men. When they're little, they dream about the NBA or the NFL or Major League Baseball. Women don't have that." Seeking to take advantage of the opportunity, the WNBA had suspended play for a month so its stars could put on their best show.[45]

The players rose to the occasion. Staley, playing in her third Olympics, carried the U.S. flag during the opening ceremonies, an honor never before bestowed on a basketball player, male or female. Staley, Lisa Leslie and Sheryl Swoopes, all part of the watershed 1996 Olympic team, still stood out on the court. They also schooled young stars like Sue Bird, Diana Taurasi, Ruth Riley and Swin Cash in the significance of their effort back in 1996, as well as the tactics required to win at the peak of international play.

The team went on a remarkable run, barely pausing until the semifinals, when the players dug down to beat a tough Russian squad. In the gold medal game, they seized control in the fourth quarter to defeat Australia, 74–63, led by key Staley baskets when the game was on the line. All the games were televised, giving viewers a good look at the team's depth and dominance. "One game it's Lisa Leslie, another it's Tina Thompson or Diana Taurasi," wrote Chuck Schoffner of the *Indianapolis Star*. "Even the player they call Pee Wee [Shannon Johnson] can't be ignored. Playing this U.S. basketball team leaves opponents breathless, dizzy and frustrated. Because it's impossible to cover them all."[46]

The respect the younger players felt for their pioneering teammates came clear in the final two minutes of the gold medal game. As the United States was winding down the clock, Chancellor sent in substitutes for everyone but Staley, who had announced she was playing in her last Olympics. Fresh off the bench, Bird passed the ball to Staley, and when Staley moved to pass it back, Bird exclaimed, "You keep the ball!" As the buzzer went off, Bird and her teammates hoisted Staley into the air. "She's the best leader I've ever known, and probably will ever know," Taurasi said. "She willed us to win."[47]

Lisa Leslie hugs Dawn Staley after the United States won the 2004 Olympic gold medal. Ruth Riley (center) and Diana Taurasi (right) look on. PHOTO BY STUART HANNAGAN, COURTESY OF GETTY IMAGES.

The strength and confidence produced by three decades of high-level women's basketball was unmistakable. Even before the Olympics opened, sportswriter Barbara Walder had waxed eloquent over the "self-awareness and dignity" of the U.S. players, penning a column that cut to the heart of the sport's achievements. "There was a lovely expectant feeling as the Olympic team gathered for the press in New York . . . just before leaving for Athens," Walder wrote. "With many of the world's top women players crammed into a tiny Radio City Music Hall dressing room, there was a tremendous energy and presence that could barely be contained."

"It was thrilling," she continued, "to be surrounded by such magnificent, fully realized women."[48]

C O N C L U S I O N

Shattering the Glass

In the opening years of the twenty-first century, women's basketball bears little resemblance to the game of a century before. In the early 1900s, the sport was played with rules that sharply restricted women's movements and in bloomers so voluminous they took half a day to iron. Most games took place in women's colleges, where physical educators shaped the sport according to a vision of restrained and refined lady-hood. When the game expanded in the early twentieth century, it was in uneven, episodic fashion. Young women lucky enough to grow up in communities that nurtured the sport had teams to join and dreams to chase. Others struggled just to find a way to play.

Today, women play basketball in every corner of the country. Virtually every high school has a team, as do many junior high schools and even some elementary schools. Recreational programs also abound. Millions of girls and women take to the court, running and jumping and shooting with explosive energy. Some pass and practice with dreams of college scholarships or even the WNBA. Others simply revel in the moment, savoring the pleasures of movement, of camaraderie, of building skills and confidence.

This broad spread is testament to the power of combining passion with opportunity. Women have loved basketball since its invention, playing the game wherever and whenever the opportunity arose. But the chance to fully express that ardor did not come until the women's liberation movement of the late 1960s and early 1970s, when a focused assault on social inequity produced Title IX, with its promise of equal opportunity in school programs. As with many of the efforts sparked by the women's movement, progress toward athletic equity soon faltered in many quarters of American society, foundering on stiff opposition to the changes required to foster true equality. But many women, along with a few men, refused to let go of Title IX's promise and have devoted decades of effort to transforming the legislation's sweeping language into reality. Theirs has been a dual push. On one level they have fought for the equal opportunities that Title IX requires, the teams and facilities that male students enjoy. But beneath that goal lies a much broader vision: fostering generations of girls and women who possess a full range of athletic virtues—strength, teamwork, assertiveness, leadership, courage—and transcend expectations of deference and restraint that hamper women's actions, in the same way that tight corsets and long skirts once constrained their movements.

The efforts of coaches and players have produced a marvelous game. Top college and WNBA contests feature precision jump-shooting, exquisite ballhandling, effortless three-pointers, a bevy of blocked shots and ferocious rebounding—all at a level of athleticism that grows by the year and all woven into a tight fabric of teamwork. Player histories are the stuff of classic sporting legend, of injuries gutted out, setbacks overcome, challenges met. Especially important, the court has become a place where what matters most is what a woman does with her abilities, not whether she is black or white, slender or stocky, married or single, lesbian or straight.

The women's game has a large and loyal group of fans. Young girls, themselves beginning to taste the joys of the sport, revel in the energy and style of highly skilled play and dream of one day being in the spotlight. Women often take pleasure not simply in the beauty of the game, but in the dramatic display of female abilities, the speed, strength and confidence that embody both accomplishment and possibility. While many sports fans, both male and female, would rather watch the dramatic athleticism of men's basketball, many women's fans prefer the team-oriented game the women play, the passes, picks and shifting formations that delight devotees of the game's subtleties.

Today's high-level play represents a remarkable achievement. But many challenges lie ahead. While few now question women's right to play competitive sports, enthusiasm for female athletic achievements—in basketball and most other sports—remains limited. The lag is clearly visible in the way colleges spend money. Three decades after the passage of Title IX, colleges still spend, on average, 64 percent of their athletic budgets on men's sports and 36 percent on women's. More dramatically, the dearth of broad-based cultural enthusiasm can be seen in the many empty seats at most regular-season college games, as well as at many WNBA games. After a promising start, audiences for WNBA contests began to drop, falling from a peak of almost 11,000 spectators a game in 1998 to around 8,500 in 2004. Although playoffs and crucial games draw sellout crowds, even the most successful WNBA teams do not yet break even. Legislation created a crucial set of institutions and opportunities. Its power to shift popular opinion was far more limited.[1]

In part, these empty seats point to the need to further develop and promote the sport, to continue what former WNBA president Val Ackerman called "a methodical education process." But they also reflect ongoing conflicts over the nature of American womanhood. In the court of public perception, the forceful, confident woman showcased by women's basketball must compete with a range of alternate visions. The vast machinery of commercial entertainment sets forth a model of femininity that stresses high-style sexual appeal, in which female celebrities combine energy and ability with high heels, low-cut blouses and other measures focused on attracting men. The customs and institutions that shape daily life, from the especially strict curfews many families set for their daughters to the laws that bar female soldiers from combat operations, remain rife with old assumptions about female frailty, perpetuating the idea that women require protection from society's most demanding pressures. In the political realm, a conservative religious and political agenda advocates a return to a neat and "natural" division of male and female roles, nostalgically idealizing the wives and mothers of the 1950s and frequently condemning women—feminists, lesbians, mothers who pursue careers—who step beyond those bounds. No matter how well women play, for women's basketball to be widely celebrated in American culture, the version of womanhood it embodies must gain greater ground.

Evidence of these competing views of womanhood runs throughout present-day play. On one hand, many young female athletes receive more encouragement than ever. UNC Charlotte coach Katie Meier, along with many of her peers, marvels at the confidence she sees in her recruits. Back in the 1980s, when she was an Illinois high school basketball star, Meier had often curbed her energy, not wanting to be called a jock. While she played hard on the school team, when jostling with her female classmates in P.E. class, she held back. "I wouldn't block anybody's shot or do anything to embarrass them," she said. By 2004, she saw far less of that insecurity. "In recruiting in the early nineties, I could tell the ones who had played with older brothers," she said. "Now I can't tell. The girls are diving for balls, going up hard for rebounds. They have permission to be aggressive." The change also shows in the parents of the eight-year-olds that enroll in her basketball camps. "Their parents don't come out of the stands to complain about play being too rough," Meier continued. "Even in the late nineties, they did. I don't know if it's the WNBA or the Olympics, but they see women applauded for playing aggressively so they're doing it."

Still, such encouragement remains far from universal. Rutgers coach Vivian Stringer voiced her deep frustration at the indifferent training so many young female athletes still receive. While parents flock to high school administrations to demand good coaches for their sons' teams, Stringer noted, they rarely make that effort for their daughters. And far too frequently, her recruiting trips make clear that parents and coaches set lower standards for young women than young men. "Guys, I think they're taught life lessons quickly," she explained. "That is, if you earn the right, you'll be out there playing. And if you don't—well, then you'd better find another way to get it done." With women, on the other hand, coaches tend to be "a little more coddling and a little more accepting of the fact that you came up short, and that's O.K."

Female athletes also still feel the pressure of alternate models of womanhood, which set conflicting standards for womanly behavior. As Tara VanDerveer put it, women "still have to establish two identities: the athlete and the female." These persisting double standards show especially clearly in the WNBA's ongoing efforts to link the league's athletes to the conventions of fashionable sexuality. Each year the league produces an annual video called *This Is Who I Am,* for which a selected group of players enter the fantasy world of high-fashion glamour, enjoying full-fledged makeovers, flattering wardrobes and the attention of highly skilled photographers and filmmakers. The 2004 video, prominently displayed on the league's Web site and accompanied by a slide show of individual photographs, offered a blend of game action and glamour shots in which, once again, a player's ability to live up to standards of style and sexuality carried as much weight as her facility for shooting and rebounding—if not more. Although WNBA athletes "like to play rough," player Nikki Teasley noted of the 2004 production, "we are still young women and it is good that we get to show our true personalities from time to time."[2]

Players and coaches must also contend with a culture that still links female athleticism with lesbianism, prompting ongoing suspicion and disdain. Growing acceptance of gays and lesbians has encouraged some gay players and coaches to talk openly about their sexual identity, and some teams to come to terms with having both gay and straight members. But the issue more often remains the subject of whispers, innuendo and intimidation that affect both gay and straight women and impede the progress of women's sports. "I know countless women who have put their personal and professional lives on the line to call for equity for female student-athletes," Laurie Priest, athletic director at Mount Holyoke College and a lesbian herself, told a reporter in 2001. "By doing so, these women have often lived in fear that their sexuality would be called into question, in subtle and not so subtle ways." For other women, Priest continued, that fear "has often compromised their willingness to fight for equity."[3]

As in the past, the pressure to strike a balance between athletic expertise and more conventional femininity remains both an unfair demand and a precarious endeavor. Some players walk that fine line with aplomb. But far too often, athletic girls and women find that skill and dedication push them dangerously to the edge of the womanly ideals held by many of their peers. Sam Donnellon of the *Philadelphia Daily News* touched on this issue in a 2004 column that described the dilemmas faced by his sixteen-year-old, basketball-crazy daughter. The Donnellons had encouraged their daughter to play sports, thinking it would build her self-confidence. But it proved a risky strategy.

"For girls, being a jock does not, in itself, make you more attractive to high school boys," Donnellon wrote. "Often it works in reverse. Play softball year-round and you risk being called 'butch.' Play hard on the basketball court and you risk being likened to a man." Such critiques, he noted, were as likely to be voiced by girls as boys. Even with plenty of teams to play for and college scholarships to win, these pressures still affect young players. "I have seen girls, talented athletes, quit sports because of such double standards," Donnellon continued. "I have seen other female athletes not give their all, perhaps because of such wariness over what that could equate to their peers."[4]

THAT SUCH DIFFICULTIES AFFECT THE RISING GENERATION OF young athletes underscores the enormity of the task that female athletes face. Rituals that celebrate male strength have been woven deeply into the habits and experiences of generations of Americans. Sports are a prime example. Fathers and grandfathers carry children and grandchildren to see the games and teams they have followed for decades, twining the experience of male sport into family history and memory. Male sportswriters berate villains and celebrate heroes with passionate commitment, carrying on arguments and conversations they began as boys. Professional men's sports have become an integral part of American corporate culture—corporations regularly purchase luxury boxes and blocks of season tickets, using them to woo clients, reward employees and bask in prestige. All of these rituals center on a vision of confident, forceful masculinity that remains largely consistent from the boardroom to the television screen to family dinner conversations. Winning this degree of cultural support for women's sport is a tall order—especially since all too often visions of athletic masculinity encompass a contrasting emphasis on female sexuality, as personified by the scantily clad women dancing on the sidelines of most men's games or the swimsuit beauties that *Sports Illustrated* parades before its readers once a year.[5]

The ongoing success this formula enjoys means that the barriers to the spread of women's sports are not simply relics from the past, confined to crusty athletic directors fighting losing battles to protect old turf or a raft of aging fans and sportswriters who grew up with men's sports and are largely unwilling or unable to recognize women's achievements. Rather, such barriers are perpetuated by powerful cultural institutions that wield wide-ranging influence over young people and the way they view the world.

Even within women's sport itself, there are powerful incentives to accommodate, rather than challenge, constricting views of womanhood. For female athletes, sexual sensation still proves a sure-fire path to media attention. In June 2004, when Seattle Storm star center Lauren Jackson posed naked for a magazine in her native Australia, more than a hundred reporters descended on a Storm practice in pursuit of the story. For Storm coach Anne Donovan, however, the excitement distracted from her players' more substantive accomplishments. "I don't think any attention is good attention," she remarked. "I think we're well-established enough now to get basketball attention for the right reason."[6]

One of the uglier results of the growing competition for top college recruits has been the number of coaches who take advantage of parents' fears about athletic lesbians to tout their own intolerance of homosexuality and suggest that rival programs are more accommodating. As well as encouraging prejudice, this strategy undercuts the sport by perpetuating the notion that the lesbians who participate do indeed pose a threat to womanhood, and that "normal" women should proceed with caution.

FACED WITH THE INTRANSIGENCE OF SUCH OBSTACLES, MANY people connected to women's basketball have adopted a long view. Margie Hunt McDonald, a Wayland College star and pioneering University of Wyoming coach, described her own lengthening perspective on the sport's development in the spring of 2003. "I promised a group of young coaches one time—my daughter was six then—that with Title IX, by the time she got to be in high school we wouldn't have any discrimination against women in college," she explained, laughing. "Then I went back later and said: 'O.K. I have a two-year-old granddaughter. . . .' "

As she works toward a vision of athletic equality that still eludes her grasp, Vivian Stringer is often frustrated by the slow pace of change. "We always as women have to defend our worth," she noted. "It's so sad because you almost have to apologize for your existence in this whole thing, and the women have gotten a bad rap." But she focuses on the future. "You know, the thing I think we have to remember through it all— nothing was easy," she said. "It's been a process. And when you think of it, it hasn't been that long that women have even begun to play the game."

Even as supporters of the sport work hard on the details of promotion and development, they counsel patience. In terms of media coverage, women's basketball is "only ten years away from a completely different paradigm," longtime women's sport leader Donna Lopiano suggested. "Today the forty-two-year-old father who grew up accepting women in sport doesn't yet run the radio or TV station. He's still ten to fifteen years away from getting that job. That's where the sea change is going to happen. He'll say: 'This is fun, I love this. My daughter plays. I want to broadcast or publish this.' " The WNBA's Val Ackerman took a similar tack. "It may take a generation," she surmised, pointing to the kids who are growing up with professional women's games. "Maybe it will take them growing up to be the paying customers and parents of their own children for the effects of what we have done to be felt. That's kind of what's happened in men's sports. Men's sports has been fueled over the decades in large part because fathers and grandfathers take their sons and grandsons to games. That's it. That's all it takes. Those boys grow up, and they are still a Red Sox fan, a Yankees fan, etc. It just takes sometimes a long time for that to happen."

For their part, many players express a sense of optimistic determination. Phoenix Mercury guard Diana Taurasi is keenly aware that support for women's basketball lags well behind that of men's. "If you're a woman, you're screwed," she remarked to one reporter. "It's the world we live in."[7] But she feels the game belongs as much to her as to any man. "The way I look at it, if you're on the court, an athlete's an athlete," she said. "A basketball player is a basketball player is a basketball player." Like many other players, she places her faith in devoted effort. "We've got to work at it," she said. "We're young, so there's still room for a lot of improvement. It'll come. If we keep playing great basketball . . . it will get there."

The history of the sport makes it clear that such progress cannot be taken for granted. Historically, support for women's basketball has depended not simply on how well women have played but also on the degree to which strength, competitive zeal and assertive confidence have meshed with popularly prevailing views of how women should act and how society should be run. The sport has made its greatest gains when institutional support has been bolstered by views of womanhood grounded in female strength and by a strong commitment to equality. When those links break, it has declined. Competitive women's basketball took off in the 1920s, peaked in the 1940s, and then was undercut by the conservative retrenchment of the Cold War era. Congress passed Title IX in 1972, a time when women's opportunities were expanding in many fields. A decade later, amid another wave of cultural conservatism, the Supreme Court gutted the legislation, stalling the game's development. Only after a sustained political and legal effort—coupled with the dedicated persistence of coaches, players and supporters—did the game begin to grow again.

The sport's history shows the importance of ongoing work on many fronts. Bringing women's basketball this far took many efforts, addressing many issues. Physical educators forcefully challenged assumptions about female frailty. High school and AAU coaches and players in turn defied physical educators' limits on women's competition. Activists and legislators promoted equity through federal law, and their successors used the courts to make sure those laws were enforced. Coaches and administrators who believed in equal opportunity went through the step-by-step process of building institutional foundations and a marvelous game. Many of these labors took place amid unfavorable circumstances. In the 1930s, African American women built programs that affirmed black female skill despite the racism that raged about them. In the 1960s, a core of dedicated women pioneered college competition with virtually no institutional support. Throughout the 1980s, when Title IX was under siege, coaches and players kept working to enrich the game. Such dedicated labor meant that in those precious moments when the cultural climate shifted, shattering old barriers and creating opportunities such as Title IX, women were ready to seize them.

The achievements of women's basketball also have broad ramifications. Athletic success does not represent the pinnacle of human achievement. Pursued to excess, competition has a darkly troubling side. But competitive athletics also embody many of this society's most cherished virtues, among them leadership, sacrifice, resilience and teamwork. The athletic rituals that play such significant roles in our society—the gathering of crowds, the building excitement of league and tournament play, the praise heaped on successful teams and individuals—are a collective celebration of these virtues, whether the athletes in question are tiny tots just learning to play or professional performers dazzling onlookers with their skills. The dedicated efforts that have placed female achievement at the center of some of these cultural rituals have established women's hold on these virtues in especially dramatic fashion. Whether or not a broad public is ready to respond, the message remains a forceful assertion of women's abilities and an inspiration to others. Tara VanDerveer pointed to this powerful influence while describing the joyfully confident skills of 1996 Olympians Teresa Edwards, Katrina McClain and Ruthie Bolton. "When Teresa bounced a no-look pass to Katrina," she wrote, "or when Ruthie stripped the ball from her opponent and glided down the court for a seamless layup, maybe a woman watching at home felt her limitations give way just a little."[8]

THE CHALLENGE OF PRESSING FORWARD IS NOW FALLING TO A NEW generation of coaches, fans and players. The revolution sparked by Title IX is more than three decades old, and the women and men who laid the sport's crucial groundwork are moving on. Many pioneering coaches have recently retired, among them Sue Gunter, Marian Washington,

Chris Weller and Leon Barmore. A new generation is moving into their places: Carolyn Peck, whose Purdue team took the 2000 national title; Muffet McGraw, who won with Notre Dame in 2001; and Anne Donovan, who in 2004 became the first female head coach to win a WNBA title.

Many key players are also hanging up their shoes. The 2004 Olympic team featured three veterans from the pivotal 1996 campaign—Dawn Staley, Lisa Leslie and Sheryl Swoopes. The Athens Games were the last for Staley, and perhaps for all of them. But a new generation stands in the wings, inspired by their determined accomplishments and ready to step into their roles, looking not just to the present but to the future.

"It's a ladder," rookie Olympian Swin Cash said a week after the United States brought home the gold medal. "You just keep pulling other women up. You lay a foundation down, and you just kind of roll from there. . . . I feel a lot of gratitude to Dawn, to Lisa, to Sheryl, all of them. Hopefully, at some point, I can do just as much as them and have other girls looking up to me."

ACKNOWLEDGMENTS

First and foremost, we would like to thank all of the people who so generously shared their memories with us. Although they are too many to list here, they can all be found in the list of oral history interviews. They are the true keepers of women's basketball history, and we greatly appreciate their willingness to share their experiences and insights. We hope we have done them justice. We regret that space did not allow us to include many more players, coaches and programs; there is far more to tell.

Interest in women's basketball history has grown enormously in recent years, and a raft of dedicated researchers have provided us a treasure trove of work to draw from, as well as valuable advice. Susan Cahn, whose wide-ranging analysis of American women's sports inspired this project, provided us with several of her own oral history interviews. The sections on black women's basketball in the 1930s would not have been possible without Rita Liberti's pioneering research into this sparsely documented subject, and Rita shared both interviews and insights as the project progressed. Bob Ikard provided us with advance material from his recently published history of women's AAU basketball. Gary Newton generously sent us a copy of his unpublished manuscript on

Hazel Walker, which helped bring life to our description of this remarkable star. Karra Porter shared insights and material from her soon-to-be-completed history of the WBL. We also got help from Max McElwain, author of a thoughtful work on Iowa high school ball, and Ursula Smith who, with Linda Peavy, has helped revive interest in the Fort Shaw 1904 championship team.

We received encouragement and advice from many other people. First and foremost, we owe thanks to the members of our writing group, Jerma Jackson and Jill Snider, who read over every chapter with meticulous care and gave us endless help, feedback and inspiration. Marc Favreau, our editor at The New Press, was a grand supporter of the project from the start, and provided many useful insights. Christine Grant read the sections on Title IX and the AIAW, and corrected some key errors. As well as sharing her memories, Paula McGee helped us conceptualize the section on USC's championship teams. Barbara Hollingsworth, Pauline Tulson, Robert Heyward and Carol Sawyer all read chapters and provided tremendous advice. Thanks to Helen Wheelock for her terrific work on the Women's Basketball Online Web site and to Mariah Burton Nelson for running the "Frankies" women's sports list, which kept us up on developments in the field. Many of the concepts in this book were originally developed in projects funded by the dissertation, postdoctoral and small grant programs of the remarkable Spencer Foundation, and some of the original research was sponsored by the Levine Museum of the New South here in Charlotte.

Archivists and librarians helped us tremendously with contacts, resources and ideas. We would especially like to thank Nan Elrod at the Women's Basketball Hall of Fame for going above and beyond the call of duty to help us. Thanks also go to Joe Gutekanst and everyone else at the Davidson College Library; Pat Ryckman at the University of North Carolina at Charlotte; Nanci Young at Smith College; Karen Mason, Janet Weaver and Jun-Nicole Matsushita of the Iowa Women's Archives at the University of Iowa; Charlene Harris in Caroline County, Virginia; Patricia White at Stanford University; Susan Tucker from the Newcomb College Center for Research on Women at Tulane University; Jim Bantin at the University of Nevada at Reno; Jason Eslinger at the Iowa Girls High School Athletic Union; Sandra Peck at Tuskegee University; Stacy

Jones, Trashinda Wright and Karen Jefferson at the Atlanta University Center Archives; Pat O'Donnell at Swarthmore College; Carolyn Marr at the Museum of History and Industry in Seattle; Gilbert Hom of the Chinese Historical Society of Southern California; J. Stephen Catlett of the Greensboro Historical Museum; Ellen Thomasson at the Missouri Historical Society; Teresa Young at Wayland Baptist University; Joan Williams at Bennett College; Tom Hanchett and Ryan Sumner of the Levine Museum of the New South and Patricia Smitz at the Institute for Research on Women and Gender at the University of Michigan. Thanks also to researchers Erin Kaufman at the University of Iowa and J.R. Duke at the University of Mississippi.

We are indebted to many individuals for providing access to players, coaches, games, information, photos and other resources: Heather Brocious and Dawn Buckner at Rutgers University; Chennelle Miller and Ina Wiggins of N.C. State University; Karen Kase of the Charlotte Sting; Amy Yakola of the Atlantic Coast Conference; John Maxwell with the WNBA; Rob Turner and Brian Davis of the University of Tennessee; Bob Schranz of the Houston Comets; Carol Hudson of Old Dominion University; Robby Lockwood, Malcolm Butler and Scott Boatright of Louisiana Tech University; Joe Carvalhido at Louisiana State University; Karen Bryant and Liam O'Mahoney of the Seattle Storm; Rebecca Vick of Western Carolina University; Meg Miller of the Dallas Fury; Paul Hickey of the Detroit Shock; Kenton Edelin of Edelin Sports & Entertainment; Bill Tavares of the Connecticut Sun; Angelica Figueroa of the Women's Sports Foundation; Barbara Reres of Senator Birch Bayh's office; Larry Torres and Camille Currie of the New York Liberty; Joe Amati of NBA Photos; Chris Rash of Elon University; Shirley Renaldi of the German-Masontown Library; Randy Press of the University of Connecticut; James Dixon of Stephen F. Austin University; Barb Kowal of the University of Texas; Felicia Hall of Felicia Hall and Associates; Brent Stastny of the University of North Carolina at Charlotte; Tom Di Camillo of West Chester State; Lydia Szyka of Immaculata University; Steve Rourke of UCLA; Vicky Hammond of the University of Southern California; Beau White of the University of Kansas; and Caroline Williams of USA Basketball.

Thanks also to the following people, who provided encouragement and support of many kinds along the way: Bijan Bayne, Jim and Celia Carnes, Nina Cloaninger, Lynne Emery, Sarah Fan, Nadene Hammond, Tom Hanchett, Raye Holt, Sarah Sue Ingram, Erin Kellen, Barbara Lau, Larry Malley, Jan Marrs, Patsy Neal, Welch Suggs and Jon Zimmerman.

On the home front, this book would never have been written without generous amounts of support, tolerance and encouragement from those we love the best. Endless thanks to Melissa, to Peter and to Parker Lee, who gave up many family evenings and weekends so we could finish. We hope you enjoy having us back.

APPENDIX

National Champions

1926   Pasadena Athletic and Country Club 11, Anaheim Athletic Club 10

1929   Shepp's Aces (Texas) 28, Golden Cyclones (Texas) 27

1930   Sunoco Oilers (Texas) 27, Sparkman Sparks (Ark.) 24

1931   Golden Cyclones 28, Wichita Thurstons 26

1932   Oklahoma Presbyterian College 35, Golden Cyclones 32

1933   Oklahoma Presbyterian College 49, Golden Cyclones 39

1934   Tulsa Business College Stenos 32, Oklahoma City Cardinals 22

1935   Tulsa Stenos 28, Holdenville Flyers (Okla.) 16

1936   Tulsa Stenos 23, El Dorado Lions (Ark.) 22

1937   Lewis & Norwood Flyers (Ark.) 17, Galveston Anicos 10

1938   Galveston Anicos 13, Wichita Thurstons 8

1939   Galveston Anicos 21, Lewis & Norwood Flyers 8

1940   Lewis & Norwood Flyers 23, Nashville Business College (NBC) 13

1941   Lewis & Norwood Flyers 16, NBC 15

1942   American Institute of Commerce (Iowa) (AIC) 42, Lewis & Norwood Flyers 25

1943   AIC 41, American Institute of Business (Iowa) (AIB) 31

1944   Vultee Bomberettes (Tenn.) 23, AIB 16

1945   Vultee Bomberettes 22, Little Rock Dr. Pepper 20

1946   Cook's Goldblumes (Tenn.) 26, Dr. Swett's (Iowa) 20

1947   Atlanta Sports Arena Blues 26, Goldblumes 22 (OT)

1948   Goldblumes 21, Atlanta Blues 18

1949   Goldblumes 35, NBC 17

1950   NBC 29, Goldblumes 28

1951   Hanes Hosiery (N.C.) 50, Wayland Baptist College (Texas) 34

1952   Hanes Hosiery 49, AIC 23

1953   Hanes Hosiery 36, Wayland 28

1954   Wayland 39, Kansas City Dons 38

1955   Wayland 30, Commercial Extension Comets (Neb.) 21

1956   Wayland 39, NBC 33

1957   Wayland 36, Iowa Wesleyan College 33

1958   NBC 46, Iowa Wesleyan 40

1959   Wayland 42, NBC 37

1960   NBC 48, Wayland 29

1961   Wayland 39, NBC 29

1962   NBC 63, Wayland 38

1963   NBC 45, Wayland 41

1964   NBC 58, Wayland 46

1965   NBC 47, Wayland 42

1966   NBC 59, Wayland 33

1967   NBC 47, Raytown Piperettes (Mo.) 39

1968   NBC 56, Raytown Piperettes 43

1969   NBC 69, John F. Kennedy College (Neb.) 36

1970   Wayland 58, Ouachita Baptist College (Ark.) 53

1971   Wayland 59, Raytown Piperettes 43

NATIONAL COLLEGE INVITATIONAL

1969   West Chester State 65, Western Carolina 39

1970   California State Fullerton 50, West Chester State 46

1971   Mississippi College for Women 57, West Chester State 55

AIAW

1972   Immaculata 52, West Chester State 48

1973   Immaculata 59, Queens College 52

1974	Immaculata 68, Mississippi College 53
1975	Delta State 90, Immaculata 81
1976	Delta State 69, Immaculata 64
1977	Delta State 68, Louisiana State 55
1978	UCLA 90, University of Maryland 74
1979	Old Dominion 75, Louisiana Tech 65
1980	Old Dominion 68, University of Tennessee 53
1981	Louisiana Tech 79, Tennessee 59
1982	Rutgers 83, University of Texas 77

NCAA

1982	Louisiana Tech 76, Cheyney State 62
1983	USC 69, Louisiana Tech 67
1984	USC 72, Tennessee 61
1985	Old Dominion 70, University of Georgia 65
1986	Texas 97, USC 81
1987	Tennessee 67, Louisiana Tech 44
1988	Louisiana Tech 56, Auburn 54
1989	Tennessee 76, Auburn 60
1990	Stanford 88, Auburn 81
1991	Tennessee 70, University of Virginia 67 (OT)
1992	Stanford 78, Western Kentucky 62
1993	Texas Tech 84, Ohio State 84
1994	University of North Carolina 60, Louisiana Tech 59
1995	University of Connecticut 70, Tennessee 64
1996	Tennessee 83, Georgia 65
1997	Tennessee 68, Old Dominion 59
1998	Tennessee 93, Louisiana Tech 75
1999	Purdue 62, Duke 45
2000	Connecticut 71, Tennessee 52
2001	Notre Dame 68, Purdue 66
2002	Connecticut 82, University of Oklahoma 70
2003	Connecticut 73, Tennessee 68
2004	Connecticut 70, Tennessee 61

NOTES

INTRODUCTION

1. By far the best examination of the tensions between womanhood and athletics in the twentieth century is Cahn, *Coming on Strong*. Many of the concepts that guide this narrative were originally articulated in Cahn's work. We also draw heavily on the ideas in Festle, *Playing Nice*. Many of the concepts related to African American women and athletics come from Liberti, " 'We Were Ladies.' "
2. *Sporting News,* June 2004, 10.

1: COLLEGE LADIES ON THE COURT

1. Hill, "Senda Berenson," 662.
2. Berenson, "Basketball for Women," draft 1 [transcript], 98. Series 6, Senda Berenson Papers, Smith College. http://clio.fivecolleges.edu/smith/berenson/6speeches/ (accessed June 2003).
3. *The Scroll,* January 1900, 12–13.
4. *Bulletin of Atlanta University,* December 1899, 1.
5. Webb, *The Basketball Man,* 57–67.
6. Naismith, *Basketball,* 57.
7. Spears, "Senda Berenson Abbot," 22–24.
8. Samuels, *Bernard Berenson,* 2–14. The subsequent description of Berenson's youth is drawn from this section as well.
9. Smith-Rosenberg, *Disorderly Conduct.*

10. *Charlotte Observer,* 7 April 1907, sec. 2, 23.
11. Samuels, *Bernard Berenson,* 87.
12. Berenson, "Basketball for Women," 97.
13. Larrabee, "Women and Cycling," 90. See also: Verbrugge, *Able-Bodied Womanhood,* 119–22.
14. Hill, "Senda Berenson," 659. The description of Homans is from Lee, *Memories of a Bloomer Girl,* 69–70.
15. Hill, "Senda Berenson," 659.
16. *San Francisco Chronicle,* 5 April 1896, 25.
17. Paul, "Clara Gregory Baer," 37–48; *Daily Picayune,* 14 March 1895, 3.
18. *Daily Picayune,* 14 March 1895, 3.
19. *Newcomb Arcade,* March 1913, 41, http://www.tulane.edu/~wc/arcade/ (accessed December 2003).
20. Emery and Toohey-Costa, "Hoops and Skirts," 141; Grundy, *Learning to Win,* 48; Lebsock, "Woman Suffrage and White Supremacy," 81.
21. *San Francisco Examiner,* 5 April 1896, 11; *San Francisco Chronicle,* 5 April 1896, 25; Lapp, "Mabel Craft Deering," 162–67.
22. *San Francisco Chronicle,* 5 April 1896, 25.
23. *Stanford Illustrated Review,* April 1924, 353.
24. For an account of Mosher's life, see Mary Roberts, "Clelia Duel Mosher— The Questioner." Folder 11, Box 1, Clelia Mosher Papers, Stanford University.
25. Summers, *Bound to Please,* esp. 87–119.
26. Mosher, *Health and the Woman Movement,* 29; Roberts, "Clelia Duel Mosher," 20.
27. *San Francisco Chronicle,* 10 April 1898, 32. This article does not bear Craft's byline, but the style is unmistakable. Information on other schools can be found in Emery and Toohey-Costa, "Hoops and Skirts," 139–40.
28. Lapp, "Mabel Craft Deering," 162.
29. *The Artemisia* (University of Nevada), 1900, 93.
30. *Stanford Alumnus,* January 1900, 93–94; *Student Record* (University of Nevada), 1 January 1900, 15.
31. Cashel, "History and Function of the Women's Athletic Association," 10–13.
32. Peavy and Smith, "World Champions," 22.
33. For accounts of the Carlisle team's endeavors, see Adams, *Education for Extinction,* 181–90; Oriard, *Reading Football,* 233–47.
34. Peavy and Smith, "World Champions," 2–3.
35. Mosher, *Health and the Woman Movement,* 10–11.
36. Berenson, "Significance of Basketball for Women," 33; Berenson, "Athletics for Women" [transcript], 20. Series 6, Senda Berenson Papers, Smith College.

37. For a fascinating account of the game's evolution, see Naismith, *Basketball,* 61–73.
38. Berenson, "Significance of Basketball for Women," 37; Beran, *Six-on-Six,* 27.
39. Baer, *Newcomb College Basket Ball Rules,* 5.
40. Paul, "Clara Gregory Baer," 42–48.
41. Cashel, "History and Function of the Women's Athletic Association," 14–18; Cahn, *Coming on Strong,* 23–27.
42. Grundy, *Learning to Win,* 230. Coleman was an early graduate of the Boston Normal School.
43. Lee, *Memories of a Bloomer Girl,* 45. Bloomers had been invented by women's rights activist Amelia Bloomer as an everyday costume. But they caused so much controversy that most women abandoned them, except for athletic wear. For Bloomer's description of the outfit and its reception, see Bloomer, *Life and Writings of Amelia Bloomer,* 65–81.
44. Grundy, *Learning to Win,* 62.
45. *The Scroll,* February 1902, 67.
46. Grundy, *Learning to Win,* 57; *San Francisco Chronicle,* 5 April 1896, 25.
47. *Stanford Alumnus,* June 1899, 4.
48. Lee, *Memories of a Bloomer Girl,* 348.
49. Ibid., 350.
50. Cahn, *Coming on Strong,* 7–9.
51. For portraits of some of these women, see Verbrugge, *Able-Bodied Womanhood,* 162–91. See also Hult, "Governance of Athletics for Girls and Women," 53–63; and Cahn, *Coming on Strong,* 100–101.

2: HIGH SCHOOL GIRLS SPUR THE SPORT

1. Beran, *Six-on-Six,* 26.
2. Grundy, *Learning to Win,* 70.
3. Cahn, *Coming on Strong,* 31–36; Pieroth, *Their Day in the Sun,* 2.
4. Zaharias, *This Life I've Led,* 28.
5. Ibid., 17, 26–27.
6. Cayleff, *Babe,* 39.
7. Zaharias, *This Life I've Led,* 14.
8. Ibid., 29.
9. Grundy, *Learning to Win,* 130–31.
10. Schwomeyer, *Hoosier HERsteria,* 209.
11. Cayleff, *Babe,* 39; Zaharias, *This Life I've Led,* 34.
12. For a detailed account of physical educators' nationwide efforts to suppress high school basketball, see Cahn, *Coming on Strong,* 55–109.
13. Beran, *Six-on-Six,* 30–31.
14. *Iowa Girls Basketball Yearbook 1948,* 31.

15. *The "H",* 1926. Folder 3, Box 3, Janice Beran Papers, Iowa Women's Archives.
16. Beran, *Six-on-Six,* 18, 37.
17. Ibid., 39.
18. Ibid., 46.
19. Because of the many variations in women's basketball rules, there is no single good source on the changes. A description of changes in the "official" rules published by the National Women's Basketball Committee (later the National Association for Girls and Women in Sports) can be found in Davenport, "Tides of Change," 83–108. A description of changes in the rules used by the AAU can be found in Ikard, *Just for Fun,* 40–41.
20. Offenburger, *E. Wayne Cooley,* 78; Beran, *Six-on-Six,* 40.
21. Offenburger, *E. Wayne Cooley,* 10, 73.
22. Beren, *Six-on-Six,* 55.
23. *Life,* 8 April 1940, 48; Beran, *Six-on-Six,* 60–62, 73–75.
24. Gems, "Blocked Shot," 141–42; Emery and Toohey-Costa, "Hoops and Skirts," 151–54; Dorothy Hom interview.
25. Emery and Toohey-Costa, "Hoops and Skirts," 151; Ikard, *Just for Fun,* 13–16.
26. Kirkpatrick and Perry, *Southern Textile Basketball Tournament,* 12.
27. Albertson, "Basketball Texas Style," 158–59; Beran, *Six-on-Six,* 156–57.
28. Zaharias, *This Life I've Led,* 3.
29. Wall, " 'We Always Loved to Play Basketball,' " 23.
30. Cayleff, *Babe,* 51; Zaharias, *This Life I've Led,* 39.
31. Cayleff, *Babe,* 51–54.
32. Zaharias, *This Life I've Led,* 41.
33. Cayleff, *Babe,* 64–72.
34. Cahn, *Coming on Strong,* 169–77.
35. *Vanity Fair,* October 1932, 36.
36. Ibid., 71; *Reader's Digest,* August 1936, 12–14. The original article appeared in *Vogue,* 15 June 1936.
37. Cayleff, *Babe,* 95.
38. Ibid., 91–92.

3: BLACK WOMEN EMBRACE THE GAME

1. *Philadelphia Tribune,* 7 April 1932, 10. In the absence of a national tournament to determine a national champion, prominent teams generally claimed their titles on the basis of overall records and opponents defeated.
2. Liberti, " 'We Were Ladies,' " 92. Much of the resurgence of interest in this era of black women's basketball is due to Liberti's pioneering research into the subject. This chapter would not have been possible without her efforts.
3. The Tribunes and the Hornets were covered regularly in the *Philadelphia Tribune.* See esp. 9 April 1931, 11; 14 January 1932, 11; 10 March 1931,

10; and coverage of the championship series in March and April 1932. For Inez Patterson, see Henderson, *Negro in Sports,* 211–15. Some of the dates in that account are inaccurate.

4. *Philadelphia Tribune,* 17 March 1932, 10. For accounts of the series games see ibid., 11 February 1932, 11; 7 April 1932, 10.

5. *Chicago Defender,* 12 March 1931. Information about Otto Briggs's baseball career can be found in Lanctot, *Fair Dealing.*

6. Dennis, *Century of Greatness,* 189.

7. U.S. Census of the Population, Caroline County, Va., 1910, E.D. 17, p. 5. For information on Caroline County, including descriptions of geography, rail connections, and African American communities, see Wingfield, *History of Caroline County,* 34–35, 167–75. Because Washington was born in an era when Virginia did not require birth certificates, her exact date of birth is unclear. On her Social Security account number application, submitted in 1943, she listed January 16, 1899. Application for Social Security Account Number 183204110, April 28, 1943.

8. U.S. Census of the Population, Philadelphia County, Pa., 1920, E.D. 632, p. 8. Sparse records make it difficult to determine the exact dates of many events in Washington's life. This description relies on recollections of Lenora Washington's son, J. Bernard Childs. See Childs interview. For a more detailed account of Washington's background and career, see Grundy, "Ora Washington."

9. Details in the following descriptions of Philadelphia's African American community are drawn from the rich material provided in Hardy, "Race and Opportunity," esp. 15–16, 41–59, 208–21.

10. Ibid., 441–46.

11. Felix, "Committed to Their Own," 128.

12. Young, *Negro Firsts in Sports,* 194. A number of details in Young's account of Washington's life are inaccurate, making it a problematic source. But the dates of Washington's tennis debut correspond with the death of Georgia Washington in Virginia, making this particular story seem credible.

13. For details on all of Washington's tennis titles, see Ashe, *Hard Road to Glory,* 448–49, 452–53, 455.

14. Ruth Glover Mullen interview (Liberti); *Chicago Defender,* 29 April 1933, 9. For descriptions of the tour, see *Philadelphia Tribune,* 22 March 1934, 10.

15. *Philadelphia Tribune,* 9 February 1933, 10; Liberti, " 'We Were Ladies,' " 89.

16. *Greensboro Daily News,* 9 March 1934, 12.

17. For a discussion of the expanding numbers of black high schools, see Anderson, *Education of Blacks in the South,* 202–3.

18. Alice Coachman Davis interview (Cahn).

19. Liberti, " 'We Were Ladies,' " 83–84.
20. Ibid., 83–86.
21. Alice Coachman Davis interview (Cahn).
22. Ruth Glover Mullen interview (Liberti); Amaleta Moore interview (Liberti); Liberti, " 'We Were Ladies,' " 87.
23. Amaleta Moore interview (Liberti).
24. Ashe, *Hard Road to Glory,* 45–48. For a description of the development of the Harlem Renaissance team, see Kuska, *Hot Potato,* 120–80.
25. Alice Coachman Davis interview (Cahn).
26. For a detailed description of the development of female track teams at black colleges, including the Tuskegee team, see Cahn, *Coming on Strong,* 117–25.
27. Sherman, *Lure and the Lore,* 125–26.
28. Alice Coachman Davis interview (Cahn).
29. Young, *Negro Firsts in Sports,* 195.
30. Alice Coachman Davis interview (Cahn). For a more detailed description of the dual worlds black athletes inhabited, see Cahn, *Coming on Strong,* 123–25.
31. Young, *Negro Firsts in Sports,* 195.

4: CROWNING NATIONAL CHAMPIONS

1. *Amateur Athlete,* May 1951, 7.
2. For a lively, comprehensive account of AAU play, including detailed descriptions of many teams and tournaments, see Ikard, *Just for Fun.*
3. The AAU was not consistent in the number of All-Americans it chose or on the separation into first and second teams. With the exception of Hazel Walker, who always included her three second-team designations in her All-American totals, only first-team designations are counted in assessing the number of times an individual received an award. For full rosters of All-Americans, see Ikard, *Just for Fun,* 201–14. Alline Banks also appears in records as Alline Banks Pate and Alline Banks Sprouse. Margaret Sexton is Margaret Sexton Petty and Margaret Sexton Gleaves.
4. Undated clipping, Alline Banks Sullivan Award Nomination Scrapbook, Women's Basketball Hall of Fame.
5. Ikard, *Just for Fun,* 53–58.
6. Following the 1946 championship, Alline Banks and Doris Weems left the Goldblumes for the Atlanta Sports Arena Blues. In 1947 and 1948, the Goldblumes and the Blues met in the AAU finals—the Blues won in 1947 and the Goldblumes in 1948. Ikard, *Just for Fun,* 59–64.
7. Bishop and Fulton, "Shooting Stars," 51. Information on Hanes can also be found in Grundy, *Learning to Win,* 145–52. For a comprehensive account of the Southern Association Textile Tournament, see Kirkpatrick and Perry,

Southern Textile Basketball Tournament. For an account of another top textile team, Chatham Manufacturing, see Wall, " 'We Always Loved to Play Basketball.' "

8. *Amateur Athlete,* April 1953, 25. For a description of the rules changes see Ikard, *Just for Fun,* 40–41, 63.

9. Bishop, "Amateur Athletic Union," 15.

10. *Chicago Defender,* 9 April 1921, 11.

11. Bishop, *Road to Respect.*

12. Ikard, *Just for Fun,* 96–103, 129, 186–88.

13. For details about the Wayland Flying Queens' early years, see Redin, *Queens Fly High,* 9–17. For basketball at Iowa Wesleyan, see Beran, *Six-on-Six,* 155–56.

14. Neal, *Basketballs, Goldfish and World Championships,* 50.

15. *Tennessean,* 10 May 1982, sec. C, 6. For a longer description of White and her career, see Ikard, *Just for Fun,* 135–46.

16. *Tennessean,* 10 May 1982, sec. C, 6.

17. Ibid.

18. Redin, *Queens Fly High,* 172.

19. All of Hazel Walker's quotes and much of the information in this section come from Gary Newton, "Hazel Walker: Miss Basketball," Hazel Walker Nomination, Women's Basketball Hall of Fame. We are indebted to Newton for his painstaking work on Walker's history.

20. For a description of the Redheads, see Ford, *Lady Hoopsters,* 95–103. For the Globetrotters and the Renaissance, see George, *Elevating the Game,* 33–56. More information on the Renaissance can be found in Kuska, *Hot Potato,* 120–80.

21. West Virginia Sports on the Net, http://www.sportsmediainc.net/wvspn/index.cfm?func=showarticle&newsid=41 (accessed August 2003).

22. Ibid.; Bishop, *Road to Respect.*

23. Bishop, *Road to Respect.*

5: A MAN'S GAME

1. Nadler, "Developmental History," 80. The following description is from pp. 79–84.

2. The statement, by University of Southern California coach Sam Barry, is quoted in McCallum, *College Basketball, U.S.A.,* 62.

3. Radar, *American Sports,* 270.

4. Wall, " 'We Always Loved to Play Basketball,' " 39.

5. For a fascinating and wide-ranging analysis of these social shifts, see May, *Homeward Bound.*

6. *Philadelphia Tribune,* 9 February 1933, 10; undated clipping, Eunies Futch scrapbook, book 3, p. 2, Women's Basketball Hall of Fame.

7. Sherman, *Lure and the Lore,* 122.

8. *Amateur Athlete,* September 1954, 10.

9. Undated clipping, Alline Banks Sullivan Award Nomination Scrapbook, Women's Basketball Hall of Fame.

10. Fanny Holdar Rendtorff to Hazel Walker Nominating Committee, 20 June 1996; Mala Hill Waller to Nominating Committee, 19 July 1996. Both in Hazel Walker Nomination, Women's Basketball Hall of Fame.

11. For a thoughtful analysis of this "apologetic" behavior and its implications, see Festle, *Playing Nice,* 45–52. For Nera White. see Sherman, *Lure and the Lore,* 123.

12. This argument comes from the thoughtful and expansive examination of the issue in Cahn, *Coming on Strong,* 164–84.

13. Festle, *Playing Nice,* 22.

14. *Clark Panther,* 30 April 1951, 9. Copy located in Robert W. Woodruff Library, Atlanta University. Bennett College, which had fielded such dominant teams in the 1930s, had taken this step even earlier. Bennett held its first play day in 1940. It dropped varsity competition soon afterward. Grundy, *Learning to Win,* 234–39.

15. Grundy, *Learning to Win,* 239. A more detailed account of the debate over the tournament, as well as its demise, can be found on pp. 239–41.

16. *Greensboro Daily News,* 11 April 1952, sec. 4, 4.

17. *Greensboro Daily News,* 18 March 1951, 7.

18. Grundy, *Learning to Win,* 245–54; Adams and Betts, *Cheerleader!* 111–22.

6: KEEPING THE FLAME ALIVE

1. Festle, *Playing Nice,* 98. A discussion of federal efforts to encourage sports, as well as the Cold War politics that inspired them, can be found on pp. 83–97.

2. Ibid., 105–7; Carson, *In Struggle,* 147–48.

3. For a vivid description of the movement and its events, see Brownmiller, *In Our Time.*

4. Pierce, *"Let Me Tell You What I've Learned,"* 51.

5. *Sports Illustrated: Sport/Women,* Spring 1997, 99–100.

6. "About Women on Campus," Spring 1997 (newsletter of the National Association of Women in Education), http://www.bernicesandler.com/id44 .htm (accessed November 2003).

7. Ibid.

8. *Honolulu Advertiser,* 29 September 2002.

9. *Chronicle of Higher Education,* 21 June 2002, sec. A, 38.

10. Title IX of the Education Amendments of 1972 (discrimination based on sex or blindness), 20 U.S. Code, §§1681–1688 (1994), www.ed.gov/pubs.

11. Bunny Sandler e-mail communication to Susan Shackelford, 4 January

2005. Welch Suggs e-mail communication to Susan Shackelford, 28 April 2004.

12. "About Women on Campus," Spring 1997, http://www.bernicesandler.com/id44.htm.

7: THE FIGHT FOR TITLE IX

1. *Ms.*, December 2002/January 2003, http://www.mariahburtonnelson.com/Articles/WomenSportsMsTitleIX.html (accessed May 2004).
2. Summitt, *Reach for the Summitt,* 21–23.
3. *Chronicle of Higher Education,* 21 June 2002, A38.
4. For expenditure figures, see Cahn, *Coming on Strong,* 250.
5. Festle, *Playing Nice,* 127–28.
6. Ibid., 131.
7. Ibid., 131–33.
8. Title IX of the Education Amendments of 1972, 34 Code of Federal Regulations §§106.1–106.71 (1988). (Nondiscrimination on the basis of sex in education programs or activities receiving federal financial assistance). Specifics on athletics are in 106.41. HEW would issue an additional policy interpretation on December 11, 1979.
9. Summitt, *Reach for the Summitt,* 11–12.
10. Schwomeyer, *Hoosier HERsteria,* 288.
11. VanDerveer, *Shooting from the Outside,* 31.
12. Ibid., 73.
13. *College Park Magazine,* Summer 2002, http://www.inform.umd.edu/cpmag/summer02/inbounds.html (accessed September 2004).
14. Ibid.
15. VanDerveer, *Shooting from the Outside,* 68–69. Hutchison, "Women's Intercollegiate Basketball," 309–11.
16. For a comprehensive account of basketball at Immaculata, see Byrne, *O God of Players.*
17. Ibid., 184.
18. *Scholastic Coach and Athletic Director,* March 1997, 76.
19. Walters, *Same River Twice,* 212.
20. *New Orleans Times-Picayune,* 6 April 2004; Byrne, *O God of Players,* 194.
21. *New Orleans Times-Picayune,* 6 April 2004.
22. Byrne, *O God of Players,* 174–75.
23. Hutchison, "Women's Intercollegiate Basketball," 314.
24. Trekell and Gershon, "Title IX, AIAW, and Beyond," 405. For an overview of Wade's career, see *Coaching Women's Basketball,* March/April 1997, 14–19.
25. For the civil rights movement in Greenwood, see Payne, *I've Got the Light of Freedom,* 132–79; for the Mississippi State incident, see Henderson, "Mississippi State University Basketball Controversy."

26. *Coaching Women's Basketball,* March/April 1997, 19.

27. O.W. Reily Jr. interview.

28. *Sports Illustrated,* 5 April 1976, 50.

29. Ibid.; *Sports Illustrated,* 4 April 1977, 59.

30. Kyvallos, "Queens College," 361.

31. For an overview of international play, see Ikard, *Just for Fun,* 95–103, 147–53.

32. *Coaching Women's Basketball,* March/April 1997, 22; *Basketball Quarterly,* 2004, http://www.abqmag.com/magazine/2004/1st_Quarter/w_summit.php (accessed September 2004).

33. *Sports Illustrated,* 18 August 1976, 35; *Coaching Women's Basketball,* March/April 1997, 21.

34. Kyvallos, "Queens College," 365.

35. *Chronicle of Higher Education,* 21 June 2002, sec. A, 38.

36. Lannin, *History of Basketball,* 89; Festle, *Playing Nice,* 249.

8: GROWING PAINS

1. Lieberman-Cline, *Lady Magic,* 28.

2. Ibid., 15.

3. Ibid.

4. Ibid., 33.

5. *Atlanta Journal-Constitution,* 6 April 2003, D1.

6. *Sports Illustrated,* 3 December 1979, 106.

7. *Sports Illustrated,* 31 March 1980, 14–15.

8. Lieberman-Cline, *Lady Magic,* 78.

9. *Commonwealth: The Magazine of Virginia,* April 1983, 49.

10. Festle, *Playing Nice,* 122–23.

11. Ibid., 199–207. Starting in 1975, the NCAA made several offers to absorb the AIAW, but was rebuffed.

12. Ibid., 203, 209.

13. Ibid., 210.

14. *Lady Vols Contenders,* 2002–03 Tennessee Lady Volunteers media guide, 206; Festle, *Playing Nice,* 210.

15. Festle, *Playing Nice,* 211–14.

16. Ibid., 215.

17. *Sports Illustrated,* 11 April 1988, 41.

18. *Sports Illustrated,* 8 April 1985, 90.

19. *Scholastic Coach and Athletic Director,* March 1997, 76; Byrne, *O God of Players,* 201–3; Walters, *Same River Twice,* 214.

20. Festle, *Playing Nice,* 248–52.

21. Lieberman-Cline, *Lady Magic,* 108–10.

22. Nelson, "Paid to Play a Game," 92; Festle, *Playing Nice,* 254–58.

23. *Sports Illustrated,* 6 April 1981, 33–34.

24. Ibid.

25. Nelson, "Paid to Play a Game," 91.

26. Ibid., 93.

27. For a detailed account of the league's struggles, see Festle, *Playing Nice,* 252–64. Festle offers an especially thoughtful description of the league's double bind. For a comprehensive account of WBL history, see Porter, *Mad Seasons.*

28. *Ruston* (La.) *Daily Leader,* 14 January 2003.

29. For the "momma" quote see *New York Times,* 30 March 1984, sec. A, 24; Lieberman-Cline, *Lady Magic,* 92–93.

30. *Women's Basketball Hall of Fame 2003 Induction Ceremony,* videotape, Women's Basketball Hall of Fame, 2003.

31. *Sports Illustrated,* 19 November 1986, 112; *Women's Basketball Hall of Fame 2003 Induction Ceremony.*

32. *Sports Illustrated,* 19 November 1986, 110.

9: DAZZLING MOVES, SPINNING WHEELS

1. *Sports Illustrated,* 11 April 1983, 24–25.

2. Ibid., 24.

3. For a description of the McGees' background, see *Sports Illustrated,* 22 February 1982, 35.

4. Cooper, *She Got Game,* 45.

5. Ibid., 72.

6. *Sports Illustrated,* 11 April 1983, 25; Cooper, *She Got Game,* 100.

7. Cooper, *She Got Game,* 74; *Sports Illustrated,* 9 April 1984, 46–48.

8. *Sports Illustrated,* 22 February 1982, 35.

9. *Sports Illustrated,* 9 April 1984, 48.

10. Ford, *Lady Hoopsters,* 131.

11. Cooper, *She Got Game,* 58, 83.

12. Festle, *Playing Nice,* 216–19.

13. Ibid., 196–97

14. Ibid., 196.

15. For a brief discussion of civil rights law, see "Civil Rights: An Overview," http://www.law.cornell.edu/topics/civil_rights.html (accessed January 2005).

16. Festle, *Playing Nice,* 220–22.

17. *Coaching Women's Basketball,* March/April 1998, 13–14.

18. Pierce, *"Let Me Tell You,"* 47; *New York Times,* 15 April 1990, sec. 10, 3.

19. Pierce, *"Let Me Tell You,"* 46.

20. *Sports Illustrated,* 17 December 1990, 80.

21. Ibid., 80, 82.

22. *Sports Illustrated,* 7 April 1986, 94.

23. Pierce, *"Let Me Tell You,"* 48–50.
24. *Sports Illustrated,* 7 April 1986, 95.
25. Festle, *Playing Nice,* 278. The Grove City case had an effect well beyond Title IX—the reasoning that the Supreme Court adopted had also undercut a wide range of other federal mandates, including civil rights measures. The Restoration Act thus covered a wide range of federal programs.
26. *Austin Chronicle,* 18 September 1998, http://www.austinchronicle.com/issues/vol18/issue03/pols.UTcoach.html (accessed November 2004).
27. VanDerveer, *Shooting from the Outside,* 104; *New York Times,* 15 April 1990, sec. 10, 3.
28. VanDerveer, *Shooting from the Outside,* 104; *New York Times,* 30 March 1990, sec. A, 26; *New York Times,* 6 April 1990, sec. A, 27.
29. *New York Times,* 15 April 1990, sec. 10, 3.
30. *Chronicle of Higher Education,* 23 October 1991, sec. A, 38.
31. The suit was *Franklin v. Gwinnett County Public Schools.* See *Chronicle of Higher Education,* 21 June 2002, sec. A, 38.
32. Tyler's remarks come from a White House–sponsored roundtable on equal pay, held 7 April 1999. See http://clinton4.nara.gov/WH/New/html/19990407-4101.html (accessed September 2004).
33. *Austin Chronicle,* 18 September 1998.
34. *Chronicle of Higher Education,* 28 July 1993, sec. A, 33.
35. For a brief summary of the case, see "Appellate Decisions Noted," July 1999, http://www.appellate-counsellor.com/newsletter/9907.htm#Stanley (accessed October 2004). The case was Stanley v. University of Southern California, 1999 WL 346615 (9th Cir. June 2, 1999).
36. Kessler, *Full Court Press,* 294–301.

10: MARSHALING MOMENTUM

1. VanDerveer, *Shooting from the Outside,* 249.
2. For a more detailed description of Swoopes and her career, see Corbett, *Venus to the Hoop,* 1–8.
3. Strasser and Becklund, *Swoosh,* 534–40.
4. For an assessment of factors influencing the game's development, including an account of UConn's rise, see *New Orleans Times-Picayune,* 4 April 2004.
5. Corbett, *Venus to the Hoop,* 45.
6. Detailed and insightful accounts of the Olympic team's organization, as well as its year of competition can be found in Corbett, *Venus to the Hoop.*
7. VanDerveer, *Shooting from the Outside,* 11.
8. Corbett, *Venus to the Hoop,* 59–63.
9. Ibid., 213; *Philadelphia Daily News,* 9 July 2004, 138.
10. *Women's Basketball,* July/August 2002, 18–20; VanDerveer, *Shooting from the Outside,* 14.

11. Corbett, *Venus to the Hoop,* 207–8, 261–62.

12. Ibid., 245.

13. *Creative Loafing,* 27 February 1999, 21.

14. Ford, *Lady Hoopsters,* 147.

15. *USA Today,* 20 June 1997, sec. E, 1–10; *New York Times Magazine,* 16 August 1998, 42–65.

16. Cooper, *She Got Game,* 194, 205–6; Savage, *Nothin' But a Champion,* 160–65.

17. *Creative Loafing,* 27 February 1999, 21–25.

18. Ibid., 21.

19. *San Jose Mercury News,* 24 January 1999, D1.

20. *Washington Post,* 16 July 2002, D1.

21. *Sports Illustrated,* 22 September 2003, 19.

22. *New Orleans Times-Picayune,* 4 April 2004.

23. Summitt, *Reach for the Summitt,* 156–58.

24. Ibid.; Summitt, *Raise the Roof,* 15, 280.

25. Summitt, *Reach for the Summitt,* 115–16, 239; *Philly's Final Four,* 81.

26. *New York Times,* 9 January 1996 43; Summitt, *Reach for the Summitt,* 51; *New York Times,* 9 January 1996, 43.

27. Summitt, *Raise the Roof,* 46.

28. *New York Times,* 26 March 1998, 1; Summitt, *Raise the Roof,* 56; *Sports Illustrated,* 2 March 1998, 92.

29. *New York Times,* 26 March 1998, 1; Summitt, *Raise the Roof,* 281.

30. Summitt, *Raise the Roof,* 280.

31. *New York Times,* 24 February 1998, C3.

32. *New York Times,* 18 March 2002, D1.

33. Ibid.; *Hartford Courant,* 17 November 2003.

34. *Philly's Final Four,* 63, 66.

35. *New York Times,* 18 April 2004, sec. 14, 1.

36. Ibid.

37. *Sports Illustrated,* 8 April 2002, 46; *New York Times,* 20 March 2002, sec. D, 3.

38. *Hartford Courant,* 17 November 2003.

39. Walters, *Same River Twice,* 83, 91, 32.

40. Ibid., 182; Page 2, *ESPN.com,* 2 January 2001, http://espn.go.com/page2/s/rizzotti/010201.html (accessed November 2004).

41. *Sports Illustrated,* 8 April 2002, 44–47.

42. Walters, *Same River Twice,* 185; *New Yorker,* 8 March 2004, 42.

43. *Sports Illustrated,* 24 November 2003, 126.

44. *New Yorker,* 8 March 2004, 46.

45. *Philadelphia Inquirer,* 29 August 2004, sec. D, 1.

46. *Indianapolis Star,* 26 August 2004.

47. *Women's Basketball,* December 2004, 12; *Philadelphia Inquirer,* 29 August 2004, sec. D, 1.

48. *Newsday,* 26 August 2004, sec. A, 47.

CONCLUSION: SHATTERING THE GLASS

1. *Chronicle of Higher Education,* 14 June 2004, sec. A, 1; *News and Observer* (Raleigh, N.C.), 5 July 2001; John Maxwell e-mail communication to Susan Shackelford, 25 October 2004.

2. VanDerveer, *Shooting from the Outside,* 60; *This Is Who I Am,* http://www.wnba.com/features/this_is_who_i_am_2004.html (accessed October 2004).

3. *NCAA News,* 8 October 2001, http://www.ncaa.org/news/2001/20011008/active/3821n03.html (accessed January 2005).

4. *Philadelphia News,* 9 July 2004, 138.

5. For a fascinating analysis of the ways gender plays out in American sporting rituals, see Messner, *Taking the Field.*

6. *Seattle Post-Intelligencer,* 22 June 2004, http://seattlepi.nwsource.com/wnba/178960_storm22.html (accessed October 2004).

7. *New Yorker,* 8 March 2004, 46.

8. VanDerveer, *Shooting from the Outside,* 141.

BIBLIOGRAPHY

INTERVIEWS

Note: Because the text refers to the maiden names of many of the women interviewed, the interviews are alphabetized by first name. Unless otherwise noted, interview tapes are in the possession of the interviewer.

Alice Coachman Davis. Interview by Susan Cahn, 7 April 1992, Tuskegee, Ala.

Alice Coachman Davis. Interview by Pamela Grundy (with Lula Hymes Glenn), 26 February 2004, Tuskegee, Ala. Southern Historical Collection, Wilson Library, University of North Carolina, Chapel Hill, N.C.

Alice "Cookie" Barron. Interview by Pamela Grundy (with Carla Lowry, Kaye Garmes, Lee Ann Waddell South and Margie Hunt McDonald), 10 May 2003, Knoxville, Tenn. Southern Historical Collection, Wilson Library, University of North Carolina, Chapel Hill, N.C.

Alline Banks Sprouse. Interview by Pamela Grundy, 9 May 2003, Knoxville, Tenn. Southern Historical Collection, Wilson Library, University of North Carolina, Chapel Hill, N.C.

Amaleta Moore. Interview by Rita Liberti (with Ruth Glover Mullen), 30 July 1995, West Cape May, N.J.

Amaleta Moore. Interview by Pamela Grundy (with Ruth Glover Mullen), 7 October 2003, West Cape May, N.J. Southern Historical Collection, Wilson Library, University of North Carolina, Chapel Hill, N.C.

Anne Donovan. Interview by Susan Shackelford, 30 July 2003, Seattle, Wash.

Betty Jaynes. Interview by Susan Shackelford, 1 December 2003, Lilburn, Ga.

Betty Peele. Interview by Susan Shackelford, 23 June 2004, telephone.

Betty Westmoreland Suhre. Interview by Susan Shackelford, 25 June 2004, telephone.

Bill Bost. Interview by Pamela Grundy, 15 March 1993, Catawba, N.C. Special Collections, J. Murray Atkins Library, University of North Carolina, Charlotte, N.C.

Bill Laimbeer. Interview by Susan Shackelford, 4 September 2004, Charlotte, N.C.

Birch Bayh. Interviews by Susan Shackelford, 10 and 13 March 2003, telephone.

Carla Lowry. Interview by Pamela Grundy (with Alice "Cookie" Barron, Kaye Garmes, Lee Ann Waddell South and Margie Hunt McDonald), 10 May 2003, Knoxville, Tenn. Southern Historical Collection, Wilson Library, University of North Carolina, Chapel Hill, N.C.

Carrie Graf. Interview by Susan Shackelford, 1 July 2004, Charlotte, N.C.

Chris Weller. Interviews by Susan Shackelford, 6 and 18 March 2004, Greensboro, N.C., and telephone.

Christine Grant. Interview by Susan Shackelford, 26 November 2003, telephone.

Dawn Staley. Interviews by Susan Shackelford, 12 August 2003 and 4 September 2004, Charlotte, N.C.

Debbie Ryan. Interviews by Susan Shackelford, 29 October 2003 and 6 March 2004, Greensboro, N.C.

Diana Taurasi. Interview by Susan Shackelford, 1 July 2004, Charlotte, N.C.

Donna Lopiano. Interview by Susan Shackelford, 18 July 2003, New York, N.Y.

Doris Coleman Guillory. Interview by Pamela Grundy, 22 June 2003, telephone.

Dorothy Hom. Interview by Pamela Grundy, 19 January 2005, telephone.

Eckie Jordan. Interview by Susan Cahn (with Eunies Futch), 18 July 1988, Winston-Salem, N.C.

Elizabeth Stratford Newitt. Interview by Pamela Grundy and Peter Felkner, 7 December 1992, Charlotte, N.C. Special Collections, J. Murray Atkins Library, University of North Carolina, Charlotte, N.C.

Eunies Futch. Interview by Susan Cahn (with Eckie Jordan), 18 July 1988, Winston-Salem, N.C.

F. Jay Taylor. Interview by Susan Shackelford, 24 August 2004, telephone.

Harley Redin. Interview by Pamela Grundy, 10 May 2003, Knoxville, Tenn. Southern Historical Collection, Wilson Library, University of North Carolina, Chapel Hill, N.C.

J. Bernard Childs. Interview by Pamela Grundy, 31 July 2003, telephone.

Jenny Boucek. Interview by Susan Shackelford, 6 March 2004, Greensboro, N.C.

Jerry Murphy. Interview by Susan Shackelford, 29 October 2004, telephone.

Jim Jarrett. Interview by Susan Shackelford, 23 August 2004, telephone.

Joan Crawford. Interview by Pamela Grundy, 10 May 2003, Knoxville, Tenn. Southern Historical Collection, Wilson Library, University of North Carolina, Chapel Hill, N.C.

Judy Rose. Interview by Pamela Grundy, 19 April 1993, Charlotte, N.C. Special Collections, J. Murray Atkins Library, University of North Carolina, Charlotte, N.C.

Katie Meier. Interview by Susan Shackelford, 22 June 2004, Charlotte, N.C.

Kay Yow. Interview by Susan Shackelford, 8 September 2003, Raleigh, N.C.

Kaye Garmes. Interview by Pamela Grundy (with Alice "Cookie" Barron, Carla Lowry, Lee Ann Waddell South and Margie Hunt McDonald), 10 May 2003, Knoxville, Tenn. Southern Historical Collection, Wilson Library, University of North Carolina, Chapel Hill, N.C.

Lee Ann Waddell South. Interview by Pamela Grundy (with Alice "Cookie" Barron, Carla Lowry, Kaye Garmes and Margie Hunt McDonald), 10 May 2003, Knoxville, Tenn. Southern Historical Collection, Wilson Library, University of North Carolina, Chapel Hill, N.C.

Leila Perry Glover. Interview by Susan Cahn, 8 April 1992, Atlanta, Ga.

Leon Barmore. Interview by Susan Shackelford, 16 August 2004, telephone.

Lewis Hill. Interview by Pamela Grundy, 9 August 2003, telephone.

Lucille Townsend. Interview by Rita Liberti, 6 August 1995, Richmond, Va.

Lula Hymes Glenn. Interview by Pamela Grundy (with Alice Coachman Davis), 26 February 2004, Tuskegee, Ala. Southern Historical Collection, Wilson Library, University of North Carolina, Chapel Hill, N.C.

Lusia Harris-Stewart. Interview by Georgene Clark, 18 December 1999, Greenwood, Miss. Center for Oral History and Cultural Heritage, University of Southern Mississippi, Hattiesburg, Miss.

Margaret Sexton Gleaves. Interview by Susan Cahn, 6 July 1988, Nashville, Tenn.

Margie Hunt McDonald. Interview by Pamela Grundy (with Alice "Cookie" Barron, Carla Lowry, Kaye Garmes and Lee Ann Waddell South), 10 May 2003, Knoxville, Tenn. Southern Historical Collection, Wilson Library, University of North Carolina, Chapel Hill, N.C.

Mariah Burton Nelson. Interview by Susan Shackelford, 22 January 2004, telephone.

Mary Alyce Alexander Clemmons. Interview by Pamela Grundy, 2 September 1993, Charlotte, N.C. Special Collections, J. Murray Atkins Library, University of North Carolina, Charlotte, N.C.

Mary Donovan Grabb. Interview by Susan Shackelford, 30 September 2003, telephone.

Melissa Miles. Interview by Susan Shackelford, 11 January 2004, Charlotte, N.C.

Mildred Little Bauguess. Interview by Pamela Grundy, 14 May 1993, Claremont, N.C. Special Collections, J. Murray Atkins Library, University of North Carolina, Charlotte, N.C.

Missouri Arledge Morris. Interview by Pamela Grundy, 16 March 2004, Durham, N.C.

Nancy Lieberman. Interview by Susan Shackelford, 27 February 2004, telephone.

O.W. Reily Jr. Interview by Perry Barrett, 19 August 1999, Cleveland, Miss. Center for Oral History and Cultural Heritage, University of Southern Mississippi, Hattiesburg, Miss.

Patsy Neal. Interview by Susan Shackelford, 17 December 2003, telephone.

Paula McGee. Interview by Pamela Grundy, 20 October 2004, telephone.

Rebecca Lobo. Interview by Susan Shackelford, 20 April 2004, telephone.

Rose Marie Battaglia. Interview by Susan Shackelford, 13 February 2004, telephone.

Ruth Glover Mullen. Interview by Rita Liberti (with Amaleta Moore), 30 July 1995, West Cape May, N.J.

Ruth Glover Mullen. Interview by Pamela Grundy (with Amaleta Moore), 7 October 2003, West Cape May, N.J. Southern Historical Collection, Wilson Library, University of North Carolina, Chapel Hill, N.C.

Ruth Riley. Interview by Susan Shackelford, 4 September 2004, Charlotte, N.C.

Sheryl Swoopes. Interview by Susan Shackelford, 21 May 2004, Charlotte, N.C.

Sue Gunter. Interview by Pamela Grundy, 10 May 2003, Knoxville, Tenn.

Swin Cash. Interview by Susan Shackelford, 4 September 2004, Charlotte, N.C.

Trudi Lacey. Interview by Susan Shackelford, 21 January 2004, Charlotte, N.C.

Val Ackerman. Interview by Susan Shackelford, 10 March 2004, Charlotte, N.C.

Vivian Stringer. Interview by Susan Shackelford, 28 January 2004, telephone.

Vivian Stringer. Interview by Pamela Grundy, 3 November 2004, telephone.

MANUSCRIPT COLLECTIONS

Robert W. Woodruff Library, Atlanta University Center, Atlanta, Ga.

Jan Beran Papers, Iowa Women's Archives, University of Iowa Archives, University of Iowa, Iowa City, Iowa.

Scrapbook Collection, Hazel Walker Nomination, Women's Basketball Hall of Fame, Knoxville, Tenn.

Senda Berenson Papers, College Archives, Smith College, http://clio.fivecolleges.edu/smith/berenson/, Northampton, Mass.

Clelia Mosher Papers, Department of Special Collections, Stanford University, Palo Alto, Calif.

SECONDARY REFERENCES

Adams, David Wallace. *Education for Extinction: American Indians and the Boarding School Experience, 1875–1928.* Lawrence: University Press of Kansas, 1995.

Adams, Natalie Guice, and Pamela J. Betts, *Cheerleader! An American Icon.* New York: Palgrave MacMillan, 2003.

Albertson, Roxanne M. "Basketball Texas Style, 1910–1933: School to Industrial League Competion." In Hult and Trekell, *A Century of Women's Basketball,* 155–66.

Anderson, James. *The Education of Blacks in the South, 1860–1935.* Chapel Hill: University of North Carolina Press, 1988.

Ashe, Arthur R., Jr. *A Hard Road to Glory: A History of the African-American Athlete. Vol. 2, 1919–1945.* New York: Amistad Press, 1993.

Baer, Clara Gregory, ed. *Newcomb College Basket Ball Rules for Girls and Women.* New Orleans: Tulane Press, 1911.

Beran, Janice. *From Six-on-Six to Full Court Press: A Century of Iowa Girls' Basketball.* Ames: Iowa State University Press, 1993.

Berenson, Senda. "The Significance of Basketball for Women." In *Basketball for Women,* edited by Senda Berenson, 31–45. New York: American Sports, 1903.

Bishop, Elva E. "Amateur Athletic Union Women's Basketball, 1950–1971: The Contributions of Hanes Hosiery, Nashville Business College, and Wayland Baptist College." M.A. thesis, University of North Carolina at Chapel Hill, 1984.

Bishop, Elva E., and Katherine Fulton. "Shooting Stars: The Heyday of Industrial Women's Basketball." *Southern Exposure* 7 (Fall 1979): 50–54.

Bishop, Elva E., prod. *Women's Basketball: The Road to Respect.* University of North Carolina Public Television, 1997.

Bloomer, D.C. *Life and Writings of Amelia Bloomer.* St. Clair Shores, Mich.: Scholarly Press, 1976.

Brownmiller, Susan. *In Our Time: Memoir of a Revolution.* New York: Dial Press, 1999.

Byrne, Julie. *O God of Players: The Story of the Immaculata Mighty Macs.* New York: Columbia University Press, 2003.

Cahn, Susan. *Coming on Strong: Gender and Sexuality in Twentieth-Century Women's Sport.* New York: Free Press, 1994.

Carson, Clayborne. *In Struggle: SNCC and the Black Awakening of the 1960s.* Cambridge, Mass.: Harvard University Press, 1981.

Cashel, Patricia. "History and Function of the Women's Athletic Association at Stanford University." M.A. thesis, Stanford University, 1946.

Cayleff, Susan E. *Babe: The Life and Legend of Babe Didrikson Zaharias.* Urbana: University of Illinois Press, 1996.

Cooper, Cynthia, with Russ Pate. *She Got Game: My Personal Odyssey.* New York: Warner Books, 1999.

Corbett, Sara. *Venus to the Hoop: A Gold Medal Year in Women's Basketball.* New York: Anchor Books, 1998.

Davenport, Joanna. "The Tides of Change in Women's Basketball Rules." In Hult and Trekell, *A Century of Women's Basketball,* 83–108.

Dennis, Denise. *A Century of Greatness, 1900–1999: The Urban League of Philadelphia's Tribute to the Outstanding African-American Philadelphians of the Twentieth Century.* Philadelphia: Urban League of Philadelphia, 2002.

Emery, Lynne Fauley, and Margaret Toohey-Costa. "Hoops and Skirts: Women's Basketball on the West Coast, 1892–1930s." In Hult and Trekell, *A Century of Women's Basketball,* 137–54.

Felix, Stephanie Yvette. "Committed to Their Own: African American Women Leaders in the YWCA of Germantown, Philadelphia, Pennsylvania, 1870–1970." Ph.D. diss., Temple University, 1999.

Festle, Mary Jo. *Playing Nice: Politics and Apologies in Women's Sports.* New York: Columbia University Press, 1996.

Ford, Linda. *Lady Hoopsters: A History of Women's Basketball in America.* Northampton, Mass.: Half Moon Books, 2000.

Gems, Gerald R. "Blocked Shot: The Development of Basketball in the African-American Community of Chicago." *Journal of Sport History* 22 (Summer 1995): 135–48.

George, Nelson. *Elevating the Game: The History and Aesthetics of Black Men in Basketball.* New York: Simon & Schuster, 1992.

Griffin, Pat. *Strong Women, Deep Closets: Lesbians and Homophobia in Sport.* Champaign, Ill.: Human Kinetics, 1998.

Grundy, Pamela. *Learning to Win: Sports, Education and Social Change in Twentieth-Century North Carolina.* Chapel Hill: University of North Carolina Press, 2001.

———. "Ora Washington: The First Black Female Star." In *Sport and the Racial Mountain,* edited by David Wiggins. Fayetteville: University of Arkansas Press, forthcoming.

Hardy, Charles Ashley. "Race and Opportunity: Black Philadelphia During the Era of the Great Migration, 1916–1930." Ph.D. diss., Temple University, 1989.

Henderson, Edwin Bancroft. *The Negro in Sports.* Revised edition. Washington, D.C.: Associated Publishers, 1949.

Henderson, Russell J. "The 1963 Mississippi State University Basketball Controversy and the Repeal of the Unwritten Law: 'Something more than the game will be lost.'" *Journal of Southern History* LXIII (November 1997): 827–54.

Hill, Edith Naomi. "Senda Berenson: Director of Physical Education at Smith College, 1892–1911." In "Pioneer Women in Physical Education." Supplement to *The Research Quarterly*. Washington, D.C.: American Association for Health, Physical Education, and Recreation, October 1941.

Hult, Joan S. "The Governance of Athletics for Girls and Women: Leadership by Women Physical Educators, 1899–1949." In Hult and Trekell, *A Century of Women's Basketball*, 53–82.

Hult, Joan S. and Marianna Trekell, eds. *A Century of Women's Basketball: From Frailty to Final Four*. Reston, Va.: American Alliance for Health, Physical Education, Recreation and Dance, 1991.

Hutchison, Jill. "Women's Intercollegiate Basketball: AIAW/NCAA." In Hult and Trekell, *A Century of Women's Basketball*, 309–34.

Ikard, Robert W. *Just for Fun: The Story of AAU Women's Basketball*. Fayetteville: University of Arkansas Press, 2005.

Kessler, Lauren. *Full Court Press: A Season in the Life of a Winning Basketball Team and the Women Who Made It Happen*. New York: Penguin, 1997.

Kirkpatrick, Mac C., and Thomas K. Perry. *The Southern Textile Basketball Tournament*. Jefferson, N.C.: McFarland Company, 1997.

Kuska, Bob. *Hot Potato: How Washington and New York Gave Birth to Black Basketball and Changed America's Game Forever*. Charlottesville: University of Virginia Press, 2004.

Kyvallos, Lucille. "Queens College: Success with No Frills." In Hult and Trekell, *A Century of Women's Basketball*, 355–66.

Lanctot, Neil. *Fair Dealing and Clean Playing: The Hilldale Club and the Development of Black Professional Baseball, 1910–1932*. Jefferson, N.C.: McFarland Company, 1994.

Lannin, Joanne. *A History of Basketball for Girls and Women: From Bloomers to Big Leagues*. Minneapolis: First Avenue Editions, 2000.

Lapp, Rudolph M. "Mabel Craft Deering: A Young Woman of Advanced Ideas." *California History* (September 1987):162–69.

Larrabee, Lisa. "Women and Cycling: The Early Years." In Frances Willard, *How I Learned to Ride the Bicycle*, edited by Carol O'Hare, 81–97. Sunnyvale, Calif.: Fair Oaks 1991.

Lebsock, Suzanne. "Woman Suffrage and White Supremacy: A Virginia Case Study." In *Visible Women: New Essays on American Activism*, edited by Nancy A. Hewitt and Suzanne Lebsock, 62–100. Urbana: University of Illinois Press, 1993.

Lee, Mabel. *Memories of a Bloomer Girl, 1894–1924*. Washington, D.C.: American Alliance for Health, Physical Education, and Recreation, 1977.

Liberti, Rita. " 'We Were Ladies, We Just Played Like Boys': African-American Womanhood and Competitive Basketball at Bennett College, 1928–1942." In *Sport and the Color Line: Black Athletes and Race Relations in Twentieth-Century America,* edited by Patrick B. Miller and David K. Wiggins, 81–99. New York: Routledge, 2004.

Lieberman-Cline, Nancy, with Debby Jennings. *Lady Magic: The Autobiography of Nancy Lieberman-Cline.* Champaign, Ill.: Sagamore Publishing, 1991.

McCallum, John D. *College Basketball, U.S.A., Since 1892.* New York: Stein and Day, 1980.

McElwain, Max. *The Only Dance in Iowa: A History of Six-Player Girls' Basketball.* Lincoln: University of Nebraska Press, 2004.

May, Elaine Tyler. *Homeward Bound: American Families in the Cold War Era.* New York: Basic Books, 1988.

Messner, Michael A. *Taking the Field: Women, Men, and Sports.* Minneapolis: University of Minnesota Press, 2002.

Mosher, Clelia. *Health and the Woman Movement.* New York: National Board of YWCAs, 1916.

Nadler, Sylvia F. "A Developmental History of the Wayland Hutcherson Flying Queens from 1910 to 1979." Ph.D. diss., East Texas State University, 1980.

Naismith, James. *Basketball: Its Origin and Development.* New York: Association Press, 1941.

Neal, Patsy. *Basketballs, Goldfish and World Championships.* Bybee, Tenn: Playbacks, n.d.

Nelson, Mariah Burton. "Paid to Play a Game." In *SportsDykes: Stories from On and Off the Field,* edited by Susan Fox Rodgers, 87–94. New York: St. Martin's Press, 1994.

Offenberger, Chuck. *E. Wayne Cooley and the Iowa Girl: A Celebration of the Nation's Best High School Girls Sports Program.* South Riding, Va.: N&K, 2002.

Oriard, Michael. *Reading Football: How the Popular Press Created an American Spectacle.* Chapel Hill: University of North Carolina Press, 1993.

Paul, Joan. "Clara Gregory Baer: Catalyst for Women's Basketball." In Hult and Trekell, *A Century of Women's Basketball,* 37–52.

Payne, Charles M. *I've Got the Light of Freedom: The Organizing Tradition and the Mississippi Freedom Struggle.* Berkeley: University of California Press, 1996.

Peavy, Linda, and Ursula Smith. "World Champions: The 1904 Girls' Basketball Team from Fort Shaw Indian Boarding School." *Montana: The Magazine of Western History* (Winter 2001): 2–25.

Philly's Final Four: UConn Rocks the Cradle of Women's Basketball. Philadelphia Inquirer Staff. Philadelphia: *Philadelphia Inquirer,* 2000.

Pierce, PJ. *"Let Me Tell You What I've Learned": Texas Wisewomen Speak.* Austin: University of Texas Press, 2002.

Pieroth, Doris H. *Their Day in the Sun: Women of the 1932 Olympics.* Seattle: University of Washington Press, 1996.

Porter, Karra J. *Mad Seasons: The Story of the First Women's Professional Basketball League.* Lincoln: University of Nebraska Press, forthcoming 2006.

Radar, Benjamin G. *American Sports: From the Age of Folk Games to the Age of Televised Sports.* Fourth Edition. Upper Saddle River, N.J.: Prentice Hall, 1983.

Redin, Harley J. *The Queens Fly High.* Edited by J.P. Woodward. Privately printed, 1958.

Samuels, Ernest. *Bernard Berenson: The Making of a Connoisseur.* Cambridge, Mass.: Belknap Press, 1979.

Savage, Tom A. *Nothin' But a Champion: The Story of Van Chancellor, Three-Time WNBA Coach of the Year.* The Woodlands, Texas: Harman Sports, 2000.

Schwomeyer, Herb. *Hoosier HERsteria: A History of Indiana High School Girls Basketball.* Greenfield, Ind.: Mitchell-Fleming Printing, 1985.

Sherman, George. *The Lure and the Lore of Basketball in Missouri.* Virginia Beach, Va.: Donning, 1994.

Smith-Rosenberg, Carroll. *Disorderly Conduct: Visions of Gender in Victorian America.* New York: Alfred A. Knopf, 1985.

Spears, Betty. "Senda Berenson Abbott. New Woman: New Sport." In Hult and Trekell, *A Century of Women's Basketball,* 19–36.

Strasser, J.B., and Laurie Becklund. *Swoosh: The Unauthorized Story of Nike and the Men Who Played There.* New York: HarperBusiness, 1993.

Summers, Leigh. *Bound to Please: A History of the Victorian Corset.* New York: Berg, 2001.

Summitt, Pat, with Sally Jenkins. *Raise the Roof: The Inspiring Inside Story of the Tennessee Lady Vols Undefeated 1997–98 Season.* New York: Broadway Books, 1999.

Summitt, Pat, with Sally Jenkins. *Reach for the Summitt: The Definite Dozen System for Succeeding at Whatever You Do.* New York: Broadway Books, 1999.

Trekell, Marianna, and Rosalie M. Gershon, "Title IX, AIAW, and Beyond: A Time for Celebration!" In Hult and Trekell, *A Century of Women's Basketball,* 401–26.

VanDerveer, Tara, with Joan Ryan. *Shooting from the Outside: How a Coach and Her Olympic Team Transformed Women's Basketball.* New York: Avon Books, 1998.

Verbrugge, Martha H. *Able-Bodied Womanhood: Personal Health and Social Change in Nineteenth-Century Boston.* New York: Oxford University Press, 1988.

Wall, Kathryn L. " 'We Always Loved to Play Basketball:' A Window of Opportunity for Working-Class Women's Sports, Winston-Salem and Elkin, North Carolina, 1934–1949." M.A. thesis, University of North Carolina, Chapel Hill, 1994.

Walters, John. *The Same River Twice: A Season with Geno Auriemma and the Connecticut Huskies.* New York: Gunkerhalter Press, 2002.

Webb, Bernice Lawson. *The Basketball Man, James Naismith.* Lawrence: University of Kansas Press, 1973.

Wingfield, Marshall. *A History of Caroline County Virginia from Its Formation in 1727 to 1924.* Baltimore: Clearfield, 1997.

Young, A.S. "Doc." *Negro Firsts in Sports.* Chicago: Johnson, 1963.

Zaharias, Babe Didrikson, as told to Harry Paxton. *This Life I've Led: My Autobiography.* New York: A.S. Barnes, 1955.

INDEX

Note: Page numbers in italics indicate photographs.